INCLUDING AESTHETICS IN ART CURRICULUM PLANNING

CARMEN L. ARMSTRONG

PROFESSOR EMERITA

NORTHERN ILLINOIS UNIVERSITY

ABAFA Systems

Copyright © 1999 by Carmen L. Armstrong. All rights reserved. No part of this book may be reproduced, stored in a retrieval system, or transcribed, in any form or by any means, electronic, mechanical, photocopying, recording or otherwise, without the prior written permission of the author.

Published by ABAFA Systems, Box 92, Sycamore, IL 60178
Printed by Northern Illinois University Printing Services, DeKalb, Illinois

ISBN 0-9670402-0-5

CONTENTS

List of Tables

List of Figures

Preface

Acknowledgments

1. **INTRODUCTION** 1

    Practical beginnings 1

    Teaching elementary and secondary art

    Teaching art methods and curriculum development to pre-service and in-service teachers

    Field testing and research on the aesthetics resource 3

    Reform in art education 4

    Summary 5

2. **COMPREHENSIVE CONTENT OF ART EDUCATION** 7

    Knowledge content of the art disciplines 7

    Behavioral content from the art discipline role models 12

    Elements, principles, subject matter, media, processes 13

    Aesthetics: An art discipline for many age groups 15

3. **AESTHETICS AS A STRUCTURAL COMPONENT OF ART CURRICULA** 19

    Rationale 19

    Goals

    Art in general education

    Meaning

    A teaching aid 21

    Planning with implementation in mind 22

    Breadth

    Planned comparison

    Knowledge content

    Summary 24

4. THE PROCESS OF PLANNING VISUAL ARTS CURRICULA   25

Overview   25
Sections

Definitions: Aims to Objectives, Curriculum

Scope: Basic considerations   28
Context of art education

    Goals or learner outcomes: national, state, district, department

    Student characteristics

Aesthetics theories

Curriculum theories: Non-sociological; Sociological

Connecting with the community   45

Structure   46
Advance organizers

Aesthetics generalizations as structure

Synthesizing the components   55
Identifying subsets of the basic considerations

A duality: The Universal Aesthetics Themes curriculum

Sequence   65
Vertical sequence

Horizontal sequence

5. PLANNING THE COMPONENTS OF MEANINGFUL ART ENCOUNTERS   71

Definitions   71

A Universal Aesthetics themes encounter   72

Collaboration: Planning interdisciplinary encounters or units   77

6. CURRICULAR EXAMPLES USING AESTHETICS GENERALIZATIONS   83

  Structuring aesthetics behaviors within a K-5 art program   83

  An art encounter structure for grade two   84

  A third grade, 36 week, curriculum structure   86

  A three unit, twelve week sixth grade art structure   88

  Vertical sequence of generalizations for units in a four year high school art program   90

  A high school Art and Spanish collaboration   93

  Integrating the art disciplines in an elementary education majors' art methods course   94

  Teacher comments   97

7. CURRICULUM EVALUATION   99

  Overview   99

  Documentation suggestions and models   99

    Orientation

    Basic considerations

    Alignment

    Structure and scaffolding

    Comprehensiveness or scope

    Cohesiveness

    Sequence

    Practicality

  Compatibility of means of assessment of student learning   111

  Confidence statement   112

8 AN AESTHETICS RESOURCE   115

Contents of the aesthetics resource   115

   Basic questions

   Theory-connected quotations

   Issues-connected quotations

   Generalizations

   Teacher prompt questions

The resource   147

   What is the nature of art?   147

   What is the value of art?   177

   Other issues   229

REFERENCES: TEXT   329

REFERENCES: AESTHETICS RESOURCE   335

APPENDIX: WORKSHEETS FOR PLANNING CURRICULA   343

Art/General Education Outcome Statements (Goals Grid)

Goals/Aesthetics Alignment in Encounters

Course Structure

Generalizations Merging Curriculum and Aesthetics Theories

Organizing Content within a Structure

Structure of Visual Arts Encounters

List of Tables

2.1   Knowledge content of art disciplines

2.2   Behavioral content of art discipline role models

4.1   Curricular theories, possible subsets of theories, and
        suggested unit themes based on each curricular theory

6.1   Charting grade levels at which to introduce inquiiry behaviors
        of the aesthetician

6.2   Third grade curriculum "Communities near and far"

6.3   Example of a three-unit, sixth grade art curriculum structure

6.4   Vertical sequence of generalizations in a four year
        high school art program

7.1   Schedule for a semester of a high school art course

viii

List of Figures

4.1   Components of art curriculum planning

4.2   Theoretical choices for curriculum structuring decisions

4.3   Model for structure or organization of an art curriculum

4.4   Example of a structure of a curriculum for one year

4.5   A model of subsuming and subordinate concepts

4.6   Example of an aesthetics generalization as an advance organizer of an encounter

4.7   Learner outcomes format: Relationship between art and general education goals of school districts

4.8   Aligning puzzle pieces from basic art curriculum components with a generalization as organizer

4.9   Hypothetical example of curriculum scaffolding: Alignment from general to specific

4.10   Unit or encounter themes derived from alignment of aesthetics theories and subsets of curriculum theories

4.11	A model of an encounter as all components fit together to create an integrated picture
4.12	Hypothetical structuring of comprehensive content by an aesthetics theory and institutions curricular theory merger
4.13	Vertical sequence: A restatement of a generalization at different conceptual levels
4.14	Dividing a course into units, encounters, and activities
5.1	Plan for an art encounter that merges aesthetics and curriculum theories in its organizing generalization
5.2	Plan for an interdisciplinary encounter: Art and History
6.1	Model of a second grade encounter
7.1	Learner outcome alignment with goals, standards, and assessment on a partial goals grid
7.2	An art fundamentals course structure
7.3	Accountability model: Inclusion of subsets of the basics

Preface

This book is intended for teachers of the visual arts. It is for teachers who wish to make art more relevant for their students by creating a thematic approach in their written visual arts curriculum plan. While the book has a visual arts frame of reference, the aesthetics resource within it is useful for organizing courses related to the visual arts such as humanities, aesthetics, art appreciation, multicultural arts, interrelated arts, integrated disciplines, and art(s) history. Teachers of self-contained elementary classrooms will find this book helpful in integrating study of visual art and other subject areas. Most directly, it is designed for K-12 visual arts education curriculum development.

Components

The book consists of a review of the content of visual arts curricula, a rationale for aesthetics as major component of the structure of an art curriculum plan, guides for synthesizing the components relevant to visual arts curriculum, examples of ways art teachers have used the resource in structuring their entire art curriculum or aspects of it and ways that the curriculum planning process serves curriculum evaluation and accountability.

Chapter eight contains the aesthetics resource and an explanation of its categories and organization. the resource is composed of a) *quotations* of aestheticians, artists, art historians and art critics, or paraphrased statements about art that are classified by the philosophic theory they represent or an issue that aestheticians address; b) *generalizations* about art derived from the quotations or the paraphrased statements to serve as curriculum organizers that is, the big idea of a lesson; and c) for each set of quotation and generalization, open-ended, *sample questions* to prompt teachers in the kind of open-ended questions to ask in initiating aesthetics dialogues based on learning experiences in which students are involved. The dialogues engage students in reflective thinking and encourage serious consideration of the meaning of the art experiences and the role of art in their lives.

This text progresses from general to specific considerations in planning a written curriculum. Some basic structural components are introduced sequentially but must be considered simultaneously, such as contextual values expressed as goals or learner outcomes at the national, state or community level, aesthetics theories, curriculum theories, and the nature of the student.

Contributions

Teacher direction. The planned curriculum is part of a triad completed by instruction (implementation of the curriculum) and assessment (feedback on the effectiveness of the curriculum and instruction) (Armstrong, 1994). This book promotes a systematic approach to curriculum planning which helps teachers to meaningfully integrate art history, criticism, production and aesthetics as they plan art courses or years of art curricula. This systematic approach enables art teachers to synthesize the complex content of visual arts education. The process is complicated, but a written structured and sequential curriculum contributes direction for the teacher, avoids undue redundancy and internal inconsistency, and provides for focus in the separate activities experienced by the students. Focus, or a point to be recognized, prepares students to *explain* the importance of their art experiences, not just *describe* them. Recognizing the focus of an activity enables seeing relationships and deriving meaning from an art encounter.

<u>An aid to relevance</u>. For half a century, art teachers have expressed dismay because their "communities did not value art." Effective ways must be sought to reach the children or grandchildren of the parents who were our art students after the mid 20th Century. This book encourages curriculum planning where the focus of the big idea of the encounter helps students make connections between art activities of the encounter and to perceive the relevance of art to life. Identifying major learnings for each lesson facilitates encourage serious study of the nature and value of art, vision of artists, and influences on them as revealed in their artistic creations. Better curriculum planning should help today's art education move art from the fringes of schooling and place it in the mainstream of the 21st century--from former conceptions of art as an entertaining activity to serious consideration of art's critical role and purpose in the big picture of life.

<u>Clarifies aesthetics</u>. The classification of quotations and generalizations in the aesthetics resource facilitates clarity and differentiation to enable teachers to make reasonable choices as they create curriculum plans. The suggested questions contribute to students' ease in synthesizing the point of their art experiences in classroom discussions.

<u>Accommodates new methods and activities</u>. The visual arts curriculum recommendations of this book also help teachers to consciously expose their students to multiple views of aestheticians through the curriculum plan. Innovative activities and methods advanced by art educators and philosophers for meaningful integration of the four art disciplines in art lessons, and inquiry approaches related to each discipline, can be planned within the structure of a curriculum based on aesthetics.

While this book is about structuring a big plan for inclusion of aesthetics as a major component in art curriculums, it also emphasizes the need for comprehensive consideration of artists' intents, art criticism, and art history in contexts of cultures, periods of history, and the many forms, processes, techniques, and skills associated with the creative production of art.

Exclusions

Curriculum planning in the context of this book does not cover instructional methods or techniques. There are many resources developed that deal with specific aesthetics activities that can be employed **within** a curriculum that has aesthetics as the core (Battin et al,1989; Erickson and Katter,1986; Lankford,1992; Stewart,1997, and others). To give equal attention to instructional strategies and the other art disciplines is beyond the scope and intent of this book.

Although the aesthetics resource includes suggestions for the types of question for teachers that could initiate an aesthetics dialogue, they are based on possible activities that the author visualized, but intentionally did not explain as a lesson. They are inspired by the generalization and intended only as prompts that will aid the teacher in formulating the types of questions that modified, would relate to lesson components that he or she has planned. Teachers are urged to simplify questions appropriately for the conceptual level of the group of students. They are urged to modify questions appropriately for the particular historical, critical and production experiences of the encounter.

General recommendations

In reading and applying the curriculum planning recommendations, teachers are encouraged to take small steps. Teachers may find generalizations that make the point of some lesson that has been successful in previous years. They can chart what is already taught to see if the major points of the lessons represent different philosophic positions. They can look for ways to plan related parts of encounters (extended lessons) or a unit of encounters before tackling a whole year. As when venturing into any challenging project, planned reinforcement goes a long way in developing the confidence and expertise to gradually develop a comprehensive curriculum for multiple grade levels.

xvi

Becky A.

Acknowledgments

The aesthetics resource provided within this book was made possible through the cooperation of approximately seventy-five publishers of journals and books. Each publisher is recognized under the pertinent quotation(s), but I wish to formally thank all of the publishers who so generously and patiently responded to my requests for copyright permission. In some cases, quotations were considered public domain or fair use by the publisher. In spite of extensive research to locate the holder of copyright, regrettably, some quotations had to be paraphrased. Some long passages were also paraphrased.

The Getty Education Institute for the Arts is acknowledged for providing educational services and opportunities for university faculty and art educators at all levels to become familiar with Discipline Based Art Education (DBAE) and to interact with each other. The Getty disseminated information in unprecedented ways to familiarize educators and stakeholders about DBAE which paved the way for change in art education and the appropriateness of this book and its aesthetics resource. Specifically, the author is grateful to the Getty Institute for providing support, under the auspices of a preservice discipline-based art education grant (Armstrong, 1990a), which enabled progress in the early development of the aesthetics resource idea.

The author also acknowledges the major contribution of William Tolhurst, Department of Philosophy at Northern Illinois University, as a consultant in early stages of this project. His assistance is appreciated especially for differentiating theoretical positions in the field, advice in categorizing theorists, and for identifying major issues addressed by aestheticians. In addition, he has been a helpful critic and evaluator of the author's efforts. Most of all, he is appreciated for his willingness to contribute to a project that extends beyond philosophy per se.

This book and its aesthetics resource originated out of the author's art teaching experience from kindergarten through graduate level courses, the development of a curriculum planning resource (Armstrong, 1979) and research in art teacher questioning strategies (Armstrong, 1977, 1986, 1993). The idea benefited from the experience and concern shared by other professionals whose ideas blended with that experience. I am indebted to many fellow art educators who have been exploring means of teaching aesthetics in art education in publications and conference presentations.

I am also grateful to my graduate and undergraduate students at Northern Illinois University who have patiently field-tested the aesthetics resource in curriculum planning courses. Many undergraduate and graduate students in curriculum classes have successfully used the aesthetics resource in its various stages of development to select advance organizers for the lessons they planned and/or taught. Art teachers who planned curricula, conducted pilot tests, videotaped instructional episodes, and evaluated the resource and its ability to help them integrate aesthetics into their art curriculum and/or teaching plans from kindergarten to senior high school visual arts education include: Noel Bunt Anderson, Tom Beck, Charrie Colwell, Lisa Galich Mack, Sally Hazelton, Patricia Herrmann, Rhonda Levy-McQueen, Robin Russell, Marilyn Schnake, and Darlene Williams. Cynthia Bickley-Green used an early prototype of the aesthetics resource to structure her university level course in humanities. I also acknowledge the help of Elizabeth Jonasson, who, as my graduate assistant, helped in checking the accuracy of quotations from original sources. Her conscientious searching, judgment, and reasonable suggestions attest to her sensitive grasp of my intent.

The editing and comments of Debbie Smith-Shank, and suggestions for consideration by Stanley Madeja were appreciated. I thank the Northern Illinois University (NIU) Art Education faculty for assuming extra responsibilities during my sabbatical semesters, and the administration and secretarial staff of the NIU School of Art for assistance in a variety of ways.

Finally, I am deeply grateful to my husband, Dr. Nolan Armstrong, Professor Emeritus of Leadership and Educational Policy Study at Northern Illinois University for insightful editorial contributions. I appreciate his expertise in critiquing the model questions in the aesthetics resource for their potential to facilitate higher order thinking. Acknowledgement words are inadequate in expressing appreciation for his patience and understanding as first reader of chapters, long term support and encouragement, and role flexibility at home.

To thoughtful art teachers and students everywhere

1. INTRODUCTION

Some goals in life seem beyond reach, but those that are worth the effort have their rewards for the conscientious. Such is the experience of many art teachers who have tackled the challenge of writing a comprehensive and theoretically sound art curriculum. Experience and changes in art education theory provide reasons for careful attention to written art curricula.

Practical beginnings

Art teachers learn from formal education, omissions of formal education successes and mistakes. The recommendations brought to the reader in this book reflect of years of art classroom teaching experience over a backdrop of principles of what constitutes a sound approach to planning curriculum. The teaching experience reinforced the validity of the principles.

Teaching elementary and secondary art

Imagine yourself in this scenario. Eager to teach a carefully planned lesson, the new art teacher's introduction of it to a class was met with the groan "We did that last year". That was motivation enough to send the teacher off to find out what each grade level did in art for previous years. The search for "curriculum" began.

Experience soon taught the teacher that she could not teach everything about line (or balance, or Romanticism, or texture, or emotive facial features) in one lesson. These concepts or ideas (e.g. line) have many more specific aspects called subordinate concepts (e.g. weighted line) that help make the point for a particular lesson and some are more appropriately introduced at one grade level or another. The curriculum task began with that insight. A spider web began to emerge as items on lists of art concepts, processes, historical exemplars were connected by lines. Eventually the lists were cut apart and stacks of related items from the lists were clustered as "lessons". Stacks were then sorted to build on art knowledge as students progressed through grades K to Six.

Not all schools include art in the academic curriculum. It might help if students could take home a simple message about what they learned in art. Art, which takes up time and a sizable part of the school's budget, should make its critical importance to the education of each child quite evident. Reflection on that note once led to variations of an overriding theme in teaching and bulletin board displays of "Art as part of life." Students and parents were continuously engaged with variations of the theme that "art and aesthetic decision-making has been essential to quality human existence and change throughout history and continues to be in contemporary life" For students to understand the theme, the subordinate concepts of elements and principles, art exemplars and production supported each lesson's big idea.

Teaching art methods and curriculum development to pre-service and in-service teachers

Many future elementary education teachers are inexperienced and insecure about teaching art or devalue it in relation to other subjects they learn to teach. It was apparent that some good reasons are needed to guide the art education experience. That led to the curricular decision of formulating unit themes or statements about the role of art in life labeled as aesthetics generalizations (Armstrong, 1990b). All content selected for the unit activities in some way contributed to the students' ability to understand that generalization. The concepts developed in lead-in experiences contributed to effective culminating unit projects. In art criticism experiences, the stage of interpretation was addressed not only by observing internal cues within works of art and by comparison and contrast with works of similar subject matter, but also from art historical inquiry into the contextual influences. Students found their aesthetics dialogues helpful in meaningfully connecting their experiences in art criticism, production, and history and observations from other subject areas of life.

The unit aesthetics generalizations approach helped shape the author's expectations for art education students' development of a curriculum plan. Curricular theories provide choices from which to decide on a philosophical "platform" on which to base an internally consistent curriculum--a pragmatic theory. A study of a community, representative of one in which the art education student would like to teach, helped select an appropriate platform. Aesthetics generalizations, or big ideas about art, help organize each encounter. Students plan all components of the curricular structure to contribute to the rationale developed based on the theoretical platform. Students are challenged by this task, but develop a sense of pride and commitment as the curriculum takes shape and they see the "big picture" of art education that they created.

Field testing and research on the aesthetics resource

The aesthetics resource in chapter 8 was field tested with art teachers who incorporated aesthetics in art curriculum planning at elementary and secondary school levels, executing their plans in instruction, and videotaping aesthetics dialogues. In addition, an integrated Spanish and Art curriculum unit was planned and taught. Teachers noted recommendations as they did their planning and review of the resource.

The language of prompt questions was empirically tested for appropriateness of the wording of the teacher questions suggested for the four conceptual levels of students. In some cases, the art teachers field testing the resource felt that the language of the suggested teacher questions would need to be simplified by art teachers for the grade level indicated. One high school teacher said she started with the less complex prompt questions and worked up to the more challenging ones for high school as the aesthetics dialogue progressed.

Reform in Art Education

At the 1965 Seminar on Supervision and Curriculum Development, Barkan who is known for his assertion that role models for art education are artists, art historians and critics also stated, " The art educator...must synthesize the knowledge in art of the artist, and the knowledges about art of the aesthetician, the critic, and the historian" (1966, p.243)*. Comments at the same meeting by Tumin, Foshay and McFee seem to support aesthetics as one of the basic art education disciplines.

By 1970, Barkan, Chapman, and Kern had assembled definitions of behaviors that characterize inquiry in each of the fine arts and quotations that exemplified concepts pertaining to works of art in those same modes. This compilation was titled Guidelines: Curriculum development for aesthetic education and was the basis for CEMREL's elementary level aesthetic education curriculum (Madeja and Onuska, 1977). Subsequently, aesthetic education emerged as an interrelated arts direction that dominated the interpreted use of "aesthetics" in visual arts education from 1970 to at least 1985.

*In E. Mattil (Project Director). A seminar in art education for research and curriculum development. (pp.240-255). University Park, PA: The Pennsylvania State University, Department of Art Education. By permission.

In the years that followed, research reports by art educators dealing with the effect of focused experiences in art history and criticism indicated positive attitudinal effects of that focus (Day, 1985, 1987). Wilson (1988) reported no statistically significant differences in what students knew about art and artists in general when students, who had production-oriented art education, were compared to students who were not enrolled in art classes.

With the support of the Getty Center for Education in the Arts (now The Getty Education Institute for the Arts), art education reform was strengthened through training seminars, research, broad dissemination of information, regional institutes and grants to universities for improvement of pre-service discipline-based art education.

Summary

Practical experience teaching art, research, and art education conceptual changes justify an expanded conception of visual arts education. Thirty years of teaching curriculum development has provided ample opportunity to assess and improve the curriculum development process recommended in this book and the aesthetics resource. Carefully considered changes have been made in response to feedback from pilot testing and changes in the field of art education.

A written curriculum plans ahead for meaningful integration of the appropriate changes described in art education reform and aesthetics needs more than casual attention. With a few exceptions, emphasis related to philosophic aesthetics is placed on instructional strategies rather than comprehensive exposure to differing views of aesthetics theoreticians. Art teachers need to plan what to incorporate from aesthetics, how to plan for its inclusion in the curriculum, and how to include aesthetics in their art instruction. With least preparation in the discipline of aesthetics, the categorized content of the aesthetics resource in this book will help teachers differentiate the content and incorporate an aesthetics component in structuring their comprehensive visual arts curriculum plan.

2. COMPREHENSIVE CONTENT OF ART EDUCATION

If asked what an art teacher teaches, the person inquiring should be prepared to listen awhile. The content specific to the visual arts is vast and complex. One could start listing all the art forms, or the media used by artists, or historical evidence of art in people's lives, or principles by which artists appear to compose elements of art in their work or big truths about art. More organized and encompassing ways of referring to the content is by the disciplines that cross the study of art styles, forms, behaviors, media, cultures, etc.

"Discipline", used in the context of this book and discipline-based art education, refers to fields of study that have conceptual structure and modes of inquiry (Clark, Day & Greer, 1987). According to King and Brownell (1966), a discipline has been defined as (a) a defined area of study, (b) the network of facts, writings, and other works of scholars associated with the field, or (c) a community of individuals whose task is the gaining of meaning. The disciplines that make critical contributions to a general education in art-- aesthetics and art history, criticism, and production--seem to adequately fall within these definitions. This chapter includes a brief overview of the most familiar disciplines. Because the focus of this book, more attention is devoted to aesthetics. Each discipline is addressed as having knowledge content--what information is to be discovered-- and behavioral content-- approaches to inquiry that characterize persons engaged in that discipline.

Knowledge Content of the Art Disciplines

Art History

Art history verifies the role of art in the lives of people across time and cultures. It is a rich source of ideas and information. By comparing and contrasting how artists have chosen to portray subjects that still concern humans today, students are presented with choices. They benefit from recognizing the reasons for the attitudes, styles, and choices of media used by others. They perceive art as occurring within a context--differing social, political, economic, philosophical, and geographic conditions of each culture that influence art. Art students utilize this information as is, recombine it, or be inspired to vary from it in ways meaningful to their personal interpretation and relevance to today.

Art Criticism

Whereas art history deals with the context of works of art--place, time, period, style, media, theme, function, cultural setting and values, etc.--criticism looks at the work of art itself. When teachers involve students in art criticism, students describe the indisputable objects, elements, or facts of the work, the specific visual qualities and spatial organization of the work, and how these contribute to the interpretation(s) one can make about its meaning. Qualities internal to the work are the basis for judgments about the effectiveness of the work, but external or contextual information can enhance the interpretation and judgment.

Art Production

In a society dominated by attention to mathematical and verbal expression of intellectual ideas, there remains around the artist a mysterious aura--somewhat envied, frequently misunderstood-- that is derived from a basic lack of understanding of visual-spatial forms of intelligence. Artists portray objects or ideals and give form to ideas, attitudes and feelings that speak not only for themselves but possibly, and sometimes intentionally, for others. Artists and art students perceive what is around them generally and specifically. They relate, interpret and organize visual information as they give form to their ideas.

Meaningful art production applies concepts developed through experiments or in the study of works of art and provides a direct experience base for thinking about the meaning of that experience. Teachers can guide that conceptual acquisition by telling, or, by asking questions about visual information brought in for students to observe and discuss.

Actual involvement in art production can help increase students' understanding of art. It is a critical component of anyone's general education. Most art teachers have experienced a deep, prolonged interaction with art through studio involvement. It is not surprising then, to see that reflected in heavily art production-oriented art programs. However, while all students can become adults who are informed about art, few will become producers of art. Therefore, the extremely production-oriented art program is limited in its appropriateness for many students who need to be educated in art.

Aesthetics

In contrast to art criticism which focuses on a particular work of art, a group of works clustered for some commonality, or works brought under analysis for comparison and contrast, aesthetics deals with large encompassing questions and issues that apply to art in general.

Aesthetics (the noun) is a branch of philosophy which is concerned with theory about art, beauty, taste and related issues. It is differentiated from aesthetic (the adjective) which pertains to the science of aesthetics and is often used to describe one's description of or response to sensory qualities encountered in art. Aesthetics is also described as a process that is ever being shaped by society and values that change with cultural contexts and conditions. In the context of this work, aesthetics is the philosophy of art.

Aesthetics deals with the big ideas or rules that justify something as art. Aesthetics focuses on the critical examination of responses to questions about the nature and value of art as well as many related issues about art. It examines issues and questions in art in order to differentiate choices for describing the characteristics of art and to formulate logical or observable and generalizable reasons for determining aesthetic quality.

Aesthetics theories are attempts by philosophers to explain what constitutes art of value in such a way that the explanations comprehensively accommodate all that should be valued as art. A theory or definition of art must specify the *necessary* (must have in order to be that object) and *sufficient* (a characteristic which, if an object has it, it is a _____) conditions needed for something to be a work of art. Theories that attempt to identify the criteria that justifies something as art must have exemplars to verify positions taken, but one exemplar cannot be the basis for a theory.

A beginners' cross examination of aesthetics theories quickly reveals that each theory explains criteria that can be exemplified by time-honored works of art, yet each theory seems not to explain the acceptance that exists for other works of art. Furthermore, the same works of art frequently can exemplify more than one theory of art.

There are multiple sets of criteria for valuing works of art. Social and geographic contexts, cultural tradition or philosophies, time, and stages of political and economic development effect what has been valued and preserved as "art". Indeed, contemporary aestheticians who think deeply about art are bound to delve into the connections between artists and the context in which they create. Theory building about art is ongoing as art and contexts continue to change.

Aesthetics tends to raise more questions than answers, but there is value in thoughtful questioning. Besides conveying value by the very fact that classroom time is devoted to it, the examination process will uncover ideas, perceived relationships, choice of value criteria, openmindedness toward logical modifications in positions about art, complex thoughts, and worth of art that is otherwise overlooked.

Table 2.1 summarizes the knowledge content of the art disciplines.

Table 2.1. KNOWLEDGE CONTENT OF ART DISCIPLINES

ART HISTORY	ART CRITICISM	AESTHETICS	ART PRODUCTION
KNOWLEDGE			
ALL DISCIPLINES: Sensory qualities of elements, formal principles, technical qualities, expressivness			
artists	journalistic	questions	media
art works	pedagogical, academic	issues	tools
eras	popular, personal	theories:	equipment
dates	scholarly	imitation	processes
styles		expression	techniques
countries		formalism	concepts: art/life
influences:		institution	art forms, alternatives
political		pragmatism/	
philosophic		instrumentalism	
social		non-western	
economic		no-theory	
geographic			
art world			

Behavioral Content of the Art Discipline Role Models

Recognition of the importance of encouraging behaviors in art is not new. As role models, the artist, art critic, art historian and aesthetician behave or inquire in ways that are noteworthy. Kaelin (1989) noted art behaviors as skills of observation, linguistic capabilities, conceptualization, judgment, reflection, and criticism.

Several questioning structures exist for teacher's use in facilitating students' behaving as their art critic role models. Feldman's (1967) scholarly art criticism structure is probably most widely used. Since a work of art has much information to be observed and related, by using small individual or large poster-size reproductions of works of art, every student can make appropriate observations in response to the teachers' well-phrased questions. With Hamblen's (1986) addition of a "Speculate" category, students can respond to some "What If" questions and have a creative interchange with the work of art that goes beyond it, perhaps leading to a production experience.

Manipulative skill leading to technical quality has traditionally been content associated with art production. The Inquiry in Art Production questioning strategy provides help for the teacher to facilitate an inductive approach to students' forming concepts, making decisions, and evaluating their art within the nine behaviors associated with creating art (Armstrong, 1986, 1993).

Aestheticians reflect about art and logically think through all that is necessary and sufficient to carefully construct position about the nature and value of art and related issues which has no internal inconsistencies.

Art historians research works of art to establish facts about their time place, method or technique, cultural context, and maker. The contextual information helps them explain causes, meanings, influences and rules that link a work to others in the same or vastly different time periods or cultures.

Table 2.2 on page 14 summarizes behaviors that characterize the inquiry of role models from each discipline. In <u>Designing assessment in art</u>, Armstrong (1994) consolidated these behaviors of role models that are common across the disciplines into seven-- know, perceive, organize, inquire, value, manipulate, and interact/cooperate. Art lessons can be structured that focus also on these behaviors as well as on the knowledge content of art.

Although attention to behaviors in art has been recommended, few curriculums focus on development of those behaviors and assess evidence of the students' acquisition of those intellectual skills. Armstrong (1994) shows how application of the recommendation for assessing evidence of acquired *behaviors* critical to learning associated with all art disciplines is possible. Teaching for behavioral outcomes means modeling, encouraging, facilitating, and rewarding those behaviors. Teaching for the behaviors of each discipline eases the transition to evaluation of outcomes of learning which are expressed in observable, behavioral terms.

Elements, principles, subject matter, media, processes

Traditionally in art education, students learn about the elements and certain principles of art and their application in art production, but role models from each discipline use these terms to talk about art whether in reference to individual works or art in general. The artist arranges elements (line, color, etc.) according to some principles (design, composition), manipulating subject matter and media by processes and utilizing techniques

Table 2.2 **BEHAVIORAL CONTENT OF ART DISCIPLINE ROLE MODELS**

ART HISTORY	ART CRITICISM	AESTHETICS	ART PRODUCTION
INQUIRY PROCESS BEHAVIORS			

establish documentary facts:
  attribute
  describe
  reconstruct
interpret:
  from the work
  research re:time
explain:
  influences, traditions
  discover regularities
    leading to rules
    operating in the work
	describe
	formally analyze
	interpret
	judge
		reflect
		compare
		contrast
		relate
		synthesize
		question
			set a direction
			discover
			visually analyze
			classify
			personalize
			  hypothesize
			reorder
			synthesize
			evaluate

to accomplish an intent. Historians refer to these components as they classify artworks by style, period, etc. The critic observes qualities that result from the artist's manipulation and organization of the elements, seeks meaning, and evaluates the work. The aesthetician considers those qualities in the context of all art in deciding whether objects such as these could be reasoned as "art".

Elements of art are inherent in any aspect of art education just as verbs, nouns, commas are to verbal communication. Principles of design, organization or composition are like rules for sentence structure in a language. Organization of parts of speech is critical to verbal communication in a language. Like in verbal communication, elements and principles of art play an **enabling** role--a means to the end of creating meaning--not the end in itself. **They are not appropriate inclusive organizers for structuring curriculum.**

Aesthetics--An art discipline for many age groups

Young children tend to mimic the values to which they are exposed. Children's reactions to art reflect the informally acquired attitudes of their homes at very early ages. Possibly, even the absence of art on the walls of their homes, influences young children to come to school with some contextually influenced ideas about art. If basic values of children are generally established by age ten (Massey,1976) then they likely have been enculturated into value systems operating in regard to art also. Children make choices as to what is beautiful on the basis of their experiences.

Art education can introduce aesthetics experiences that help explain, expand upon and/or change children's naive value judgements by taking the time to discuss ways that people regard art. Thus, art education exposes children to a widened base for developing conceptions, attitudes and values of art. Early exposure to alternative views, in simplified but accurate form, may deter narrow, premature closure on values regarding art. The aesthetics experience invites students to sort through specifics and to think critically about the comprehensive or general ideas about art. Generalizations drawn from aesthetics provide choices of criteria by which one can entertain accepting even new or unfamiliar works as "art". Aesthetics can be meaningfully included in the art curriculum and, in turn, is understood better by its integration with the concrete referents of the other content areas of the art education curriculum.

As in any subject, aesthetics can be introduced to young students at their conceptual level. Rather than imposing a too sophisticated subject on children, Battin (1988) suggests devising puzzles and problems that intrigue young students, for it is not the challenge of deep thinking that is inappropriate for them, but rather someone's approach that is beyond their conceptual level. Young students respond to thinking deeply about their own concrete experiences or scenarios that they can vividly picture.

Results of a study with fifth and sixth grade students having experiences guided by teacher questioning about aesthetics issues, suggest that students of this age do have the intellectual potential to improve in their verbal reasoning about defining art (Russell, 1988) even after having four years of art education. Russell cites other studies that exist on the positive results of the Philosophy for Children program on children's reasoning and mental maturity. Moore (1995) and Parsons and Blocker (1987) reasonably argue that aesthetics should not be denied to young students who surprise adults with their thinking ability when the content is introduced reasonably close to their conceptual level. Even primary level students can find that listening and thinking can lead to their important big ideas about art. Well-phrased teacher questions prompt students to emulate the aesthetician's behaviors, i.e. to develop cognitive strategies that lead to the higher order intellectual skills (Gagne' and Briggs, 1974) that characterize the aesthetician.

Appropriately considering student's interest in games, Erickson and Katter (1986) have created a series of art games (now commercially available from Crizmac). These authors have presented content from the four disciplines of art in intriguing formats. However, incorporating the game or puzzling scenario that is meaningfully integrated with the total art experiences of an encounter, is still the responsibility of curriculum planners.

In the aesthetics resource in Chapter 8, appropriateness of the questions designed to prompt the teacher's facilitation of an aesthetics dialogue has been checked out against experience and knowledge of the conceptual levels of children by art teachers. The Lorge formula for estimating the readability of text and/or other appropriate instruments was used on the questions associated with ten percent of the quotations. Analysis of this ten percent sample of the questions demonstrated that questions suggested for teachers to ask of students at a particular level should be comprehended by students at that level (Armstrong,1992).

Children can verbalize simplified versions of great thoughts. Given practice in explaining why art is important for a variety of reasons, even young students will share signficant information with persons at home about their art education. As in parallel situations with other subjects, the teachers' comprehension is enhanced by trying to truthfully simplify sophisticated, complex abstract thoughts. The teacher benefits by greater insight into the generalization by having the aesthetician's quotation with each generalization in the aesthetics resource. By reaching all students through a truly comprehensive general art education, the desired outcome of a society of informed adults who value the role of art in our lives is possible.

18

3. AESTHETICS AS A STRUCTURAL COMPONENT OF ART CURRICULA

Aesthetics is not only a source of legitimate content for art education. Its pervasive ideas and broad applicability of statements made by aestheticians suggest it as a structural component of art in curriculum plans. Aesthetics serves as a bridge to the world of choices-- a more informed basis for qualitative decisions about art. Without art education, people make value judgements about art; but the choices or decisions of worth may based on limited exposure or vague notions of possible considerations in determining aesthetic worth.

Rationale

Goals

In the early 1980's some significant commonalities resulted almost simultaneously from different arenas in art education. The National Art Education Association developed a list of goals for art education. The goals about content areas of art education included aesthetics. Researchers produced evidence that the dominant production model fell short of assumptions about what art students were learning in art.

Art as general education

The continuing existence of art throughout history and in most cultures testifies to the validity of its study for being an educated person. Discipline-based art education (DBAE) advocates the education of a citizenry that is well-informed about art. It promotes art as a vital part of human activity that is worthy of study for all who would be "educated".

Aesthetics is the art discipline that particularly looks at the big picture of life and reasons for the value of art in human life. Since in our system of public education, schooling is for the general education of all students, the argument for educating for an adult who is generally informed about all of life's endeavors would especially support selecting significant ideas from aesthetics as a major component for structuring plans for teaching art.

Meaning

The generalizations from aesthetics serve as organizational and culminating bridges to understanding. Seeing relationships and synthesizing learning from different experiences encourages development of higher order intellectual skills and cognitive strategies which prepare students for decision-making roles in life.

One of the recently approved national visual arts standards supports the importance of connectedness for students' grasp of meaning in art. One standard specifically addresses connecting art to other disciplines. Connections need to be made at a high level of abstraction or generalizations from two disciplines. General statements are the starting point and can be broken down into more specific ideas in curriculum planning.

Aesthetics increases meaning of art-related course experiences by facilitating transfer to life values. In all of our attention to a discipline orientation, one cannot forget the challenge of facilitating a student's excitement about learning in art. Intrinsic motivation in art can evolve from learning that is organized around human concerns. A student sees a purpose to learning if it fits with life concerns that he/she recognizes. Woodruff (1975) maintained that more extensive learning is produced by the curriculum that calls for in-life, want-serving behavior of the student. Bruner (1963) urged that a basic group of human plights provide the organizing principles of study to enable students to relate facts to a generic organization. He maintained that this generic learning is the only way to cross the barrier from learning to thinking. Stewart (1986) also included "the universe" as one of the foci of aestheticians on theorizing about art (in addition to the artist, viewer, and the work) which suggests inclusion of a broader context than art per se.

Meaningful learning experiences, translated appropriately to the conceptual level of the child and related to real life, and, taught by a teacher with a sense of direction from a planned curriculum, will go far in meeting the goal of having students value art and the educational experience through which they learned about art.

A teacher aid

Typically art teachers have less formal education in aesthetics than in the other art disciplines. How can teachers be expected to plan and teach something which seems vague? Teachers may tend to give aesthetics less attention as a result. Formally and informally acquired philosophic views operate as art teachers make curricular and instructional decisions. The philosophic basis for such decisions may not be a conscious one on the part of the teacher.

Like other people, art teachers have comfort zones and may repeatedly rely on good, reliable examples and expressions. Sometimes in art exhibits of several schools, the teachers' favorite styles, techniques, media or orientations to subject matter or art forms predominate in their students' work. It is also very likely that teachers have leanings toward certain aesthetic theoretical positions even though they may not recognize them by name.

Busy art teachers with variable knowledge of aesthetics may be helped by a concise, simplified organization of that field. The aesthetics resource in Chapter 8 is designed for use by art teachers who want to expand their information base about aesthetics. It assists them in differentiating the theoretical source of generalizations about art. The organization of the resource enables the teacher to be accountable for comprehensiveness in planning the exposure of theoretical choices to students rather than unwittingly supporting a limited or biased viewpoint. The resource brings to mind (and ultimately exposes students to) views of art that emanate out of different contexts and value systems across time and cultures as teachers plan art education curriculums.

Art teachers find what they perceive as the best fit between aesthetics generalizations, art examples from history and across cultures, an art work as the subject of art criticism, and related art production experiences. Research by Silverman (1969) demonstrated that art teaching was most effective when taught by art teachers who had helped develop the curricula they taught. Participation in the decision-making process contributes to teachers' comprehension and commitment.

Planning with implementation in mind

Breadth

The breadth approach to aesthetics in curriculum planning is also designed to increase the students' knowledge base about aesthetics. Including aesthetics in curriculum planning, does not mean selecting one theory of art to teach, but rather exposing students to many rationales for valuing art and the multiple bases for such values. Art education should expose students to a choice of theories, subsets of recognized theories, positions, issues, and problems, and encourage openmindedness and logical discussions of the nature of art that consider contexts from which works emanate. The challenge is to find the most meaningful fit, expose students to a breadth of content, and avoid undue redundancy.

Planned comparison

Students in art education can be engaged in reflectively considering conflicting and overlapping positions about the nature and value of art in varying social contexts. This suggests that, rather than choosing between curricular approaches to aesthetics, a teacher may plan to contrast and compare the qualities of several approaches. A plan might be to have students consider cross-cultural, life-oriented variables that could impact commonly accepted aesthetic theories, i.e. where contexts might qualify any automatic acceptance and extend students' knowledge meaningfully. Current art education curricula should allot time to think and talk about art.

Knowledge content

General ideas about art tend to be lasting. Curriculum in art that is structured around aesthetics provides students the opportunity to explore the encompassing rationales for the continuing presence of art throughout history. Teachers may already be basing what they teach in art on some pervasive ideas about art that they consider important (Anderson and McRorie, 1997). However, it is the teacher's responsibility to help students to recognize the theoretical foundation of their encounter experiences in terms that are appropriate for each age group. Although most people make informal value judgments related to art each day, without having had an art education with a conscious focus on big ideas about art, these choices or decisions of worth may be based on vague or limited notions of possible considerations in determining quality.

Summary

An alternative to the *chance* incorporation of aesthetics content in the art curriculum is to *start* with it, that is, to draw upon aesthetics as the source of abstract general ideas to guide art lessons that can inform our everyday responses to art. Through the students' synthesis of experiences, reflection, and seeking general, tentative conclusions, they can easily extend the meaning of the art encounter into life.

4. PLANNING VISUAL ARTS CURRICULA

Overview

Chapter two focused on the knowledge and behaviors content of the four art disciplines--the *what* to teach as art education. Chapter three presented a rationale for having aesthetics generalizations as a basic component of the curriculum planning process. Chapter four is concerned with the curriculum planning process--organization and arrangement of art experiences-- i.e. *when* to teach the *what*. Instruction, in contrast to curriculum planning and beyond the scope of this book, is concerned with *how* to teach--the approach, methods, techniques or experiences employed to facilitate the acquisition of knowledge or development of behaviors in art education.

Sections

This chapter can be best understood if it is considered in three sections. After a few definitions of terms, the first section looks at the foundational considerations for planning curricula. The second considers principles of arranging curricular components by creating a structure for a year or many years. The third section shows how to break down the basic considerations into specific items that can be meaningfully connected as the teacher plans years, courses, units, and encounters

Definitions

<u>Aims, goals, learner outcomes, and lesson or encounter objectives.</u> Aims, school philosophy, or mission statements express views of what schooling intends to accomplish. A vestige of educational philosophy may appear in statements made by a school board or teacher group, but the community values of a particular district will more strongly influence the tone.

General educational goals are sometimes derived from a mission statement and stated in separate sentences for easy reference. Often general education goals for a school make reference to what makes theirs a quality program (teacher qualifications, discipline, scheduling) rather than student goals for learning or learner outcomes as a result of that quality program. When written as learner outcome statements, general education goals refer to outcomes across all disciplines of the curriculum.

Recent emphasis on learner outcomes parallels the assessment movement and recognition of the need for observable evidence of what students have achieved. Learner outcomes are usually written in reference to student performance in a discipline area, but are more general than lesson or encounter objectives. Learner outcomes in art may also be described as visual arts goals written in terms of student observable behaviors.

As can be seen, there is a progression from a general level to specificity--from encompassing aims to general education goals to art goals or learner outcomes, to encounter or lesson objectives. As part of a school district's professional staff, the curriculum planner in art must demonstrate alignment to the general education goals of the district, state arts goals or standards, and possibly to national visual arts standards.

Curriculum. Curriculum is a plan for positive educative experiences for varying periods of time--an extended lesson to a year's plan in one subject to an entire K-12 art education plan. Although curriculum may refer to the multi-subject academic curriculum of an entire school district, that conception is not the focus of this book.

Art teachers continually make informal, small scale curricular decisions. How much help is given them in making these decisions? How many times does an art teacher realize, after the fact, that there was a great opportunity to emphasize something about art that could have been introduced in a lesson? How do art teachers translate recommendations for curriculum planning in methods text books into a plan to which they are committed?

Effective curriculum planning has never been easy. Curriculum planning progresses from the general to specific--from general encompassing ideas about art, as thoughts worthy of attention, to the exemplars, explanations and applications of each organizing big idea. Compatible with recommendations for general curriculum planning, DBAE advocates a written, structured and sequential curriculum in art that has a balance of attention to the four art disciplines-- aesthetics, art history, art criticism, and art production. Note that balance of attention or value is not measured in minutes.

Curriculum plans are complex theoretical assertions of what should work. They should be comprehensive, have complete coverage of content, and be cohesive (without internal contradictions or inconsistencies). So, curriculum planning is not just a smorgasbord of lessons no matter how innovative or well-composed they are individually. It involves planned exposure to major ideas in a field, from a platform (focus, rationale, or emphasis) to guide the selections of content and experiences that will bring students to recognize the point of each lesson, unit, or course of study. The platform or focus can come from community concerns, curriculum theories, aesthetics theories, cross cultural topics, current topics, time-honored themes, or compatible combinations of these. Curriculum is the organization and building of meaning through art learning year by year--vertical sequencing--and throughout each course or year--horizontal sequencing.

Scope: Basic Considerations

Context of art education

Planning an art curriculum involves establishing the scope or breadth of what is to be introduced and vertical sequence of content for each of the four disciplines, and within art production, for each major area of art production (sculpture, painting, fiber arts, etc.). Elements and principles by which they are organized are selected to enable the student to successfully give form to the production activity and help focus attention on the generalization of each encounter. Elements and principles are important enablers, but not the main focus of art learning.

What basic considerations lie behind the observable lesson? What goals are met? What characteristics of students are considered? For what kind of community is the art curriculum planned? The art curriculum planner considers these questions while outlining the breadth of basic components of the curriculum structure. The teacher can be thinking about the most defensible fit between (a) big ideas drawn from aesthetics, (b) examplars of art historical periods, styles, cultures (c) insights to be gained from criticism of diverse examples of works of art, and (d) concepts that an experienced art teacher can anticipate will contribute to creating art in a variety of forms using a variety of media and techniques. Figure 4.1 is a model of the basic considerations, content to organize, and vertical sequencing task facing an art curriculum developer. The basics must be considered separately then simultaneously, in structuring the curriculum.

Figure 4.1. Components of curriculum planning in art

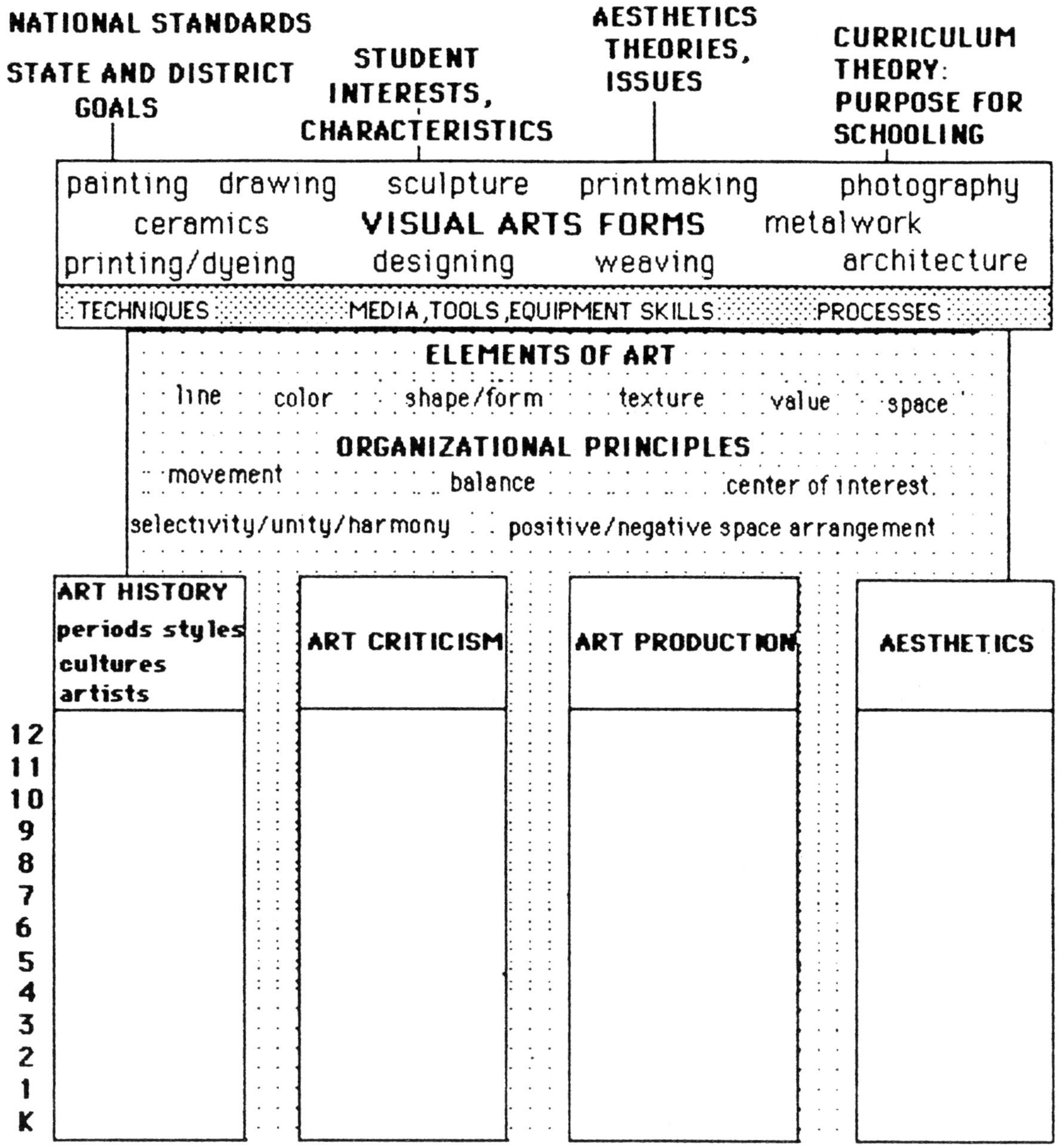

| NATIONAL STANDARDS | | AESTHETICS | |
| STATE AND DISTRICT GOALS | STUDENT INTERESTS, CHARACTERISTICS | THEORIES, ISSUES | CURRICULUM THEORY: PURPOSE FOR SCHOOLING |

painting drawing   sculpture   printmaking   photography
      ceramics   **VISUAL ARTS FORMS**   metalwork
printing/dyeing   designing   weaving   architecture

TECHNIQUES   MEDIA, TOOLS, EQUIPMENT SKILLS   PROCESSES

ELEMENTS OF ART
line   color   shape/form   texture   value   space

ORGANIZATIONAL PRINCIPLES
movement   balance   center of interest
selectivity/unity/harmony   positive/negative space arrangement

| ART HISTORY periods styles cultures artists | ART CRITICISM | ART PRODUCTION | AESTHETICS |

12
11
10
9
8
7
6
5
4
3
2
1
K

Goals or Learner Outcomes

Goals or learner outcomes may be framed by the art teacher or may be already established by the art department of a school district. Compare those existing goals with school district general education goals, state art goals or national standards. A grid chart serves this purpose well. Along one axis write key words of each general education goal. Along the other axis write key words of national standards or state fine arts goals. State fine arts goals may be written for music, dance, theater, and the visual arts. The curriculum writer's task is to find general education goals that can be met as the visual arts curriculum meets state fine arts goals. In the cell where two compatible goals intersect, the curriculum writer could write a visual arts goal which incorporates the language of both district general education goals and state fine arts goals. Careful attention to semantics is important here to clarify compatibility and the contribution of the visual arts to school goals in a **unique** way. The visual arts goals or learner outcomes thus formed should be written in observable, but general terms. For example, "Students will describe the relationship between subjects of visual art works and their cultural contexts".

Resist the temptation to try to make it appear that there is a match between every general education and state arts goal in the visual arts curriculum. Claiming that art can do everything is a weak position. Try to show that visual arts education meets most district goals in some unique way while it meets at least one of the state arts goals. It may be necessary to write more than one goal in a cell, but every visual arts goal derived by this process can be rephrased into subordinate goals aimed at different grade levels or courses later. Resolve any gaps or inconsistencies before continuing to build your curriculum with them.

Student Characteristics

Probably no one would advocate planning a curriculum without considering the nature of the student. At each grade level, there are wide differences in any group of students, but thinking in generalities helps set reasonable expectations for student capabilities. As the curriculum is being framed some categories of developmental characteristics to keep in mind are physical, social, intellectual, psychological, and graphic (Armstrong, 1979). Consideration of student interest categories such as myself, family, friends, animals, science and technology, nature and weather, fantasy, future entertainment, and beliefs can suggest topics, or motivating lesson openings. Many child and adolescent development sources plus the teachers' experience contribute to identifying age-appropriate student characteristics of which to be mindful in making curricular selections and decisions later in the process.

Aesthetics Theories

Chapter 2 included aesthetics as important content of visual arts education and Chapter 3 provided a rationale for it as a major component of the structure of visual arts curriculum planning. The aesthetics resource in Chapter 8 includes quotations from aestheticians representing a variety of aesthetics theories and issues to consider. The classification of quotations and generalizations derived from them by the aesthetics theory they represent helps in meeting the curriculum criterion of comprehensiveness and avoid a teacher's personal philosophic preference. In planning a visual arts curriculum, teachers can tally the frequency of generalizations used from each aesthetics theory to check for planned introduction of a variety of theoretical positions to students.

Curriculum Theories

Curriculum theories may be the least familiar basic component to the art curriculum planner although most have some ideas about why schools should exist. Finding a theoretical foundation to which one can have a commitment will aid in the art curriculum having a direction to which all components will contribute. A curriculum that holds together makes sense to outsiders.

Art curriculum, being a theoretical assertion of what could work, should operate from a commitment to some "platform". Platforms are positions based on beliefs about the purpose of education, and predominant focus on one helps avoid internal inconsistencies in a curriculum.

Reasons offered as the purpose of education are extensive. The slogans that exist and represent rationales for education constitute a menu of value choices. The imperative "You gotta have art" calls for art because it is a time-honored discipline without which one cannot live. "Saleable skills" suggests a sociological concern about education for the purpose of getting a job. In a shrinking world, "Multicultural education" emphasizes the understanding of the commonalities and differences between people across the globe. All of these slogans may have merit, but in some communities, emphasis on one may gain greater nods of recognition. This calls for a review of purposes of schooling to see if an art curriculum planned for a school district can be aligned with any existing curriculum theory or must formulate its own platform.

Curriculum theorists categorize conceptions of the purposes met by formal education in a variety of ways, but generally they fall into *sociological* or *contextual* and *non-sociological* or *essentialist* theories. The following paragraphs will briefly differentiate the curriculum theories shown in Figure 4.2 by their non-sociological or sociological orientations.

Figure 4.2 **Theoretical choices for curriculum structuring decisions**

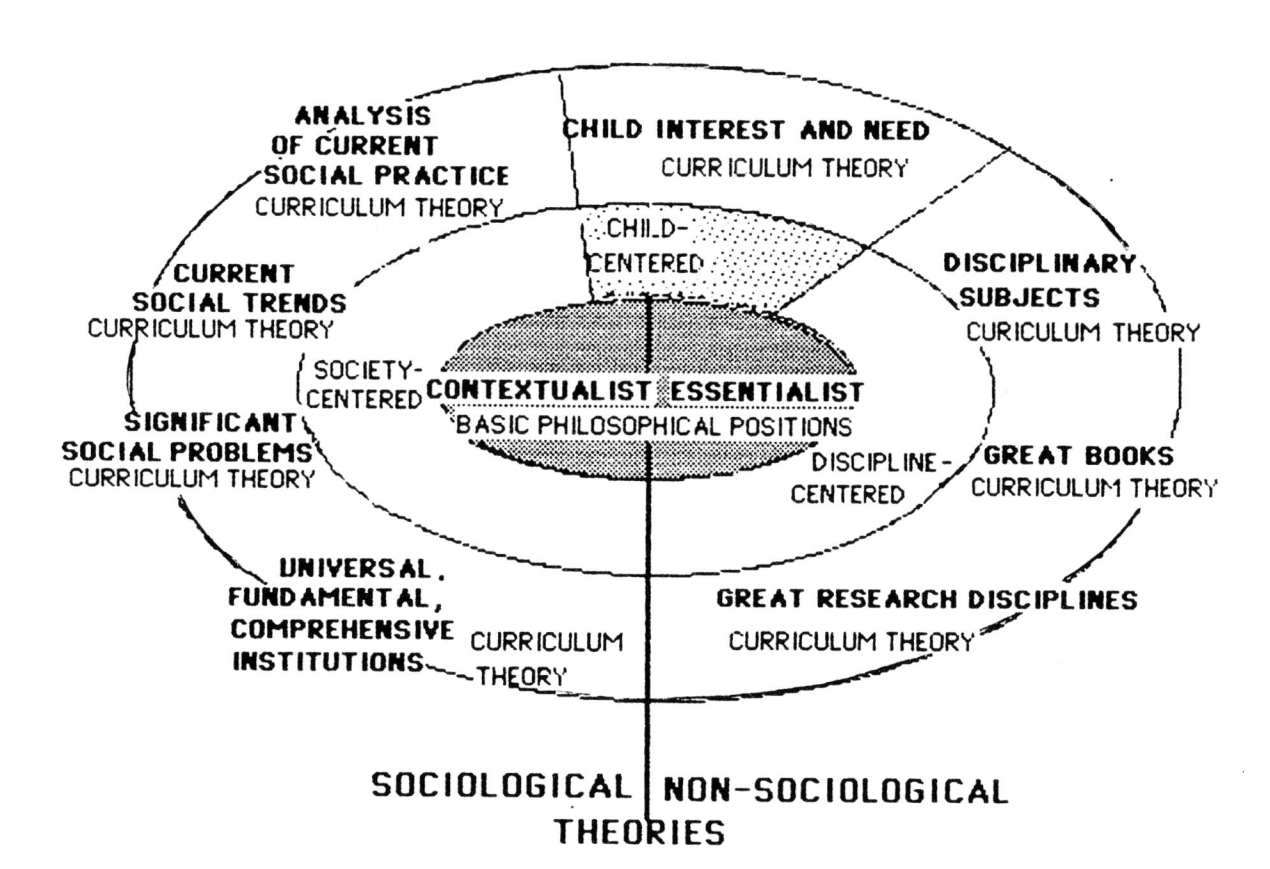

Non-sociological theories. Using the *non-sociological* categories reviewed by Smith, Stanley and Shores (1957), the visual arts could be taught as a Disciplinary Subjects where exercise and drill could develop facility in some mental or motor skill. Brainstorming classes that attempt to encourage divergent thinking for problem solving exemplify a contemporary application of this very old theory. But practicing process without meaningful application on content has questionable value. For example, in art, manipulative skills are developed to effectively operate on media to effect meaning and purpose, not as ends in themselves.

Translating the Great Books theory to great works of art, would seem to provide a good rationale for art in schools since in teaching art history we may use works of art that have achieved time-honored recognition and many served as moral values exemplars. However, a concern for relevance today and a cross time and cross cultural consideration of the visual records of peoples would disallow strict adherance to that theory. It inadequately accommodates non-traditional roles of art and a life-oriented education that reflects many values of our pluralistic society.

The Child Interest and Need theory influences choices that any curriculum writer makes. No matter which theoretical approach is chosen, the concern with the nature of the student is a variable in the process of selecting content that is appropriate for the conceptual level and interests of the student. How might an art curriculum that claims to be based on children's interests and needs consider different community values, comprehensiveness of content, and minimal state education mandates?

If art is justified as a Great Research Discipline, it might seem logical to utilize the elements and principles of art or the four art disciplines to structure art curricula. It was pointed out in Chapter two, that because the elements and principles are enablers or means to more valid ends of art education, they are inappropriate bases on which to structure curriculum.

One might assert that DBAE exemplifies a great research disciplines curriculum theory, but DBAE is not a curriculum and emphasis on (a) the meaningful integration of the art disciplines and (b) cross cultural understanding and contextual relevance rather than accumulation of knowledge would need to expand a narrow conception of the Great Research Disciplines curricular theory. Traditional Western interpretations of art would need to expand to consider the contemporary and cross-cultural context, emerging conceptions of art, and exemplars which make the study of art a rich and relevant component of life.

Art curriculum will develop manipulative skills and intellectual skills, develop concepts of the elements and principles of art, use time-honored art exemplars, and plan art that is appropriate for the nature of the student, but content taught "in the service of" does not qualify as a structural component. The exception would be if a community strongly values one of those directions. A compromise may be necessary until the community has had opportunity to expand their conception of visual arts education through the evidence of the enacted curriculum plan.

Sociological theories. The *sociological* curriculum theories (Smith, Stanley and Shores,1957) are concerned with societal relevance although they vary in perspectives. The Current Social Practice theory looks to the present status and societal needs, such as international crises, as the basis for decisions as to what to teach. In a rapidly changing society, what is relevant one day may be changed the next.

Curriculum based on the Social Trends theory, would avoid becoming stagnant and out of touch with reality, but may find it difficult to meet the constant need for change brought on by competition between nations and technological innovations. Communities would have to have a strong commitment to this purpose for education to financially support the research and technical equipment needed for a predictable future. In today's high tech world, it is difficult for schools to keep up with change, much less, accurately predict it.

Social problems command the attention of many communities. Schools may be expected to correct societal ills that spill over into school hallways and classrooms. Reactionary tactics call for policing the schools. Educational theorists ideally advocate curriculum designed to develop students' intellectual skills to prepare them to reconstruct society--to solve problems that exist or are yet to emerge.

Different sociological theories may provide appropriate rationales for art education depending on the community or world situation contexts. The sociological theories vary from those that attempt to be relevant, but are adaptive rather than progressive, to those that are impressive in the challenge they accept, but become complicated in implementation. That is hardly surprising since values of a pluralistic society confound the decisions of our greatest leaders.

The Universal, Fundamental, Comprehensive Institutions theory is a sociological theory that can accommodate the positive aspects of many theories. The complex name suggests desirable qualities of other theories--universal, fundamental, comprehensive. The sociological term "institutions" refers to means that humans have developed to meet social, economic, political, and philosophic needs. These are functional groups, customs, and characteristics of all evolving cultures that are likely to continue existing in some form in the 21st century.

The visual arts have been influenced by and have played important roles in the evolution of these institutions. Institutions influence the value attached to art forms and even contributed to the record we have of those cultures no longer in existence. Hence, value statements regarding the visual arts can be easily formulated in relation to any of the institutions and explored in terms of one or more aesthetics theories. Those value statements may be expressed in terms of (a) what artists do, (b) what they "say" in their work, (c) the subjects which they feel important enough to recreate or comment on, or (d) what has been valued as art by people at different times throughout history or in different cultures.

If one can broadly interpret these "institutions", they can contribute to the thematic structure of visual arts curricula; for throughout history, artists from all cultures have given form to ideas related to these categories of institutions and their subgroups. Sub-sets of the four institutions have been the subjects of artistic creations or have influenced art work by artists using a variety of styles, media, and interpretations of reality. With the help of the teacher, students can identify with such themes and see the translation to meaningful situations in their own lives. Table 4.1 shows some possible subsets of sociological and non-sociological curricular theories described in the preceding pages and offers suggestions for unit or encounter themes that reflect the philosophic orientation of the theory.

Table 4.1 **Curricular theories, possible subsets of theories, and suggested unit themes based on each curricular theory**

Disciplinary Subjects Theory:

Perceiving exercises	Contour drawing for seeing detail
	Perspective: Rules for showing depth
	Gesture: Seeing the whole
	Structure of the skeleton and muscles
	Figure drawing: Proportions
	Color wheel, color schemes, color moods
Deductive reasoning exercises	Combining incongruities
	New uses for common objects
	Tessellations
	Metamorphosis
Manipulative skill exercises	Wheel throwing
	Ink pen stroke variations
	Water color techniques

Great Books Curricular Theory:

Gods, supernaturals	Revered personages
	Human-god relationships
	Standards for human behavior
Heros, idols	Patriots, leaders, royalty
	Olympic champions
	Adventurers
	Physical ideals
Symbols	Role of religious symbols
	Symbols for order in daily life
	Gestures: Signals to expressions
Ideals, values:	Slaves, serfs, superiors
Work	Remuneration
	Contemplating and celebrating feelings

Table 4.1 **Great Books Curricular Theory**, continued

Family	Roles, structures
	Rules, rights, responsibilities
	Life styles
Health	Environment, food, shelter
	Care giving and social concerns
	Social concerns
raditional roles of art	Religious communication
	Patronage
	Political or Spiritual effect

Child Interest and Need Curricular Theory:

Self	Personality
	Achievement
	Physical self
	Satisfying needs in desirable ways
Nature	Tree climbing
	Spring (Fall, Summer) flowers
	Taking care of nature/Growing things
Animals	Domestic friends
	Wild animals/ Circus animals
	Animal care
	Psychic animals/ communication
Friends	Same sex/opposite sex
	Fairweather friends, popularity
	Relationships
	Clubs, organizations
Family	Family fun
	Family routines
	Extended families/ single parent families
Recreation	Outdoor activities: Winter /Warm weather
	Indoor activities
	Movies, plays, theater, dance performances
	Special lessons, competition
	Summer camps

Table 4.1 **Child Interest and Need Curricular Theory**, continued

Neighborhood or community	Annual events: Parades, festivals
	Visiting neighbors, special persons
	Cooperating, seeking commonalities
Food	Special event foods: Holiday, ethnic, favorite
	Healthy foods
	Eating out
Fantasy	Day dreams/Nightmares
	Play acting
	April fool jokes
Holidays, events	Vacations
	Easter, Halloween, Thanksgiving, Chinese New Year, Hanukkah, Christmas
Future careers	What I want to be, Individuality

Great Research Disciplines Curricular Theory:

<u>Art production</u>

Two dimensional visual arts	Drawing
	Painting: Watercolor, acrylic, and others
	Graphic arts
	Photography
	Media arts
	Printmaking
	Architectural and Interior design
	Weaving
Three dimensional visual arts	Sculpture
	Fiber arts
	Ceramics
	Architecture
	Jewelry and metal work
	Basketry
	Woodworking...furniture, objects

Table 4.1 **Great Research Disciplines Curricular Theory**, continued

Conceptual, combinations and non-traditional visual arts	Miniatures
	Performance or interactive visual arts
	Stage craft and design
	Quiltmaking and other Traditional women's visual arts, Egg art
	3-d paintings, weavings
<u>Elements and principles</u>	Variations in visual forms across cultures
<u>Art history</u>	
Cultures	Commonalities and uniquenesses
Periods, dynasties	Across time sequences of development
Civilizations	Influences on their rise and fall
Countries	Characteristic styles, symbolism, use of art
Artists, styles	Innovators, Trend setters, Refiners
<u>Aesthetics</u>	
Theories	Imitation/Expression/Formalist, Institution
Issues	Experience, process, media, semantics...
<u>Art Criticism</u>	
Types	Journalist, Scholarly, Academic, Personal
Stages or approaches	Describe, Analyze, Interpret, Evaluate

Current Social Practice Curricular Theory:

Vocational careers in art	Plans for in and around where we live
	Arranging enhancements for our homes
	Selling through art
	Graphic design/Package design
	Inviting, announcing with elegance
	Space planning (city/mall)
	Internet art
	Professional artist
	Cartoonist, Illustrator
	Art dealers, gallery directors
	Wearable art

Table 4.1 **Current Social Practice Curricular Theory**, continued

Avocational use of art	Artist
	Support the arts
	Kits and crafts
Research and writing about art	Art across time and cultures
	What's good, bad, in, and out about art?
	What is art and what is it good for?
Art education	Creatively facilitating/enlightening
	Why is art here? Explaining collections

Current Social Trends Curricular Theory:

Work	Location, gender issues, child care
Transportation	Mono rail, Bullet trains
	Stealth bomber, Supersonic Concorde
	Electric automobiles
Communication	E-mail vs. pony express
	Interactive videoconferencing
	Information highways. World wide web
	Classification systems.
Space	Cyberspace
	The undersea canopy
	Tomorrow's community: Arcosanti
	Universe: Space exploration
Entertainment: Active/Passive	Video games
	Sports

Universal Fundamental Comprehensive Institutions Theory:

Social institutions	Family
	Social group
	The artworld
	Recreation clubs
	Ethnic groups
	Folkways, customs
	Common interest or support groups
	Religious-orientation social activities

Table 4.1 **Universal Fundamental Comprehensive Institutions Theory**, continued

Political institutions	Government by the people...
	Protocol
	International relations
	Democratic process
	Citizenship means...
	Access to influence
	Court system
Economic institutions	Energy
	Food, shelter
	Workplace
	Population growth, control
	Natural resources
	Climate changes
	Money management: Budget to stock market
	Profits/losses...The bottom line
Philosophical institutions	Ethics, moral attitudes
	Supernatural beings, events
	Rituals, celebrations
	Religions, sects
	Insurgents
	Aesthetics
	Values enacted in the real world
	World power status and obligation
Social Problems Theory:	
Person in society	Alienation
	Solitude, Privacy, Interacting in a group
	Self-made person
	Inner-directed/other-directed
	Interdependent/co-dependent/independent
	Ethics: self-serving/nurturing
	Self-centered/socially-centered
	Gender specific roles or not

Table 4.1 **Social Problems Theory**, continued

Family and friends	Divorce
	Abuse
	Partners, Relationships. Marriage.
	Trust. Respect
	Responsibility. Self-control. Road rage
	Support. Safety.
	Self love, Need to be loved, Love of others
Health concerns	Aging problems/Infant death syndrome
	Contaminated food or water supply
	Epidemics
	Insect invasion
	Smoking/Drugs
	Malnutrition
	Disease: respiratory/heart/cancer/ depression
Industrialization/urbanization/ Information processing	Internet: Uses and abuses
	Labor-management relations
	International human rights/child labor
	Pollution and environmental hazards
	Unemployment, economic dislocation
	World-wide interdependency
	Group deliberation and decision-making
Group values, status and conflict	Value of life, Violence
	Prejudice; Class, race
	Cultural diversity/ pluralism/integration
	Oppression. Politics. Democracy
	Double standards
	Movie/TV rating or producer responsibility
	Community action
	We-they-us
	Competition/ Cooperation/ Consensus

Adapted from Jinayon, S. (1989). <u>Suggested themes for retrieval of art reproductions based on curricular theories</u>. M.S. Thesis in Art Education. Northern Illinois University, School of Art, DeKalb: IL 60115

Any of the sociological or non-sociological curricular theories may give primary focus to the formation of a rationale and structure of the curriculum. A curriculum which focuses on creative solutions to social problems confronting students would have different unit titles than one focusing on forms of visual art as a Great Research Discipline or units titled for jobs for which art students train as in a Current Social Practice curriculum orientation.

Discipline-based art education can operate within any of the major curriculum theories. The exemplars chosen might vary, but all art disciplines and their integration can contribute to the inferred goals of these varying views about the purpose of education. The possibility of combining generalizations from the aesthetics resource in chapter 8 with subthemes of the Universal, Fundamental, Comprehensive Institutions curriculum theory will be further developed as the "Universal Aesthetics Themes" art curriculum in this chapter and in chapter five.

Connecting with the Community

In attempting to decide on a curricular theory or platform, it is advisable to do an informal sociological analysis of the community for which the curriculum is planned. A sociological analysis uncovers, values that linger from historical backgrounds of communities; from changing composition of the population; the economic base of the community; influential power groups or individuals; community traditions or events; and social, religious, and recreational offerings. The point is to ascertain how the community can be helped to value the art program by thoughtfully presenting it to them. The art teacher can select a curriculum platform to which the community is likely to be receptive. The art program, using unit themes derived from a curriculum theory that corresponds to the community values, acknowledges the community as a stakeholder in the schools and structures an art program with integrity that is responsive to the community concerns. The program acknowledges its role to educate the students and community that is offering the art program in the schools.

Curricular theories provide the curriculum developer with choices on which to focus for a cohesive platform to guide a rationale for art in the curriculum with a consistent emphasis. A theory base helps teachers stay on track with a justification for art education to which they have a commitment.

Structure

The term "discipline", used in the context of discipline-based art education, refers to fields of study that have conceptual structure and modes of inquiry (Clark, Day and Greer, 1987). In reference to the conceptual structure of a discipline, the structure may be a set of fundamental generalizations, principles or basic abstract ideas that organize the field of knowledge in a cohesive interrelated whole, focus the investigation and inclusion of knowledge for the discipline, and provides the basis for discovering what else exists in the discipline (Saylor & Alexander, 1966). Doll (1989) calls the structure a webbing of big ideas and concepts that holds any body of subject matter together and to which all items of subject matter must connect. The definitions by both Doll, and Saylor and Alexander support the Clark, Day and Greer recommendation for structure in art education curriculum planning which seeks to integrate the four disciplines of art. Both interpretations are relevant to planning curricula in art around aesthetics generalizations that (a) serve as the webbing to relate content from the other three art disciplines in art encounters and (b) provide a picture of the overall network of ideas that can give purpose and meaning to the art activities in which we engage our students.

Structure refers to the skeleton of ideas from each essential component of curriculum planning in art. Each idea can be stated for naive levels of understanding and progress toward statements having greater sophistication. In contrast to curriculum as just a bunch of lessons, the art curriculum planner should create an ideational structure or scaffolding.

An ideational scaffolding suggests thematic courses and "units of study". Rather than start with the matching of content, teachers might decide on a structure of units which corresponds to their rationale for art as part of formal education (curricular and aesthetics theories) and units which reflect the commitment that the curriculum developer has made.

Figure 4.3 exemplifies the descending order of inclusiveness in ideational curricular structures starting with a course addressing generalizations for units which encompass encounters of integrated activities related to the four art disciplines. Each activity considers the content to be learned, such as concepts to be developed, and the instructional approach to be employed as part of an encounter activity to encourage art related behaviors.

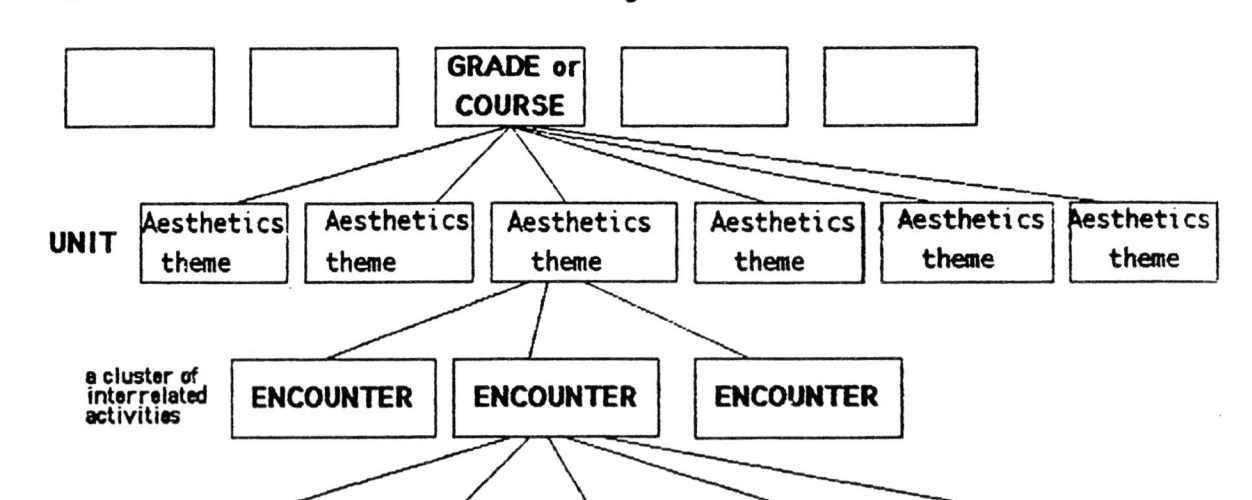

Figure 4.3 **Model for structure or organization of an art curriculum**

```
                        GRADE or
   ☐        ☐           COURSE          ☐        ☐

        Aesthetics Aesthetics Aesthetics Aesthetics Aesthetics Aesthetics
UNIT    theme      theme      theme      theme      theme      theme

a cluster of
interrelated    ENCOUNTER    ENCOUNTER    ENCOUNTER
activities

   art history   art criticism  concept-developing  art production   aesthetics
   Activity      Activity       Activity            Activity         Activity

   Inquiry       Inquiry        Inquiry             Inquiry          Inquiry
   approach      approach       approach            approach         approach
      +             +              +                   +                +
   Content       Content        Content             Content          Content
```

Adapted from Efland, A. (1977). <u>Planning art education in the middle/secondary schools of Ohio</u> Columbus, Ohio: State of Ohio, Department of Education.

Figure 4.4 is an example of ideational scaffolding as it might be realized in one encounter (Unit 1, Encounter 3 of this Grade 4 art curriculum structure). Each unit name or "big idea" is influenced by a different aesthetics theory. Each unit would involve related encounters. Each encounter includes meaningfully integrated activities that deal more specifically (less inclusively) with the knowledge and behavioral content related to the aesthetics generalization that is shortened into the theme statement.

Figure 4.4 **Example of a structure of a curriculum for one year**

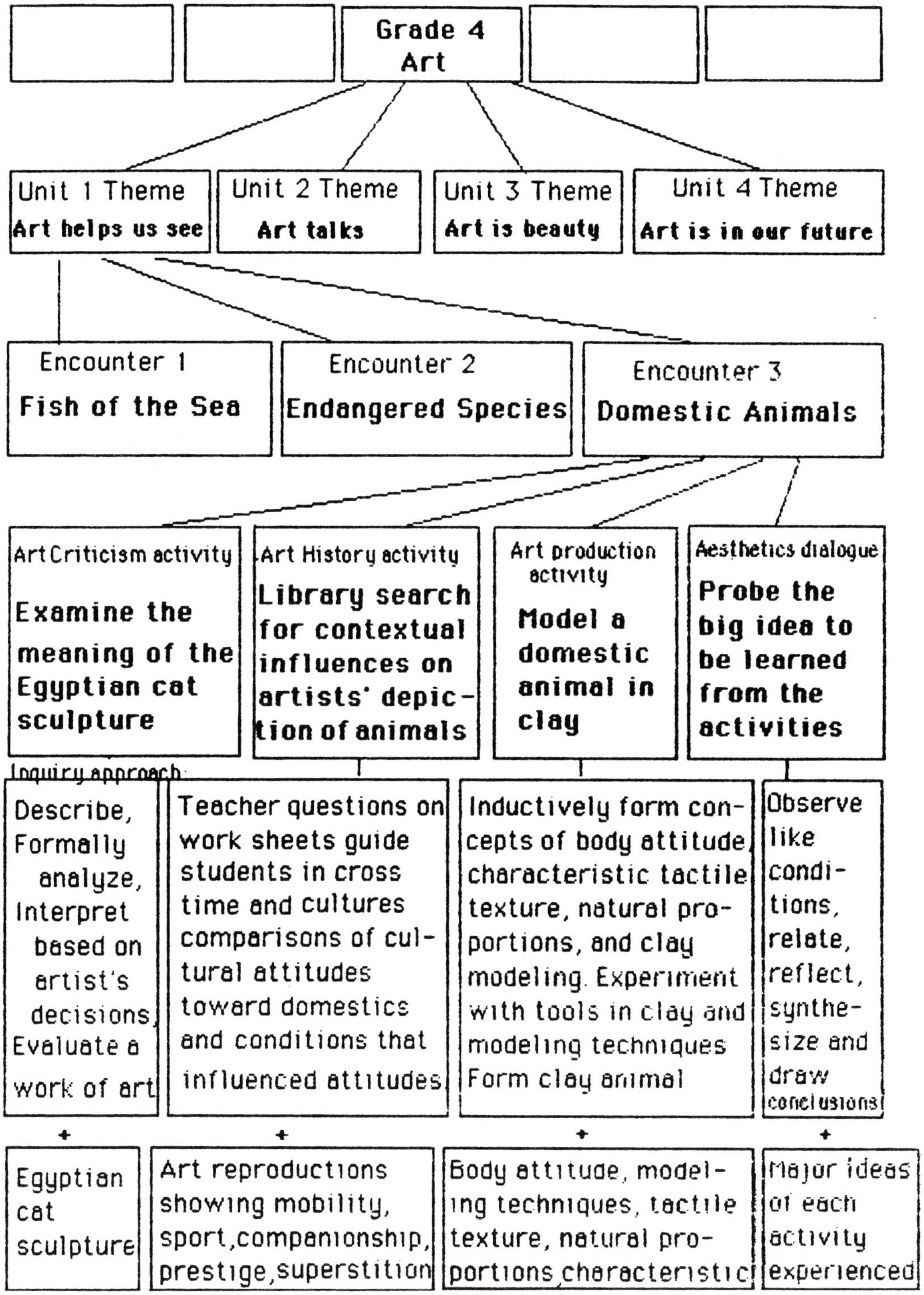

```
                            Grade 4
                             Art
         ┌──────┬─────────────┼─────────────┬──────┐
    Unit 1 Theme  Unit 2 Theme  Unit 3 Theme  Unit 4 Theme
    Art helps us see  Art talks  Art is beauty  Art is in our future
```

Encounter 1	Encounter 2	Encounter 3
Fish of the Sea	Endangered Species	Domestic Animals

Art Criticism activity	Art History activity	Art production activity	Aesthetics dialogue
Examine the meaning of the Egyptian cat sculpture	Library search for contextual influences on artists' depiction of animals	Model a domestic animal in clay	Probe the big idea to be learned from the activities

Inquiry approach:

| Describe, Formally analyze, Interpret based on artist's decisions, Evaluate a work of art | Teacher questions on work sheets guide students in cross time and cultures comparisons of cultural attitudes toward domestics and conditions that influenced attitudes | Inductively form concepts of body attitude, characteristic tactile texture, natural proportions, and clay modeling. Experiment with tools in clay and modeling techniques Form clay animal | Observe like conditions, relate, reflect, synthesize and draw conclusions |

+ + + +

| Egyptian cat sculpture | Art reproductions showing mobility, sport, companionship, prestige, superstition | Body attitude, modeling techniques, tactile texture, natural proportions, characteristic | Major ideas of each activity experienced |

Progression from general to specific learnings can apply also to a progression from inclusive advance organizers to specific concepts as illustrated by analogy to a chest of drawers. Figure 4.5 uses animals as a subsuming concept and its subordinate concepts in descending order of inclusiveness, i.e. from animals to dogs to working dogs to beagles. In this illustration, to develop specific subordinate concepts of "working dogs", a beagle would be differentiated from a St. Bernard by attention to its visual attributes. Photographs or actual objects could be the focus of teachers' questions so that students inductively form the specific concept by observing the attributes and responding to the questions (Armstrong, 1986). Out of all there is to teach, plan to select those specific concepts that help students grasp the big idea of the lesson.

Figure 4.5 A model of subsuming and subordinate concepts

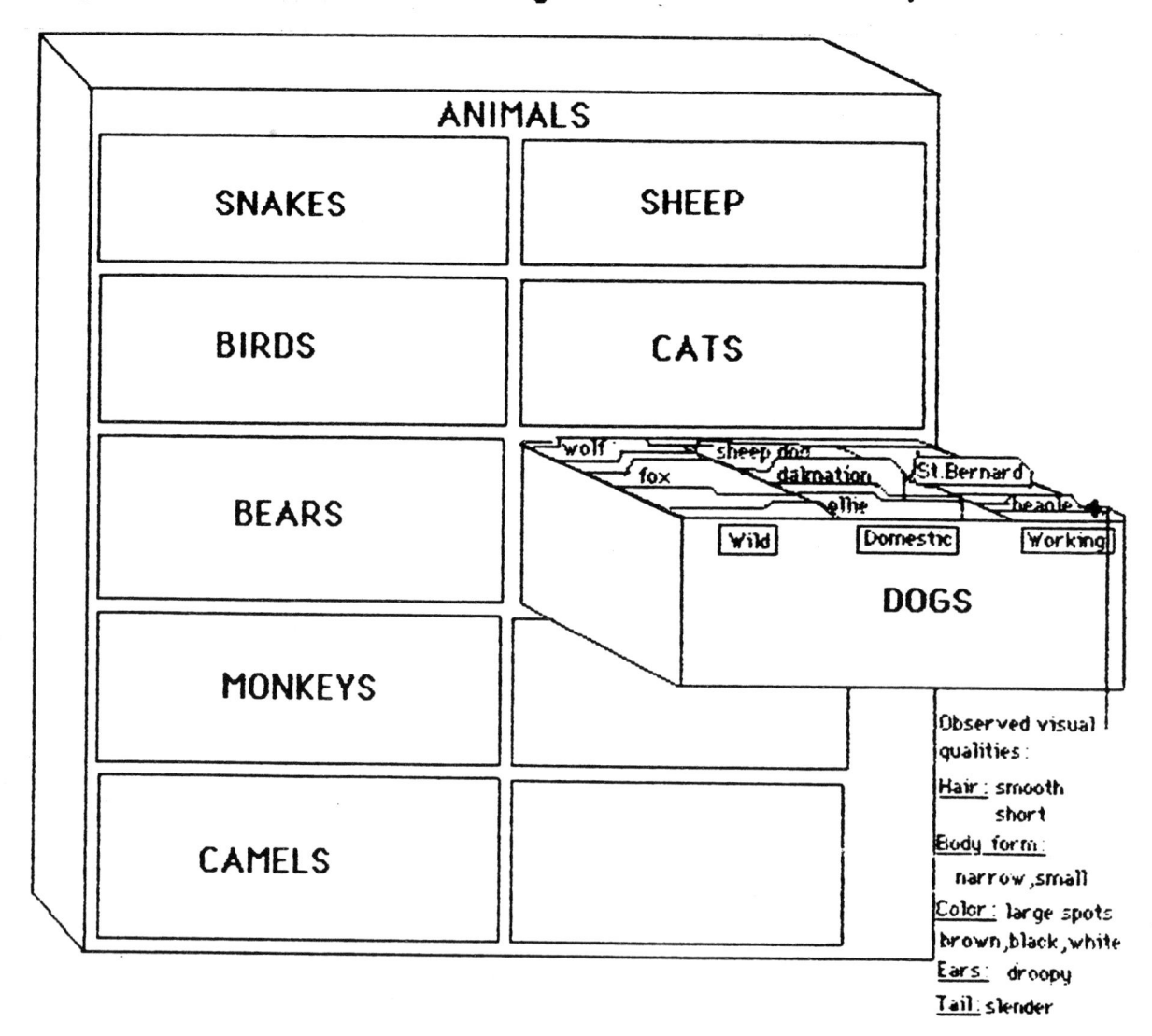

A structure of content contributes to comprehensiveness-- exposure to possible experience in art--, avoids redundancy, and outweighs fears of loss of spontaneity. Actually, greater freedom to vary exists when possibilities emerge for the teacher who knows where the unexpected can contribute to and substitute for elements in the expected, structured learning experience. Curriculum planning which proceeds from the general to the specific is less likely to leave unintentional gaps in knowledge or to neglect thinking through the application of theory into practice. It assists teachers in identifying the expected evidence of student learning.

Advance organizers

In creating a structure, the curriculum planner should identify "a hierarchical series of advance organizers (in descending order of inclusiveness), each organizer preceding its corresponding unit of detailed differentiated material" (Ausubel,1965, p.112)*. An advance organizer is a generality that is already somewhat familiar to students--experience, concept, a topic, information, a subject, or theme. Beginning a unit or lesson with an advance organizer focuses students' attention and serves as a reference point for the new information to be learned. Change the chest of drawers analogy to a chest of drawers labeled for different kinds of clothing. The teacher might say "Today we are going to explore more in our sock drawer. We know about uses of socks, but there are many new and exciting things to discover about them." Substitute a chest of "art elements" drawers and open "line" to explore how many subordinate concepts of line can be selected for introduction at different grade levels for specific activities where their expansion of "line" can serve students' ideas best.

*In R.Anderson and D. Ausubel (Eds.). Readings in the psychology of cognition. New York: Holt, Rhinehart and Winston. By permission of Harcourt, Brace & Company.

Aesthetics Generalizations as Structure

Russell (1991) describes a perspectives approach to integrating aesthetics in the art curriculum whereby students develop an understanding of different vantage points of aesthetics issues. Statements by persons in the art world (includes aestheticians) can represent aesthetics theories. Generalizations derived from such quotations can be selected for their appropriate conceptual complexity or can be simplified. Structuring curriculum using aesthetics generalizations as advance organizers of units and encounters which expose students to the variety of aesthetics theories and issues is a perspectives approach. In age-appropriate terms, the teacher calls attention to the contrasting theories to help students recognize the varying stances and accept the fact that differences exist for good reasons. For young students this means honest translation of theories to the conceptual level of the student.

A slogan or theme may be derived from a sophisticated generalization for quick communication when introducing encounters or titling displays of student work. For example from the quotations categorized as "Art as imitation", one could select any of these generalizations that vary in complexity:

Natural rules are imitated in the structures of works of art.

Art portrays a kind of truth that may not stand up to empirical investigation or may be a partial truth.

Art is based on observation of objects, but goes beyond copying.

Works of art can depict reality, or an ideal based on reality.

Art imitates to different degrees.

Art imitates nature's activity.

From the category of quotations classified as "Art as form", one could select:
> Illustrational painting, losing interest in its subject matter, ceases to be art.
>
> Some descriptive paintings may have formal significance and, therefore, qualify as works of art.
>
> Works of art have unity, complexity, and intensity.
>
> Recognizable objects in art are as important as organized elements.
>
> Organization is more important than replication.

From the category of "Art as expression", a teacher could choose:
> Artists collaborate with an assumed audience and express emotions.
>
> Artists use projection and introjection of feelings in works of art.
>
> Art represents universals by the artists' treatment of the subject.
>
> Expression of the work relates the artist and the owner.
>
> Art is a distinctive interpretation of life experiences.
>
> Art is an expression of the artist.

Statements can be selected by the curriculum writer for compatibility with other disciplines, curricular theory, art goals, available art exemplars, and logical ordering of concepts.

Hence, generalizations derived from selected statements by aestheticians can be used in structuring the art curriculum and serve as advance organizers. This would mean starting with an inclusive organizer--an aesthetics generalization such as "Functional objects are enhanced by their visual organization". One of several less inclusive organizers would be the principle "Enhance objects by relating surface to form" . This organizer, in turn subsumes concepts relating to surfaces, textures, types of forms, and ways of relating all the elements which could be developed for a successful production activity or to assist in expressing observations in the art criticism activity. A course can procede from the inclusive generalizations to specific, contributing concepts in an encounter as shown in Figure 4.6.

Figure 4.6 **Example of an aesthetics generalization as an advance organizer of an encounter**

ART MAKES THE FAMILIAR STRANGE
SO IT CAN BE SCRUTINIZED

Armstrong, C.(1997). Aesthetics Resource, Section 2.4, Item 136

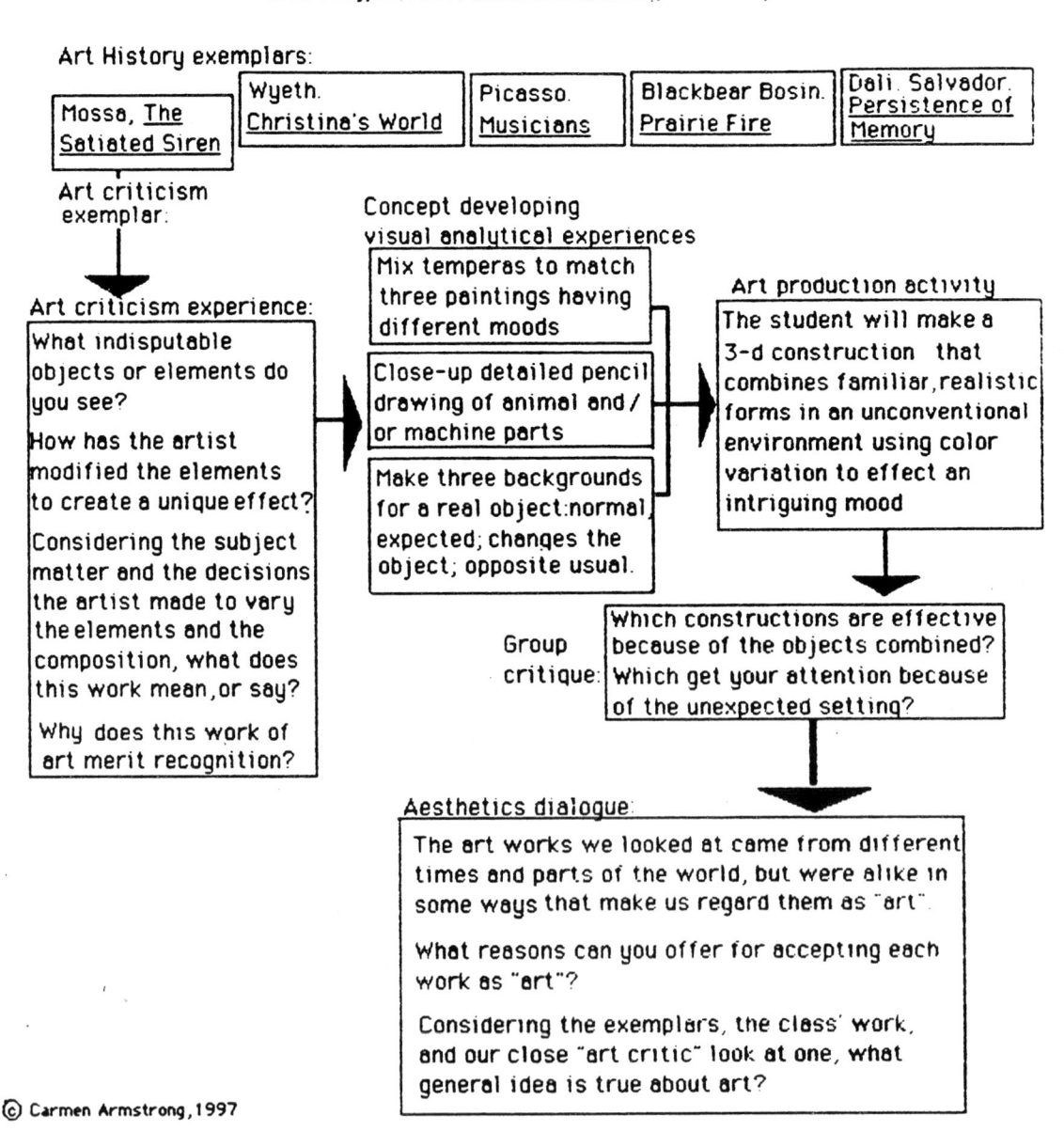

Art History exemplars:

| Mossa, The Satiated Siren | Wyeth. Christina's World | Picasso. Musicians | Blackbear Bosin. Prairie Fire | Dali. Salvador. Persistence of Memory |

Art criticism exemplar:

Art criticism experience:
What indisputable objects or elements do you see?

How has the artist modified the elements to create a unique effect?

Considering the subject matter and the decisions the artist made to vary the elements and the composition, what does this work mean, or say?

Why does this work of art merit recognition?

Concept developing visual analytical experiences

Mix temperas to match three paintings having different moods

Close-up detailed pencil drawing of animal and/or machine parts

Make three backgrounds for a real object: normal, expected; changes the object; opposite usual.

Art production activity
The student will make a 3-d construction that combines familiar, realistic forms in an unconventional environment using color variation to effect an intriguing mood

Group critique:
Which constructions are effective because of the objects combined? Which get your attention because of the unexpected setting?

Aesthetics dialogue:
The art works we looked at came from different times and parts of the world, but were alike in some ways that make us regard them as "art".

What reasons can you offer for accepting each work as "art"?

Considering the exemplars, the class' work, and our close "art critic" look at one, what general idea is true about art?

© Carmen Armstrong, 1997

Each generalization in the aesthetics resource is coded to indicate which question or issue is addressed by the quotation. The responses to the major questions are organized and coded by the theoretical position which the quotation represents. It is the curriculum planner's responsibility to expose students to the breadth of positions available for consideration as well as the idea that there may be expanded attributes that define art and more reasons for valuing art in the future. So a teacher may select at least one generalization from each of the theoretical positions which answer either the "What is art?" or the "What is the value of art?" questions and a choice of generalizations dealing with other issues for each grade level of the curriculum being planned. Some generalizations are less sophisticated and some that seem above student conceptual level can be reworded more simply by the teacher.

Synthesizing the Components
Identifying Subsets of the Basic Considerations

Curriculum planning is like laying all your cards on the table. If goals or student outcomes, aesthetics generalizations, student characteristics, and curriculum theory are basic considerations, the teacher may rightly feel that curriculum planning is still too abstract. Each of these basic considerations can be broken down into subsets. Subsets of curriculum theiries are shown in Table 4.1. Subsets of characteristics of students (e.g. physical, intellectual, psycho-social, or graphic development) each have more specific, age-related characteristics. Subsets of art history such as periods, cultures, types of art forms, or styles can each be further broken down to consider for planning the curriculum. Viewing subsets lets the curriculum planner perceive many possibilities for meaningful integration of components in encounters.

Sometimes school district goals seem far removed from art goals. The art teacher can plot them on the format in Appendix 1 and write art learning outcome statements in the spaces where two goals intersect and warrant emphasis as a goal, choosing language that merges the intent of general education goals and art goals.

Figure 4.7 Learner outcomes format: Relationship between art and general education goals of school districts

ART GOALS

General Education Goals	1 Qualities and meaning of works of art	2 Influences on artists and art	3 Processes tools and art media	4 Create art	5 Characteristics and value of art	6 Sensory environm't. awareness
1 Communicate effectively/ organize ideas						
2 Accept cultures different from own		Example of alignment and vertical sequencing: **Visual arts learner outcome 2-2** The student will describe the relationship of different cultures to human artistic contributions and their value				
3 Show positive self-concept		K-H Students recognize that people make art for many reasons or functions in a culture. 2-H Students describe themes that are common across cultures and time in art. 3-H Students identify art work from particular culture 4-H Students recognize art associated with particular artists and styles.				
4 Know about physical health and hazards		5-H Students describe influences of other cultures on the human-made environment and their own art. 7-H Students compare and contrast art from different periods of history, offering reasons for difference 7-H Students document societal influences on art.				
5 Demonstrate critical thinking / inquiry behaviors		7-H Students trace change in art styles over time.				
6 Solve problems						

As exemplified by the elaboration of where art goal #2 and general education goal #2 merge in Figure 4.7, each new art learning outcome statement can be restated as appropriate to the level of achievement anticipated for each grade level or cluster of grades. Thinking at this time in terms of planning curriculum for one year, goals or learner outcomes, can be numbered for further use for each grade level or cluster of grade levels. Hypothetically, there may be ten goals (G) addressed at one grade level which coded for use in charting them as G1 to G10.

The teacher may similarly identify six characteristics (C) of students at that grade level that need to be taken into consideration in topics introduced, instructional approaches taken, or art history exemplars chosen. They might be listed and coded as C1 to C6.

Any curriculum theory chosen as a rationale and focus for planning art curriculum can be analyzed into subsets that contribute ideas for inclusison as unit topics, or subject matter addressed in encounters. An example of subsets of each curriculum theory (T) was shown in Table 4.1. Eight subsets of the curriculum theory chosen might be coded T1 to T8 (Note: The number is a procedural suggestion and not meant to suggest the number of subsets that a teacher should choose).

In considering the basic contribution of pervasive ideas of art from aesthetics, select appropriate generalizations that represent each theory and appropriate issues for each grade level. The generalizations in the aesthetics resource are numbered, making it easy to list choices, once the decisions are made. Aesthetics generalizations (A) might be coded as A1 to, posssibly, A15.

A curriculum accountability example using the coded subsets is shown in Figure 7.3 . The teacher who goes through this procedure can document the validity, comprehensiveness, and consistency of the curriculum based on what was intended. This process of identifying and making specific use of the basic considerations in planning curriculum is the foundation for a strong rationale or mission statement and a guide for making choices.

Is there a preexisting structure of generalizations? There is no established structure which comprises a hierarchy of learning in aesthetics. Clusters of theories have been generally recognized, but they, nor the issues addressed by aestheticians, have any inherent ideational scaffolding or hierarchical order. The most defensible reason for selecting an order of generalizations and encounters is the logical building of concepts to be addressed in the encounters. For example, student success in creating patterns might be enhanced by prior understandings of "regular repeat", "unity", and "variation of shape". Pattern would fit under generalizations dealing with enhancement of visual forms which do not need to precede or follow another generalization. However, attention to basic shapes and related visual qualities might be helpful prior concepts to have grasped.

Teachers might develop a series of ideas that are important for students to understand. These may be perceived as general purposes for studying art. Which ideas should precede others? Analysis of those ideas could reveal affinity to various positions in aesthetics. By a search of the aesthetics literature or with the aid of the aesthetic resource, generalizations might be ordered to support the series of ideas.

Once the lists of subsets are created for each grade level, the task is to look for logical combinations while fitting in all subsets which the teacher intends to consider in the curriculum planning process. Curriculum planning which meaningfully integrates basic categories is like fitting together pieces from several or more puzzles where you are looking for pieces that are cut alike, but deal with different components of an art encounter, for example, aesthetics, institutions of evolving cultures, the students, and art learning outcomes. As in Figure 4.8, one would stack the pieces that are conceptually compatible and would fit together for meaningful learning. The art exemplars, forms, techniques and media become added pieces to integrate. The idea would be to create a new context of relatedness for the puzzle pieces where a stack becomes components of the art encounter plan.

Figure 4.8 **Model for aligning puzzle pieces from basic art curriculum components with a generalization as organizer**

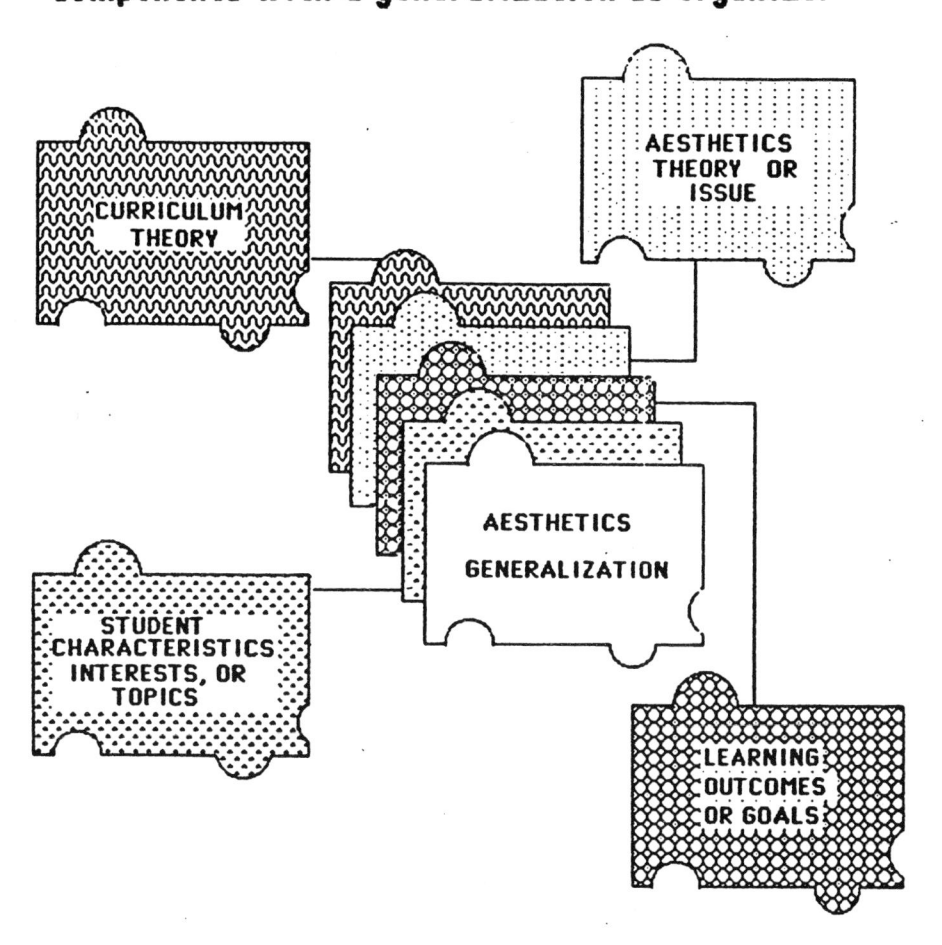

Figure 4.9 shows how one encounter, with three encounter objectives related to the art disciplines (AP, AES, AH, and AC) and the encounter generalization, enables the synthesis represented by students' big idea of the encounter (bottom grey box). Students were prepared by the art experiences planned by the teacher to formulate one or more pervasive ideas about art related to the generalization on which the teacher based the encounter activities.

Figure 4.9 Hypothetical example of curriculum scaffolding: Alignment from general to specific

Student interest in science fiction

Aesthetics Generalization
Artists invent but revisit nature to vitalize the image invented

Theme or Slogan
Art is basic to knowing

District Goal
Create with knowledge

Great research disciplines curriculum theory: Scientific inquiry in art

General art goal
The student identifies major art historical figures, periods, influences

General art goal
The student correctly uses art media and processes in art production activities

Learner outcome
The student records specific visual qualities in observations of objects from life and art

Learner outcome
The student supports conclusions about unfamiliar art with relevant reasons

AH | Encounter objective | AC
The student differentiates work by Pippen, Bellows, and O'Keeffe from Dali in terms of context and visual qualities

AP | Encounter objective
The student makes a clay surreal construction with illusionary depth and detail

AP AES | Encounter objective
The student logically synthesizes learning from criticism, history, and production activities

Concept: Perspective — Concept: Clay techniques — Concept: Detail with clay — Concept: Surrealism

Artists study the real to imagine and invent new fantasy situations.

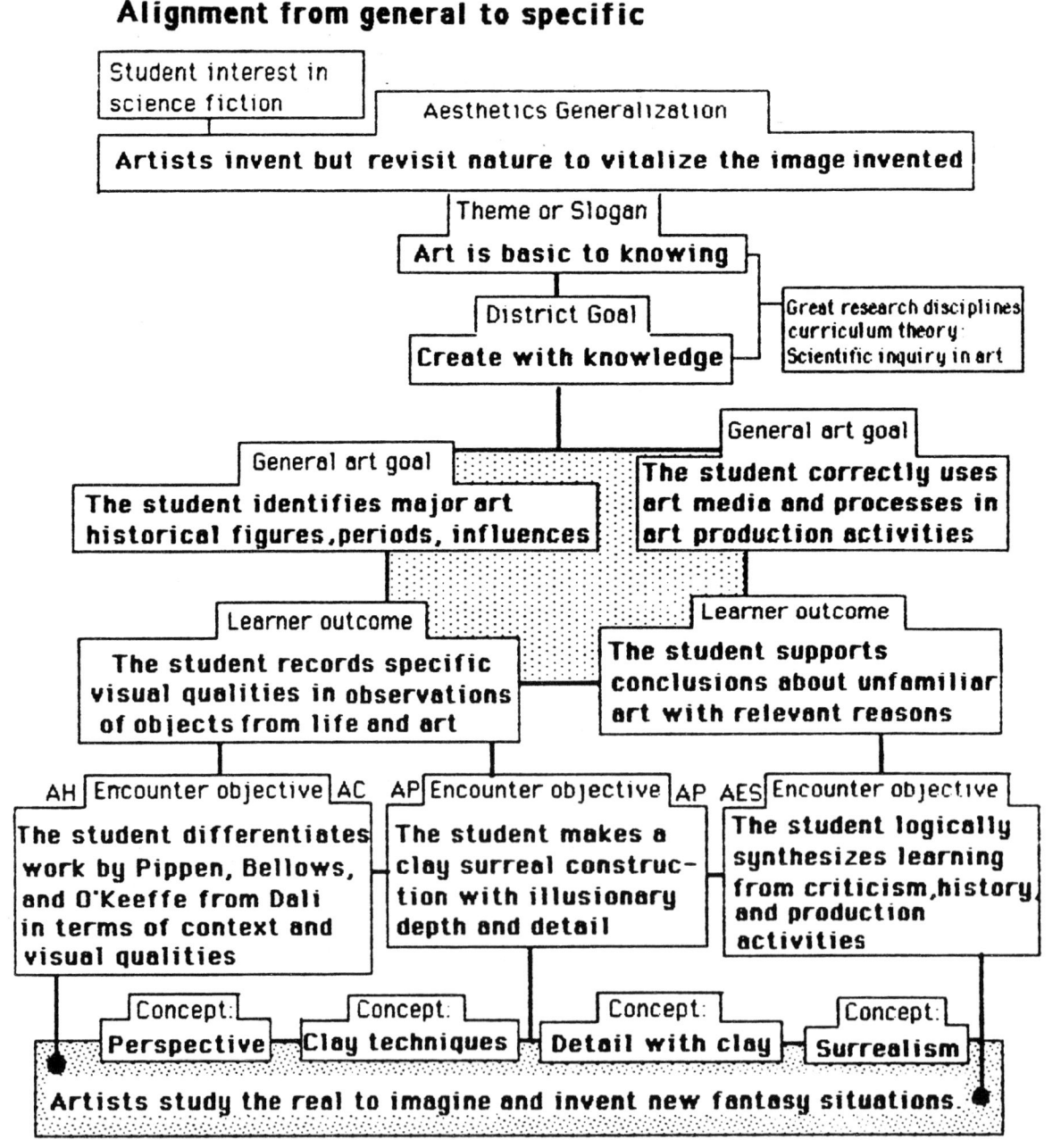

A Duality: The Universal Aesthetics Themes Curriculum

A *duality* is a state or quality of something that has dual purpose. A duality is a way to merge one's commitment to two emphases. The Universal Aesthetics Themes curriculum structure is a duality because a generalization that serves the intent of addressing aesthetics and the context that influences art is a duality. It combines theoretical roots to make serious study of art socially relevant. Hypothetically, a structure of duality generalizations as advance organizers of an art and life-oriented curriculum could be derived from (a) a perceived compatibility between the institutions of evolving cultures (Universal, Fundamental, Comprehensive Institutions theory) and (b) responses to questions about the nature and value of art from representatives of seven categories of aesthetics theories in the aesthetics resource. Armstrong (1988) explains this life-oriented modification of aesthetics generalizations by associating generalizations drawn from aesthetics with themes derived from major institutions of all evolving cultures--social, political, economic, and philosophical-- and works of art. A hypothetical part of the process is shown in Figure 4.10 with possible fits between some of the curriculum theory subsets and aesthetics theories and issues.

Selections from a hierarchical, vertical sequence of subordinate concepts related to the elements and principles of art, behaviors associated with discipline role models, as well as contemporary or historical art exemplars could be clustered meaningfully under each thematic duality. The curriculum planner would attend to how each encounter would help students meet one or more of the stated art goals.

Figure 4.10 Unit or encounter themes derived from alignment of aesthetics theories and subsets of curriculum theories

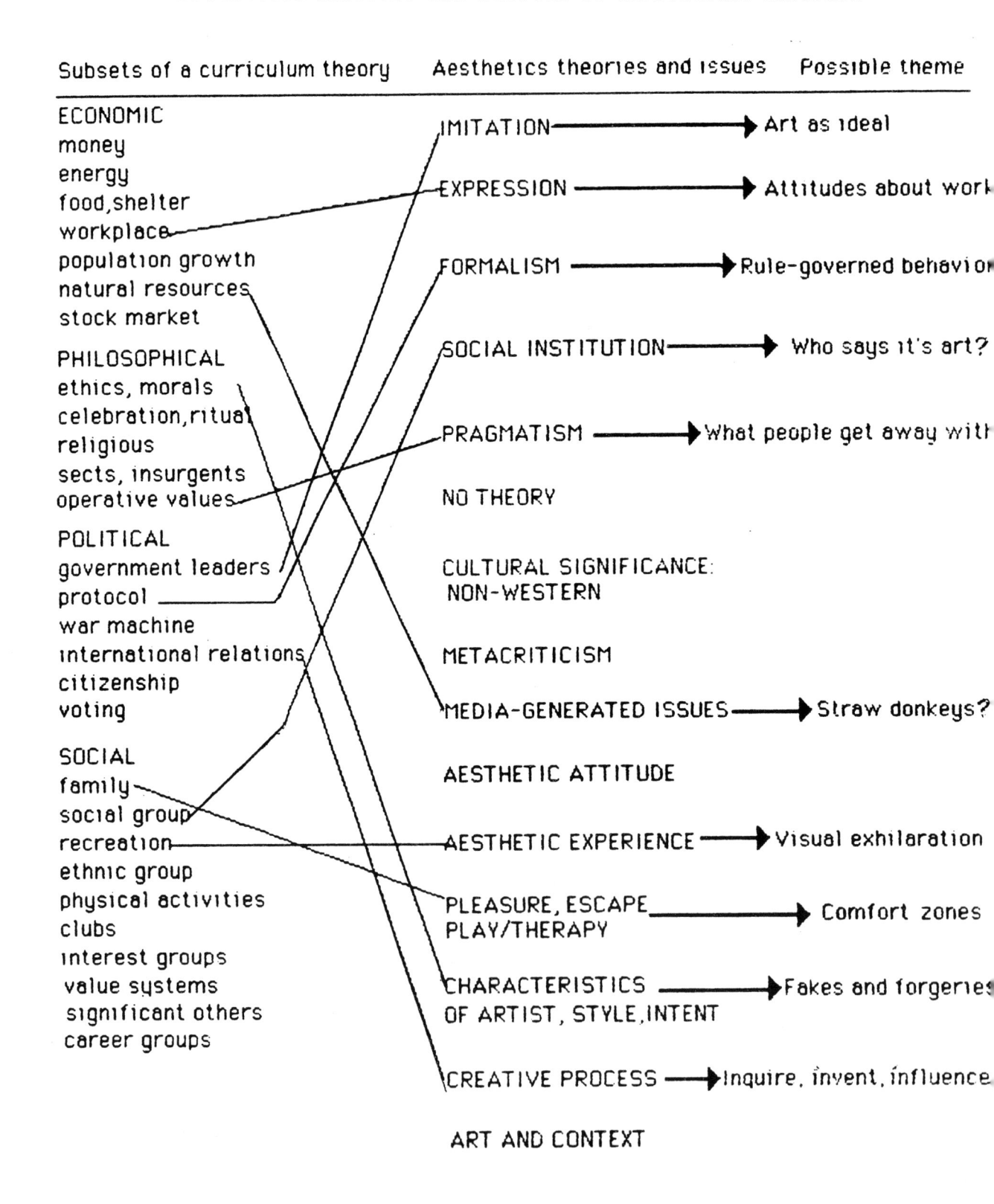

Subsets of a curriculum theory	Aesthetics theories and issues	Possible theme
ECONOMIC money energy food, shelter workplace population growth natural resources stock market	IMITATION	Art as ideal
	EXPRESSION	Attitudes about work
	FORMALISM	Rule-governed behavior
PHILOSOPHICAL ethics, morals celebration, ritual religious sects, insurgents operative values	SOCIAL INSTITUTION	Who says it's art?
	PRAGMATISM	What people get away with
	NO THEORY	
POLITICAL government leaders protocol war machine international relations citizenship voting	CULTURAL SIGNIFICANCE: NON-WESTERN	
	METACRITICISM	
	MEDIA-GENERATED ISSUES	Straw donkeys?
SOCIAL family social group recreation ethnic group physical activities clubs interest groups value systems significant others career groups	AESTHETIC ATTITUDE	
	AESTHETIC EXPERIENCE	Visual exhilaration
	PLEASURE, ESCAPE PLAY/THERAPY	Comfort zones
	CHARACTERISTICS OF ARTIST, STYLE, INTENT	Fakes and forgeries
	CREATIVE PROCESS	Inquire, invent, influence
	ART AND CONTEXT	

Most schools have a limited number of poster size art reproductions, or other art exemplars. Libraries, community artists, museums, and historic sites offer alternative sources of art works. Early in the curriculum planning, an inventory list should be made of all available art reproductions or originals. With a complete list of available art, side by side with lists of categorized aesthetics generalizations selected, and a list of subsets of your chosen curriculum theory, the best reinforcing matches can be made for meaningful integration. The grade level by grade level identification of art forms, media and processes can be another list to be consulting simultaneously with the subsets of specific concepts to be developed at one grade level. This integration process is suggested in Figure 4.12 by the lighter ovals.

Figure 4.11 shows a different comparison between curriculum plannng and putting together a puzzle, to exemplify the integration of basic considerations and content in art education for encounters. One can imagine that the puzzle pieces are subsets of each major component that, when meaningfully fit together, complete an encounter or unit.

Figure 4.11 **A model of an encounter as all components fit together to create an integrated picture**

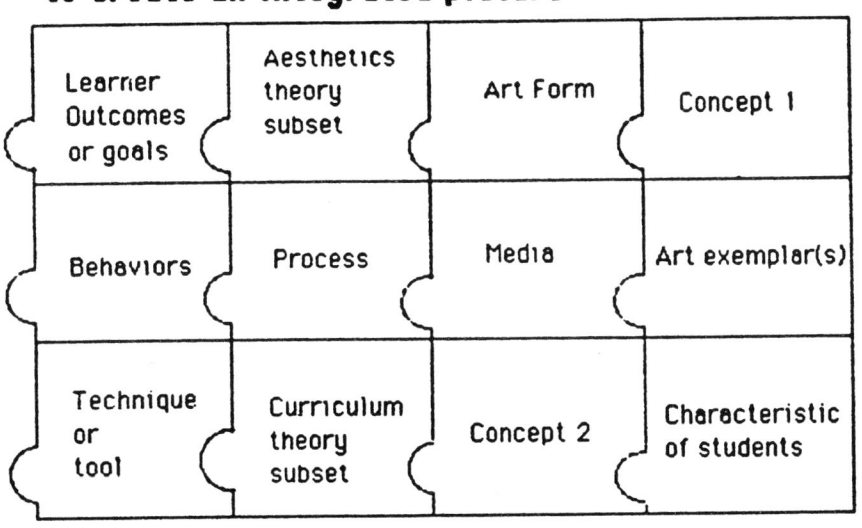

Learner Outcomes or goals	Aesthetics theory subset	Art Form	Concept 1
Behaviors	Process	Media	Art exemplar(s)
Technique or tool	Curriculum theory subset	Concept 2	Characteristic of students

In the Universal Aesthetics Themes diagram in Figure 4.12 clusters of content relate to merged aesthetics theories (light grey ovals) and institutions of evolving cultures (dark grey ovals). Each cluster represents components comprising units that focus on the generalizations that would be derived from this duality. The language of the generalizations serving as advance organizers for each unit and/or encounter would reflect the merger.

Figure 4.12 **Model for structuring comprehensive content around an aesthetics theory and institutions curricular theory merger**

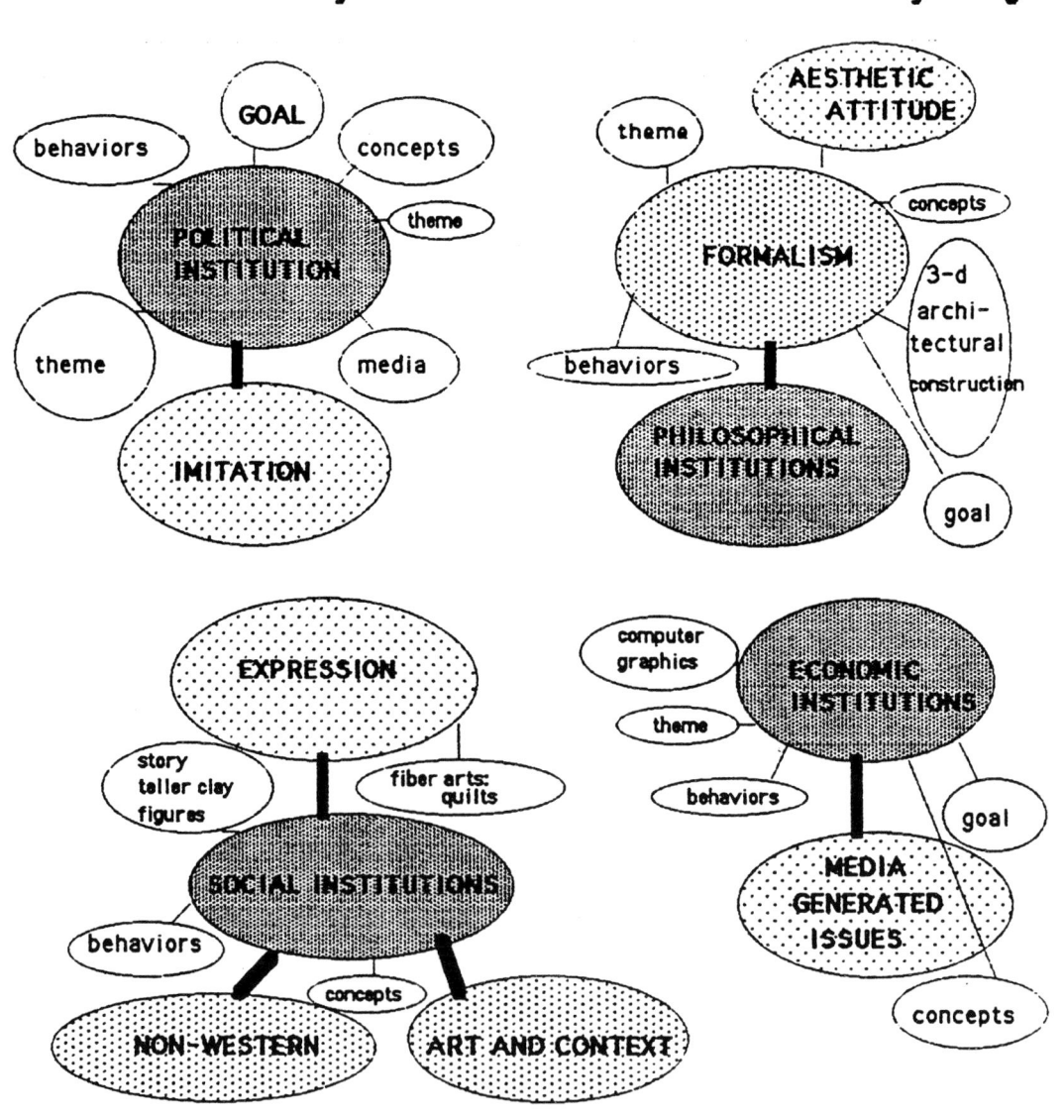

The inclusion of the major aesthetics theories exemplifies the perspectives approach (Russell,1991) to including aesthetics in curriculum planning. While each aesthetics theory should be represented by generalizations each year, subsets of aesthetics issues and institutions may be used more than once, or not at all in one year. Curriculum comprehensiveness would suggest having no significant omissions from the philosophical platform originally chosen.

Each encounter in the example in Figure 4.12 would have a theme, a translation of the generalization, that is worded for conceptual level of the student that suggests meaningful life truths. These could all focus on how artists have reacted to life situations...those universal, fundamental institutions through which all societies evolve. Addressed as deemed appropriate at various age levels, the themes could help students see art as personally relevant. The duality of the themes so derived does not isolate art from the life that has inspired so much of it. Identifying with such themes, the student can see the translation of the generalization of an encounter to situations in their own lives.

Sequence

Sequence refers to the considered arrangement of lessons which build on each other for greater meaning to the student. This may be "vertical" which refers to the ever-expanding level of sophistication developed by revisiting basic concepts of a structure as proposed by Bruner's spiral curriculum (1963) or "horizontal", i.e. from the beginning to the end of a period of study.

Vertical sequence refers to the expanding of the structure over a period of years with ever-increasing complexity which avoids redundancy. Horizontal sequence suggests a relatedness from lesson or encounter to encounter across a period of time within a unit, semester, or year. In other words students are having their prior learnings reinforced while always being challenged by expanding considerations, new variables that qualify prior simple ideas, or fine points.

Vertical sequence

In planning a year or several years of art education, the aesthetics resource helps the teacher to consciously tap a variety of answers to the basic questions asked by aestheticians which represent different theoretical positions. In keeping with philosophical inquiry, this introduces the opportunity for reflective consideration of opposing points of view.

After selecting diverse generalizations that seem to address important big ideas about art, the teacher can either (a) use the same array of generalizations at each level for curriculum planning, adapting their application appropriately for the students of specific groups, (b) select generalizations that in themselves seem to vary along a continuum of less to greater sophistication, or (c) restate generalizations into statements appropriate for the conceptual sophistication of primary, intermediate, junior high or high school levels.

The teacher would incorporate vertical sequence into the curriculum of the first option by varying the sophistication of the questions used to engage students in an aesthetics dialogue. Such instructional sequence is planned for by levels of sophistication of the "prompting" questions accompanying each generalization in the aesthetics resource. In addition, the art history and art criticism experiences, and art production activities, varied at each grade level, would provide opportunities to reinforce the generalization within any one cluster of grade levels.

In the second option, the teacher would use the more sophisticated generalizations as organizers at higher grade levels and find similar generalizations from the same aesthetic theory to introduce that theory to the lower grade levels but not necessarily in the same order. An example of this option is given under the <u>Within category hierarchies</u> section of this topic and in Figure 4.13.

Figure 4.13 **Vertical sequence: A restatement of a generalization at different conceptual levels**

High School/Adult:
> **SUBJECT MATTER DOESN'T MAKE SOMETHING ART: THE ARTIST APPROACHES THE WORLD AND HUMAN EXPERIENCES WITH A DISTINCTIVE GOAL IN MIND**

Junior High School:
> **ART EXPOSES US TO A VARIETY OF VIEWPOINTS FROM WHICH LIKE OR SIMILAR EXPERIENCES CAN BE UNDERSTOOD**

Intermediate grades (4-6):
> **ART PORTRAYS ARTISTS' VIEWS OF OUR ENVIRONMENT**

Primary grades (K-3):
> **ART SHOWS WHAT IS SPECIAL ABOUT THINGS WE KNOW**

Figure 4.13 is an example of how a teacher might restate a generalization to appropriately fit the conceptual levels of students at several grade levels. Choosing this option, the teacher might repeat the generalization suggested for each of the primary grades with different encounter activities or substitute other restatements of generalizations representing that aesthetic theory category. For example, "Artists show what it is like to be alone or with friends" is a simplification of the generalization "Artists communicate feelings about individual and group activity".

Horizontal sequence

Once teachers have decided on a number of "best fits" or art encounters, they have the task of horizontally sequencing those encounters. There may be several related encounters that cluster to form a cohesive unit. It is not implied that every encounter must flow to the next for an entire year, but it is not incorrect if it does. The basic idea of horizontal sequence is that conceptual learning from one instance should contribute to the meaningfulness or comprehension of the next over a period of time. Planning around learning periods of uninterrupted days of school helps reduce the review time necessary to get students back on track. It is a sound practice to have the school calendar at your elbow when planning. Figure 4.14 shows how a course can be divided into units of different lengths with varying numbers of encounters that are comprised of varyng numbers of activities.

Figure 4.14. **Dividing a course into units, encounters, and activities**

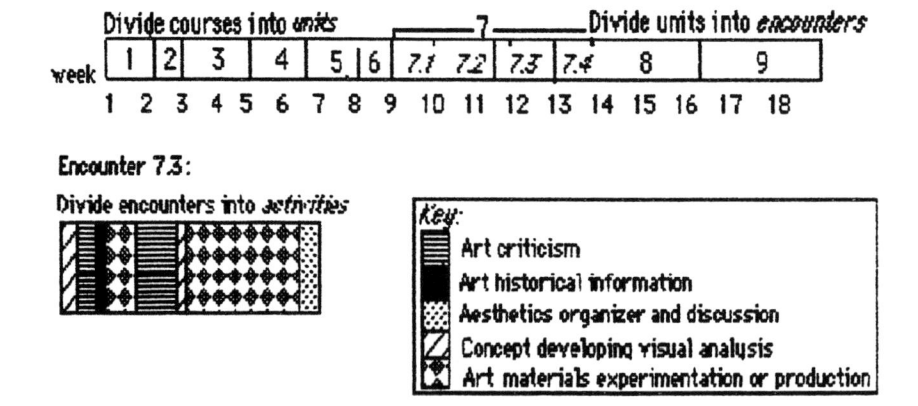

Summary

Preparation for student success is the commitment of the teacher in curriculum planning, but as large a task as it may be, it is continuous. While a basic scope and sequence may be appropriate for a number of years, specifics may change. New mandates may bring the need for modifications. Relevance of current affairs may make subject substitutions more meaningful. It is possible that school themes or collaborations with other disciplines would enter into the ordering of encounters. Student interests could be the influence on order.

School districts do not have elastic budgets nor extended school hours. New kinds of experiences planned will demand new resources, and different classroom time and physical arrangements. As teachers become more selective, they will look for the integration of activities that make <u>most sense</u> in terms of the anticipated learning outcome. Art teachers may reallocate some of the time and dollars normally spent to support art production activities. Just as exposure to art of the past is necessarily distributed throughout the K-12 art educational experience, so the exposure to any art production media, process, skill, or technique will need to be thoughtfully introduced at the best time for what it can contribute to the encounter. Individual teacher judgment may decide that charming, but shallow activities may not provide sufficient benefits to be retained. Having a meaningfully integrated art curriculum does not necessitate abandoning a teacher's existing, good art curriculum. It may just mean reshaping and expanding it. A teacher might trade off dollars and time spent for some production activities in order to give students practice in formulating their thoughts about art verbally.

The structuring of content contributes to comprehensiveness in planning and that means students are exposed to many ideas. Structure helps avoid redundancy and its attitudinal consequences for students. Structure, rather than constricting spontaneity, actually permits greater freedom to vary, because when possible alternatives appear, the teacher knows where and when the unexpected can contribute to and substitute for components in the planned curriculum. Curriculum planning which proceeds from the general to the specific is less likely to leave gaps or to neglect thinking through the application of theory into practice and recording evidence of student learning.

5. PLANNING THE COMPONENTS OF MEANINGFUL ART ENCOUNTERS
Definitions

Reference was made to encounters in previous chapters. An *encounter* is a cluster of related art experiences which (in keeping with current educational reform) includes experiences in aesthetics, art history, art criticism and art production. In contrast to a "lesson" which suggests a 45 or 50 minute class period, an encounter is an extended lesson that varies in length. For a brief example, an encounter may involve student research on Northwest Coast Native American totemic images that is related to a planned design abstraction problem. Students might be guided in an art criticism experience with actual totem poles at a museum of natural history or reproductions of them in the classroom. They may be led by the teacher into an aesthetics dialogue about the reasons why these wood carvings, that primarily had sociological value when carved, are valued as "art" today. These experiences would be an encounter--a lesson extended in time from one class period to more and that possibly occurs in different locations.

Aesthetics defies consensus concerning answers to its basic questions. Therefore the aesthetics *generalizations* must be conceived of as possible statements on which to focus in art encounters that can be exemplified by art works and are worthy of discussion. Generalizations in the aesthetics resource (chapter 8) are derived from philosophical quotations by persons of the artworld. Aestheticians spend lifetimes examining encompassing ideas about art, yet many never arrive at answers that are considered sufficient to others. The deep thinking and serious consideration of these debatable statements are worthy of class time. Conceptions of what constitutes "art" in school, can expand to include discussions that are engaging and challenging. Students have the capacity to formulate ideas that need to be heard.

The *integration* of the four art disciplines suggests an embeddedness. The encounter is not made up of an unrelated series of activities, but activities drawn from each of the four disciplines that reinforce each other and connect to the organizing generalization. The generalization might first suggest an activity related to one discipline of art then expand to include activities from the others. It could be a special art production activity that would send the teacher looking for related art history exemplars and a rationale for its relevance and value in an aesthetic theory. A cluster of historical exemplars showing common subject matter but widely differing interpretations (as exposed in the art criticism experience) could motivate the teacher and/or students to seek explanation in aesthetic theories. They could help explain the differing interpretations and contribute to valuing individual interpretation in students' art productions. The teacher might select a generalization by thinking through the point of a favorite art experience.

A Universal Aesthetics Themes Encounter

The aesthetics resource in chapter 8 helps teachers who want to structure socially relevant encounters that emerge from the study of art (Armstrong, 1988, 1990b). Figure 5.1 suggests how an art teacher can integrate aesthetics with relevant life-oriented situations. Generalizations about art reveal commonalities as well as varieties of attitudes in the art of cross cultural and across time exemplars that are concerned with similar themes or subject matter. In the example of Figure 5.1, the Economic subset of the Universal, Fundamental, Comprehensive Instititutions curricular theory is combined with the Art as Expression aesthetics theory. From this duality emerges the generalization: "Art gives form to ideas and attitudes about work as it relates to sustaining life". This generalization serves as the organizing idea of the art-in-life oriented art encounter.

Figure 5.1 Plan for an art encounter that merges aesthetics and curriculum theories in its organizing generalization

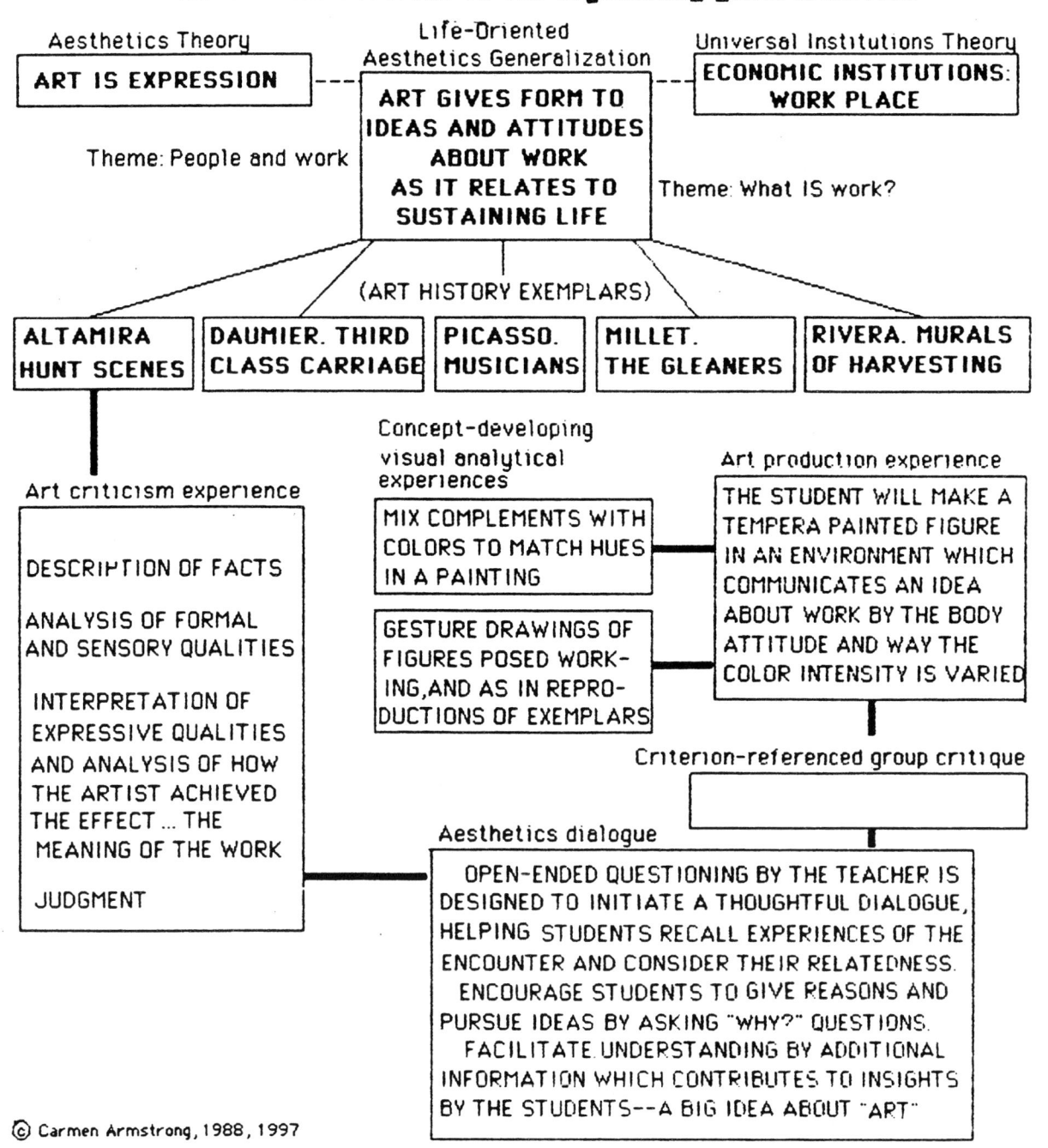

Aesthetics Theory
ART IS EXPRESSION

Life-Oriented Aesthetics Generalization
ART GIVES FORM TO IDEAS AND ATTITUDES ABOUT WORK AS IT RELATES TO SUSTAINING LIFE

Universal Institutions Theory
ECONOMIC INSTITUTIONS: WORK PLACE

Theme: People and work

Theme: What IS work?

(ART HISTORY EXEMPLARS)

| ALTAMIRA HUNT SCENES | DAUMIER. THIRD CLASS CARRIAGE | PICASSO. MUSICIANS | MILLET. THE GLEANERS | RIVERA. MURALS OF HARVESTING |

Art criticism experience

DESCRIPTION OF FACTS

ANALYSIS OF FORMAL AND SENSORY QUALITIES

INTERPRETATION OF EXPRESSIVE QUALITIES AND ANALYSIS OF HOW THE ARTIST ACHIEVED THE EFFECT ... THE MEANING OF THE WORK

JUDGMENT

Concept-developing visual analytical experiences

MIX COMPLEMENTS WITH COLORS TO MATCH HUES IN A PAINTING

GESTURE DRAWINGS OF FIGURES POSED WORKING, AND AS IN REPRODUCTIONS OF EXEMPLARS

Art production experience
THE STUDENT WILL MAKE A TEMPERA PAINTED FIGURE IN AN ENVIRONMENT WHICH COMMUNICATES AN IDEA ABOUT WORK BY THE BODY ATTITUDE AND WAY THE COLOR INTENSITY IS VARIED

Criterion-referenced group critique

Aesthetics dialogue
OPEN-ENDED QUESTIONING BY THE TEACHER IS DESIGNED TO INITIATE A THOUGHTFUL DIALOGUE, HELPING STUDENTS RECALL EXPERIENCES OF THE ENCOUNTER AND CONSIDER THEIR RELATEDNESS.
ENCOURAGE STUDENTS TO GIVE REASONS AND PURSUE IDEAS BY ASKING "WHY?" QUESTIONS.
FACILITATE UNDERSTANDING BY ADDITIONAL INFORMATION WHICH CONTRIBUTES TO INSIGHTS BY THE STUDENTS--A BIG IDEA ABOUT "ART"

© Carmen Armstrong, 1988, 1997

Art History

The aspects of discipline experiences have been introduced in this book and many other places, so focus will be on preparation for the encounter.

Historical exemplars of a common theme, "work", suggested by the generalization are drawn from across cultures and time. Contextual information is researched to plan study sheets, games, or activities. Students determine why it was important to have made the art work of the time and how it fit into the lives of people at that time and place. In class discussion of the students' findings might compare and contrast the body language from different cultures and times, e.g. Rivera's harvesting murals with Millet's The Gleaners and Daumier's Third Class Carriage. Insights to different interpretations combine information gained from external cues found in researching historical context questions with internal cues gleaned from the art criticism experience. Cross cultural comparisons can be a bridge to seeking situations that are roughly parallel in our society.

Art Criticism

Teachers can plan to engage students in art criticism experiences with one of the art historical exemplars. Teachers prepare for facilitating meaningful art criticism experiences by careful selection of works that help make the point of the generalization, by carefully analyzing the work before leading the class in the art criticism experience, and planning for the students' involvement, for example, by classroom arrangement so all students have equal opportunity to observe and respond. Since they have been selected for some commonalities, it may help students to notice qualities of the art work being discussed if teachers ask them to look for differences between it and the other art historical works.

Art Production

Although art making experiences can evolve out of the nature of the discussion. it is more responsible to plan for their relevance. Art teachers know most about art processes and forms that lend themselves to the point of the encounter. They know what media, processes, and techniques have been introduced and to what extent. The teacher analyses the anticipated production tasks and prepares for students' successes by identifying the specific (subordinate) concepts that can contribute to the effectiveness of the students' art works. Armstrong (1986) introduced a questioning strategy part of which aims to engage students inductively in forming specific concepts. With such meaningful investment in their learning, greater retention results.

Criterion-referenced group critiques

Particularly at the secondary level, some students become reluctant to be singled out to discuss their work out of fear of ridicule, self-consciousness, or any number of other reasons. There are other ways than to have a student stand in front of a group to talk about his/her own work. A way to sidestep this confrontational situation is to display all art work. The concepts which were taught and which should be evident in the art work become the criteria by which to discuss the success of the works. If the teacher asks for students to identify the *many* products by number or placement that demonstrate a certain quality with which they are familiar, attention is focused on evidence of the learning expected rather than personally on the students. By the time the group has pointed out positive evidence of learning related to each criterion, likely most students will have received at least one positive comment. The teacher's criterion-referenced assessment of the learning already noted in the group critique, comes as no surprise to the student.

Aesthetics Dialogues

Discussion during the critique can be the smooth introduction to an aesthetics dialogue. Not a casual discussion nor a teacher-dominated talk, dialogues engage a group of people who probe the importance of the encounter and validity of the production criteria, and/or the reasons why the historical exemplars are "art."

Teacher questions in chapter 8 are intended as prompts for the open-ended nature of questions appropriate to initiate dialogues. Also the teachers' questions should emanate out of the experiences students had. Information paragraphs and suggested open-ended questions could be planned, but sound reasoning is emphasized. Art concepts must be grasped in order to see relationships that contribute to comprehending the point of the encounter and generalization.

An aesthetics dialogue can evolve from discussion of the criteria by which the products are valued, such as, believably expressive body positions. It could emerge out of a discussion of the nature and importance of the art education experience in relationship to the historical visual statements and, more generally, to art in the lives of people beyond the art classroom. The activities of each of these content areas provide the ideational scaffolding which enables students to engage in aesthetics dialogues. By curriculum and encounter design, students would come to such discussions with minds prepared for extending thoughts based on their direct and concrete art history, criticism and production experiences.

Appropriate teacher prompts to relate aspects of those experiences that are meaningful today are helpful. These would be designed to encourage students' reflective thinking beyond the critique of their own experiences to a big idea that sums up the importance of their art encounter. Such summary generalizations would extend the personal, immediate experience of students to a big truth about art in general--for example, an expression of some value of art--which was arrived at inductively by the prepared mind of the student.

The open-ended questioning approach is an appropriate strategy for eliciting reflective reasoning in the aesthetics dialogue. When students are given practice in verbalizing the synthesis of experiences as a big idea of the lesson, it stands to reason that the activity of formulating that big idea would make a more lasting learning experience than hearing someone else make the same statement.

Collaboration: Planning Interdisciplinary Encounters or Units

The sixth national standard for visual arts (NAEA, 1994) emphasizes making connections between art and other disciplines. As reasonable as that standard is, visions loom into one's mind of earlier misuses of "art" in the service of illustrating facts of another discipline or busy work late in the school day when students are restless.

The idea of interdisciplinary learning is valid. If art is a part of life, it can be argued that it connects with all the other disciplines that are also part of life. Hence, the emphasis on connections is worthy of consideration. Interdisciplinary education is most effective for art teachers who have indepth expertise in a second discipline and can recognize concepts or generalizations that have application in both disciplines. Several teachers can effectively collaborate by brainstorming and pooling their separate areas of expertise. An elementary art teacher and a music teacher in the same school found that students' grasp of concepts common to music and art was significantly higher when the concepts were introduced in both subjects in the same time frame. This team approach worked better than when the concepts were taught in just one discipline or at different times in both disciplines (Russell,1985).

Although seeking worthy connections, or integration, with math, science, social studies, etc. can be challenging, a conscientious team or teacher who is well-prepared in both subjects can provide a rich and meaningful experience for students. Selection of an appropriate organizing generalization from the aesthetics resource to be the focus or big idea of an art encounter should maintain the emphases from the selected subject and on the distinctive nature and value of "art" in interdisciplinary learning.

Let us suppose that readings in history exposed a teacher to some general ideas about life which inspired works of art. Those ideas may be about relationships, authority, international confrontations, or other subjects which they feel important enough to recreate or comment on. The aesthetics resource can provide general ideas about art or art-related issues that are compatible with the general ideas about life from a historical perspective. Merging ideas of the two sources connects or synthesizes the duality into one generalization to serve as the advance organizer of the interdisciplinary encounter as shown in Figure 5.2.

Figure 5.2 Plan for an interdisciplinary encounter: Art and History

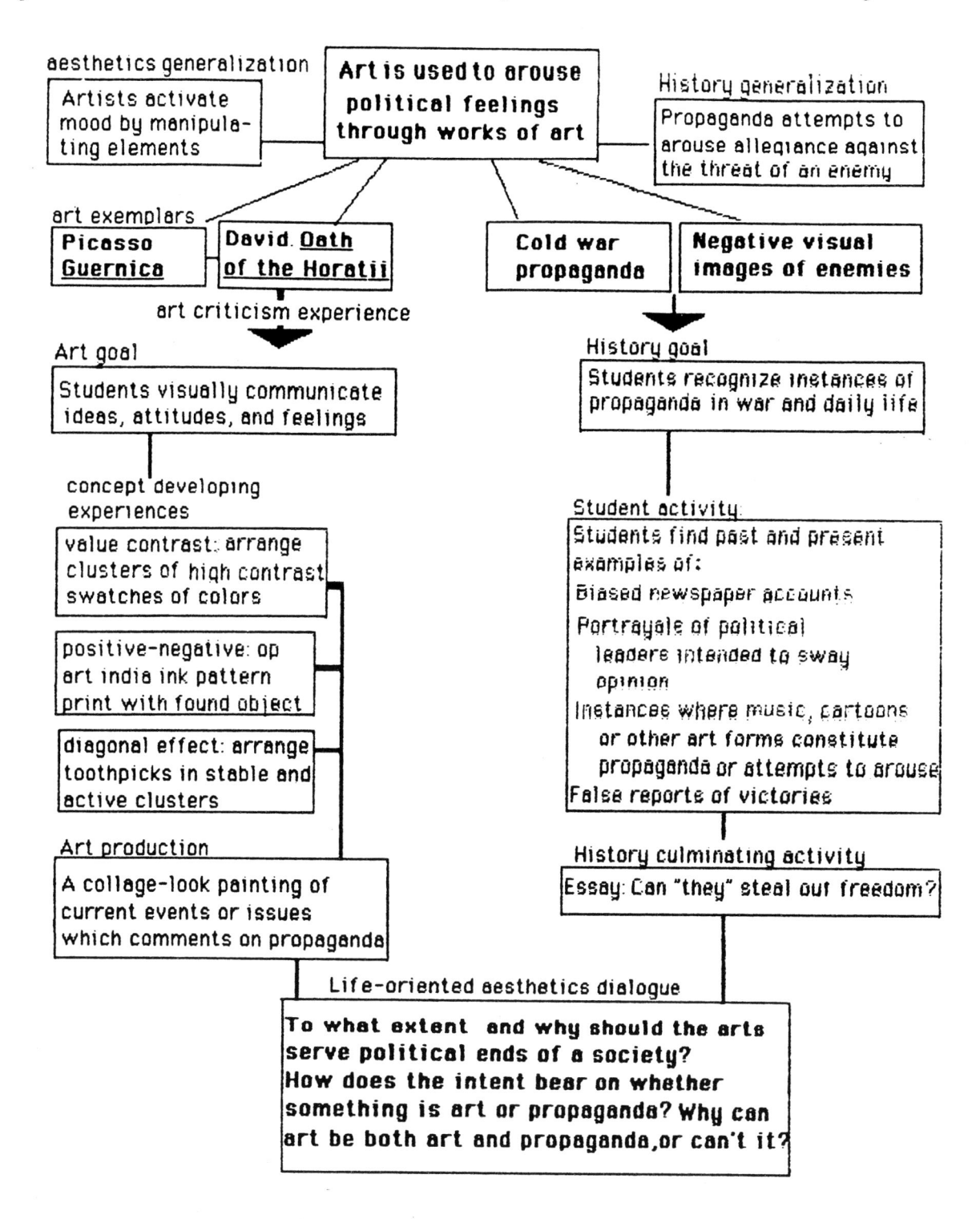

aesthetics generalization
Artists activate mood by manipulating elements

Art is used to arouse political feelings through works of art

History generalization
Propaganda attempts to arouse allegiance against the threat of an enemy

art exemplars
- Picasso Guernica
- David. Oath of the Horatii
- Cold war propaganda
- Negative visual images of enemies

art criticism experience

Art goal
Students visually communicate ideas, attitudes, and feelings

History goal
Students recognize instances of propaganda in war and daily life

concept developing experiences
- value contrast: arrange clusters of high contrast swatches of colors
- positive-negative: op art india ink pattern print with found object
- diagonal effect: arrange toothpicks in stable and active clusters

Student activity:
Students find past and present examples of:
Biased newspaper accounts
Portrayals of political leaders intended to sway opinion
Instances where music, cartoons or other art forms constitute propaganda or attempts to arouse
False reports of victories

Art production
A collage-look painting of current events or issues which comments on propaganda

History culminating activity
Essay: Can "they" steal our freedom?

Life-oriented aesthetics dialogue
To what extent and why should the arts serve political ends of a society? How does the intent bear on whether something is art or propaganda? Why can art be both art and propaganda, or can't it?

© Carmen Armstrong, 1998

Analysis of the merged generalization will suggest some concepts which the students will need to grasp in order to comprehend the point of the generalization and encounter. The point of the encounter will be more easily grasped if the students understand the relationships between the concepts introduced. The teacher will have simplified the generalization and concepts appropriately for the sophistication level of the students.

Art History

Having selected works of art and historical events that relate to the generalization, the teacher(s) will need to research historical information about the context of the art works also--why they existed or were important to have been made and how they fit into or spoke for need for change in the lives of people at that time and place. What did the geographic setting contribute? What influenced the need to create it? An art historical activity could be for students to find comic strips or cartoons that carry subtle moral or political meanings by language, context, and the visual images. Political and social contextual aspects of David's Oath of the Horatii could be researched by small groups of students and the information uncovered then shared with the class.

Art Criticism

In preparation for the art criticism experience, the teacher examines the exemplars chosen for significant objects that dominate or are part of the setting, analyzes the placement of objects, and notes modifications of shapes, colors and other elements that are consistent with each other and searches the work of art to detect cues that suggest the artist's decisions that create meaning to the work.

Art Production

The art production component may vary from the usual conception of art activities because of the connection to history without being used as illustration in the service of history. Art educators (Hurwitz and Madeja, 1977; Anderson,1973; Stewart,1988; Erickson, 1986; Erickson and Katter,1989) provide ideas for art activities which bridge any imagined gap between talk about art and student participatory activity in art learning situations. The activities may include the kinds of art products currently displayed in our school hallways, but possibly with a new twist of student statements, related historical and art historical worksheets, or teacher written objectives and concepts developed. It is also feasible that a teacher would plan to display the students' concept development exercises, such as experimental tempera painted variations of color values or intensity changes of a color on a bulletin board. One could display the traced analysis of the gestures of bodies of people, as well as the spatial relationships between them, depicted by an artist which communicate different attitudes about patriotism and fear. An art criticism assignment could be the evidence of learning displayed. A videotaped aesthetics dialogue could be played as parents mill around on parent conference night. These activities provide concrete evidence of the art learning process and enable students to recognize and employ artists' and historians' methods to effectively communicate ideas graphically and verbally about life.

Aesthetics

An aesthetics dialogue, with teacher prompts to remind students to recall the meaning of their encounter experiences should help students formulate in their own words, the big idea of the lesson--the aesthetics generalization that guided the teachers' selection of the experiences students had.

It may be obvious that the encounter examples given in this book culminate with an aesthetics dialogue. That fact reflects concern that the aesthetics dialogue emerges out of thoughts that have been cultivated so as to help get across the meaning of the integrated encounter. It does not infer that ending with the aesthetics dialogue is the only way to engage students thoughtfully and efficiently in recognizing worthy issues to discuss in art. Indeed, themes and topics derived from the aesthetics generalizations are serving as advance organizers that prime students throughout the lesson for an opportunity to synthesize the related ideas addressed in the encounter. The teacher must decide when students have enough experiences to profitably engage in a serious, reflective aesthetics discussion. A focused aesthetics dialogue that is worth the time taken for it results from a comprehensive, not redundant, planned curriculum.

6. CURRICULAR EXAMPLES USING AESTHETICS GENERALIZATIONS

Art teachers piloted the aesthetics resource in chapter 8 to see how it could assist in curriculum planning and instruction. They were asked to review the aesthetics resource, use it to plan a unit or curriculum in accord with their ongoing art program, and implement their plan in the classroom. They videotaped their students' culminating aesthetics dialogues and evaluated the entire process. Their suggestions contributed to the book and some results of the art teachers' pilot study are summarized in this chapter. The following selections rely heavily on the descriptions of the teachers.

Structuring aesthetics behaviors within a K-5 art program

Robin Russell, Art teacher, Medina, Illinois Elementary School District # 11

A structure of content in an art program is complex. The art teacher needs to identify concepts and subordinate concepts of elements and principles, art forms and their related processes, techniques, media, cross cultural and across time art history exemplars, behaviors related to each art discipline role model and aesthetics theories appropriately adapted to level of students.

As part of her curriculum planning process, Russell indicated on a chart when specific aspects of each content area would be introduced to a grade level. Some curriculum planners also code such entries with letters or a symbol to indicate when content is introduced, reinforced or extended in sophistication at different grade levels.

A simplified model of some of the aesthetics behaviors considered in Russell's curriculum planning structure follows as Table 6.1.

This type of format can be used to indicate at which grade level a behavior is expected and to what degree of achievement, for example, help build a group statement (H) individual contribution (I), or give evidence as complete thoughts (T).

Table 6.1. Charting grade levels at which to introduce inquiry behaviors of the aesthetician

Aesthetics skills	K	1	2	3	4	5
Respect and react thoughtfully	.	.	.	.	.	.
Synthesize and create own ideas	.	.	.	.	.	.
Explain reasons for themes in art and society	.	.	.	.	.	.
Discuss the value of kinds of art	.	.	.	.	.	.
Explain why we display art and where	.	.	.	.	.	.
Discuss relationships between art and customs	.	.	.	.	.	.
Explain art values that support or conflict	.	.	.	.	.	.
Justify art as "art" in formalist terms	.	.	.	.	.	.
Discuss feelings and art	.	.	.	.	.	.
Make sound judgments about art	.	.	.	.	.	.

An Art Encounter Structure for Grade Two

Sally Hazelton, Art teacher, Batavia, Illinois Elementary School District

The second grade encounter in Figure 6.1 was planned by Hazelton for two, one hour lessons. It was part of a previously determined thematic structure, but that structure was compatible with aesthetics generalizations chosen as advance organizers of encounters. Themes addressed each year with increasingly greater sophistication for the higher grade levels were "My world around me"(K), "The artist as inventor--Imagination and fantasy"(1), "Art from around the world"(2),"Art decorates my world"(3)," Seeing the world more clearly"(4)," Contemporary art and culture" (5), and"Art as communication"(6).

Figure 6.1 Model of a second grade encounter

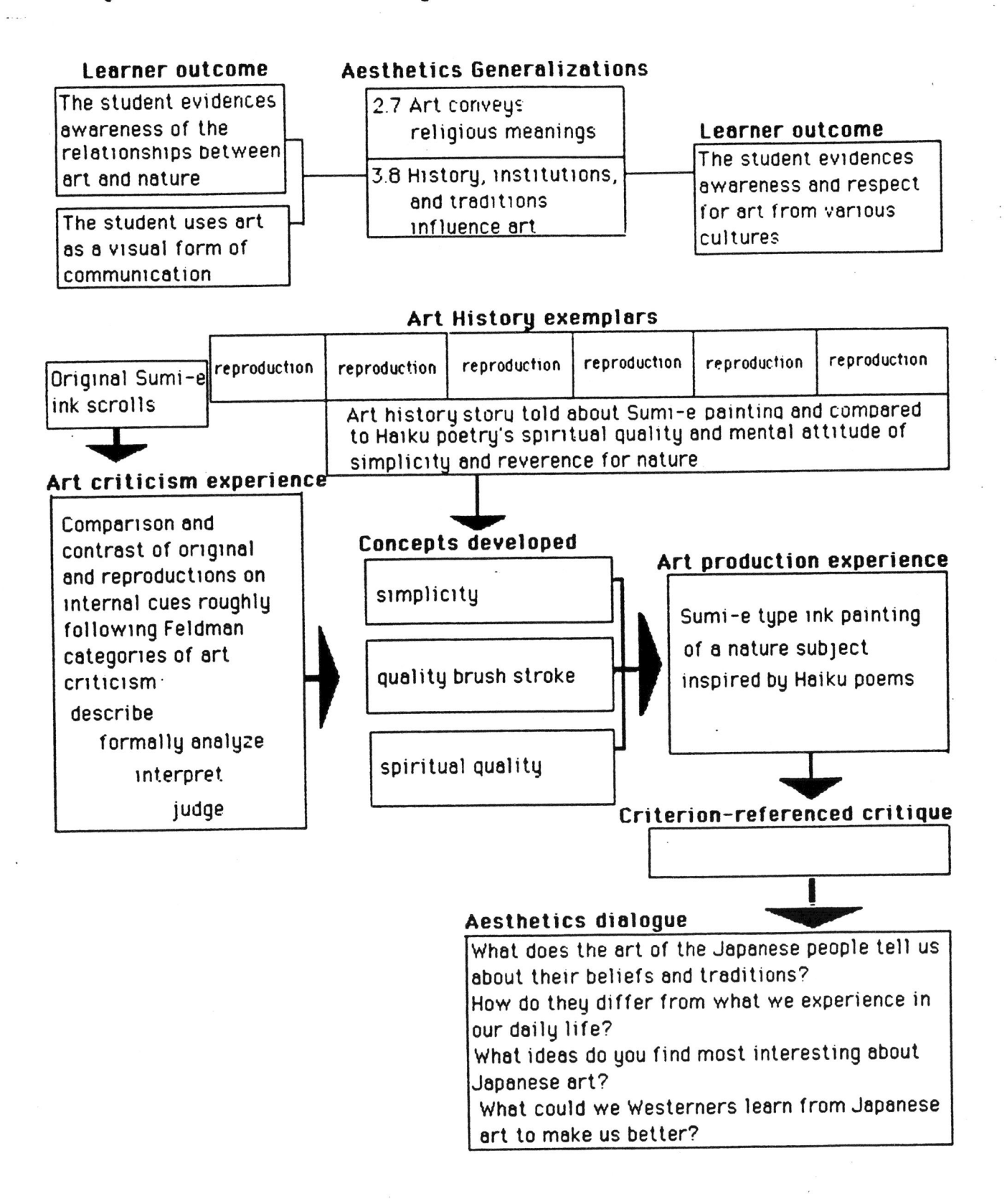

Learner outcome
- The student evidences awareness of the relationships between art and nature
- The student uses art as a visual form of communication

Aesthetics Generalizations
- 2.7 Art conveys religious meanings
- 3.8 History, institutions, and traditions influence art

Learner outcome
- The student evidences awareness and respect for art from various cultures

Art History exemplars

| Original Sumi-e ink scrolls | reproduction | reproduction | reproduction | reproduction | reproduction | reproduction |

Art history story told about Sumi-e painting and compared to Haiku poetry's spiritual quality and mental attitude of simplicity and reverence for nature

Art criticism experience
Comparison and contrast of original and reproductions on internal cues roughly following Feldman categories of art criticism:
- describe
- formally analyze
- interpret
- judge

Concepts developed
- simplicity
- quality brush stroke
- spiritual quality

Art production experience
Sumi-e type ink painting of a nature subject inspired by Haiku poems

Criterion-referenced critique

Aesthetics dialogue
What does the art of the Japanese people tell us about their beliefs and traditions?
How do they differ from what we experience in our daily life?
What ideas do you find most interesting about Japanese art?
What could we Westerners learn from Japanese art to make us better?

The two aesthetics generalizations around which the encounter shown in Figure 6.1 was organized were: "Art conveys religious meanings," and "History, institutions, and traditions influence art." Focus on these generalizations supported goals of: "The student evidences awareness of art and nature," "The student evidences awareness and respect for art from various cultures," and " The student uses art as a form of communication."

An original Sumi-e ink painting and six reproductions of Sumi-e ink paintings were the focus of the art criticism discussion based on internal cues of the works. The art historical context was introduced as a story-telling listening experience which related visual qualities of the art to the mental attitude, simplicity, reverence for nature, and spiritual reality qualities of Haiku poetry. students created ink paintings inspired by Haiku poems. Concepts of quality brush strokes, a range of values, simplicity, and spiritual quality were developed and formed the criteria of assessment of learning evidenced in the art product.

The aesthetics dialogue was facilitated by teacher questions such as: "What does the art of the Japanese people tell us about their beliefs and traditions?"" How do those beliefs differ from what we experience in our daily life?""What ideas do you find most interesting about Japanese art?" "What could Westerners learn from Japanese art to make us better people?"

A third grade, 36 week art curriculum

Charrie Colwell, Lombard, Illinois School District # 45

Art teachers find that planning curriculum must also consider learning periods, blocks of time for an encounter in order to focus on one generalization that is not interrupted by vacations-- a learning period. In

Colwell's district, art was taught once a week and units varied from two and one half weeks to almost seven weeks long. Testing days and parent conferences can subtract from time spent continuously on an encounter. Table 6.2 is a simplified form of Colwell's thorough structure and plans for encounters within it.

Table 6.2. **Third grade curriculum "Communities near and far"**

Weeks	Focus	Theory	Aesthetics Generalization
Unit 1. Rural Communities			
1-3	My school community Children at play-Recess	Expression	Works of art transmit the artist's experience to the viewer
4-9	Scarecrow sculpture	Expression	The function of art is to share feelings
9-15	Winter landscapes	Media-Gener.	Appreciating artists' choice of media as part of the creative activity is enhanced by knowing processes and expressive possibilities
Unit 2. City Communities			
16-19	Seascape	Imitation	Art represents nature as beautiful and ideal
19-21	Fish drawing	Imitation	imitative works of art can contribute to understanding
21-25	Fish stitchery	Creat.Proc.	Artists invent by changing things

Table 6.2 continued

Unit 3. City Communities

25-27	Cityscape	Formalist	Art expresses feelings by composition of its elements
28-30	City people	Expression	Artists give form to their ideas according to the way they see life
31-36	Public sculpture	Social Insti.	Works of art meet complex conditions including public acceptance

A three-unit, twelve week sixth grade art structure

Noel Anderson, Art teacher, Naperville Illinois School District #301

Anderson's structure of the twelve week course that met fifty minutes daily, was based on district-wide themes of "Communication/ Symbols", "Heroes, Idols, Superheroes, and Villains" and "Color Theory".

Table 6.3 shows how these themes were related to aesthetics and extended into discipline-based units.

The disproportionately long (9 weeks) Unit 1 wherein an aesthetics dialogue was a first time experience for both teacher and students may have negatively affected the students' ability to synthesize their experiences. Some group work and requests for hand-raising responses to restated questions helped when initial responses were spotty. Interest, enthusiasm, "on target" responses, and extension of big ideas to life situations were pervasive by the third unit aesthetics dialogue.

Table 6.3. **Example of a three-unit, sixth grade curriculum structure**

	Unit 1	Unit 2	Unit 3
Theme:	Communication/Symbols	Heroes, Idols, Villains	Color Theory
Theory:	Value of art as imitation	Art and Context	Metacriticism
Aes.Gen.:	Works of art can convey meaning	Works of art have societal influence	Form refers to the relationship between perceptible elements and it can hold a viewer's attention.
Exemplars:	Ancient Egyptian art/architecture*; cave paintings	van Eyck. Arnolfini Wedding; Picasso. Guernica; Bonheur. Col.W.F.Cody*	Demuth. Buildings; Dove. Foghorns; Mondrian. Composition No.2*

focus of art criticism experience

Concepts:	Pattern, balance technical quality unity, color/shape symbolism	texture, detail technical quality technique	primary, secondary color schemes
Lead-ins:	cartouche symbol/sign	Superman cartoon story: Buehr. Heraldry	
Production:	2-D mummy case or coat-of-arms	3-D clay people pot	2-D cut paper collage

The cooperative group work in unit two where students converged their ideas into one group response led to comments as:

"freedom of art work'

"People communicate their ideas and values through other people who have the same values, such as a sculpture with good standards"

"All different artists have different opinions on heroes, idols, superheroes, anti-idols, and villains"

"tells value...tells freedom"

It appears that some students were merging ideas from unit 1 with their following unit and that is not a negative observation.

Vertical Sequence of Generalizations for Units in a Four Year High School Art Program

Darlene Williams, Evergreen Park, IL High School District # 231

Teachers may find an entry into curriculum development by their previous successes. Williams chose to select 40 aesthetics generalizations to link with ten unit topics that were successful with her previous students. For each of the ten topics, she chose generalizations that had four different levels of complexity in consideration of the conceptual levels of her Art 1 to Art 4 students. Since Art 4 students develop individual contracts, she was mindful of their experience in selecting the aesthetics generalizations for them. Table 6.4 shows that vertical sequencing within each topic.

Table 6.4. **Vertical sequence of generalizations in a four year high school art program**

Topics	Art 1	Art 2	Art 3	Art 4
Imitation	Art is representation and invention.	Works of art create meaning through selection and composition.	Art represents Nature as beautiful and and ideal.	Abstraction moves away from the representational reality of Art.
Expression	Works of art transmit the artist's expression to the viewer.	The elements of art are expressive in themselves.	Expressive content is a fusion of subject matter and form.	Artists assimilate life experiences and give form to their interpretation.
Formal Principles	Works of art formally employ design principles.	Organization is far more important than replication.	The form of a work of art is is its most essential quality.	Form is bound together with emotion in art.
Symbols	Art is a language that we learn.	Art reinforces values by using symbols that are understood.	Art portrays uncomman qualities of common objects.	Works of art create meaning by composing with symbolic objects or elements to portray the artist's insight.

(continued)

(Table 6.4 continued)

<u>Media</u>	Expression of ideas is influenced by the media used.	Artists manipulate media and tools to capture what they want to show.	New media may present questions about the role of the viewer.	The artist chooses a medium based on the nature of the media and how it and the artist's form will unite.
<u>Cultural Context</u>	Art is related to the type of society that exists.	Art is a link between humans, the natural world and the supernatural.	Art reflects and or helps to solve the problems of a society.	Art that evokes expression may may do so inconsistently depending on the disposition of the viewer and the context.
<u>Aesthetics</u>	Art is aesthetically gratifying.	People respond to what their senses pick up and what the whole work of art makes them think about.	Subject matter and form are fused in the aesthetic experience.	Aesthetic perception involves objectivity, subjectivity, and synthesis.
<u>Art Becoming Art</u>	Great works of art tend to deal in universal values.	History, institutions, and traditions influence art.	People can read something in art but context information helps.	Art may be supported for other than artistic merit.

(continued)

Table 6.4 continued

Creativity	Artists invent by changing things.	Art begins with the artist's need to look closer.	Artists do not have a precise solution in mind but are sensitive to points of synthesis.	Creativity involves responding to the interaction between an artist and the image emerging in the medium.
Criticism	Meaning is an individual matter.	Criticism helps art communicate by noting visual qualities and relationships that create meaning.	Art criticism involves debate about and justification of the criteria used in judging works of art.	Definition of art may be specific to a culture or a time.

A High School Art and Spanish Collaboration

Rhonda Levy McQueen, Art teacher, Polaris School for Individualized Education, Oaklawn, IL Community High School District #218

In structuring units for the Art and Spanish collaboration, Levy selected two aesthetics generalizations to guide the encounters: "Artists collaborate with an assumed audience and express emotions shared by it," and "Art is a distinctive interpretation of life experience." Students were involved in this experimental learning situation on an extra credit basis with slide presentations and discussions were held after school. Students created self-portraits and studied the work of Frida Kahlo. Two additional classes participated in this unit within classtime. This encounter culminated with an aesthetics dialogue group concensus that the power to show emotions and things unique or different about oneself, whether good or bad, ...these things relate to the artist and should be expressed outwardly. People later in time will look back and see the artist as this picture. Whereas the first group engaged in the aesthetics dialogue only, the second two were assigned to write a paper based on the aesthetics discussion in Spanish.

Another theme developed for the Art and Spanish collaboration was "Day of the Dead" inspired by the exhibit of altar installation pieces at the Mexican Fine Arts Museum in Chicago. Each altar clearly reflected its message, intent, and reason for being. In their contextual research, students probed topics of:

Mayan or Aztec Indian traditions

Efect of Spanish Catholic invasion of Mexico

Mexican attitude toward life and death

Day of the Dead symbols and their meaning

Related traditions from other cultures and time periods.

Integrating the Art Disciplines in an Elementary Education Majors' Art Methods Course

Carmen L. Armstrong, School of Art, Northern Illinois University, DeKalb, IL

Elementary teachers must teach many subjects; therefore, their perception of the value of the art methods course is important. Students can be helped to connect purposes for art education to their art experiences by an emphasis on the big ideas from aesthetics.

Orienting students to art history, aesthetics, art criticism, and art production as the four disciplines most pertinent to art education is Part One of the one semester course that meets 5 or 6 hours per week for 16 weeks. Part Two is structured around five major observations about the role and value of art. These are expressed as "aesthetics generalizations" of each of the five units of Part 2 and are the basis for major goals for art, selection of concepts on which to focus, visual analytic experiences, and end product applications in each unit. The cluster of experiences, wherein each of the four disciplines are meaningfully integrated, constitute an encounter, and there may be three or four encounters in a unit.

The four generalizations that align with the major four categories of aesthetics theories and are the advance organizers of the units of the second part of the course. A fifth unit on the creative process--an issue that aestheticians address--was added. The five generalizations are:

"Artists visually record the real or create the ideal by attention to specific visual qualities,"

"Art communicates ideas, attitudes, and feelings,"

"Persons arrange what we refer to as elements of art according to principles that have purpose and meaning in their culture,"

"People and artists enhance and embellish their personal and public environments," and

"Artists break boundries by inquiring, inventing, elaborating, exaggerating, and combining incongruities."

For each encounter, historical, cross cultural works of art that exemplify the unit aesthetics generalizations are selected and one or more is the focus of group art criticism experiences. Visual analytic experiences, designed to develop concepts needed for success in producing art, precede the art production experiences. Either the art criticism activity or discussion of the student art work leads into a group aesthetics dialogue. The focus on one aesthetics theory for a unit is designed to help the elementary education major to differentiate the intent of each theory as well as recognize that there are multiple choices for considering and evaluating whether something is art-- not just one right answer, but many possible reasons why something could be art.

Curriculum planning is not feasible for the novice teacher with one semester of art methods. It makes sense to introduce pre-service students to a continuing support system to reinforce ideas learned in one fast semester. Competent art educators have published such curricula. Therefore, each unit of Part Two is introduced by the instructor with concept developing integrated experiences, then followed by two pairs of peer teachers, one team teaching a primary encounter and one an intermediate level encounter to the class. The encounter is developed from, but elaborates on, a lesson from any of several available art curriculum series. The students choose their lesson from lessons recommended by the instructor. Each student-taught encounter is two to two and one half hours long and is understood to be broken down into segments when taught to children. Each team completes and duplicates an encounter plan for the class members that includes a black and white copy of the art reproduction that was the subject of their art criticism experience.

Each team assesses the art production component of the lesson they taught in terms of rubrics for concepts taught and rate their classmates on the quality of their contributions to discussions.

Teacher comments

The opportunity to use the aesthetic resource in its early stage provided helpful feedback in refining it. The following comments suggest that new ideas may take some time to assimilate, but there are rewards for the endeavor. The teachers write:

"Realizing that 'aesthetics' is discussion and debate about art ideas, I had to keep an open mind while reading"...."Many of these ideas would probably have to be carefully presented to all students, especially young ones, prefacing their introduction with 'some people think' and ending with 'what do you think...?' "

"I also found that the more I read through the generalizations, the fewer questions I had about what each generalization meant which I attribute to increasing familiarity with the topic."

"The [graduate class] assignment led to comparisons and issues with reasons."

"...once the teacher becomes comfortable in aesthetics-based discussions, the students will also participate with ease."

"...need to organize my approach to cut out ambiguous questions."

" I feel that with practice, I will become more natural with asking the appropriate question for the generalization being learned."

"The other questions used in the aesthetics discussion were easier to write after reading the ones under the generalization."

"It takes two years to get over a production orientation. My students love the discussion."

"I really see the logic behind using aesthetics as the starting and ending

98

point of any and every art lesson taught at any level. I cannot think of any lesson I teach that could not, or should not have a basis in aesthetics."

"Daddy in church"
Becky 6½ yrs.

7. CURRICULUM EVALUATION

Overview

How good is the curriculum that an art teacher has planned? This chapter shows ways that the curriculum writer can demonstrate to others that the art curriculum planned meets recognized recommendations. If the curriculum has been developed following guidelines of this book, much of what was "process" can be presented for evaluation.

NAEA's Exemplary art education curricula: A guide to guides (1994) includes examples of curricular components planned for particular school districts. Some of them help demonstrate comprehensiveness of certain components of the curriculum. Some graphically show consideration of the nature of the students in planning when to introduce or extend development of concepts or techniques. Adaptation is always necessary but models from other schools help. Often graphics portray information and relationships that are difficult to follow in paragraph form. The Appendix includes some blank forms which may be helpful and convenient for the reader to use.

Documentation Suggestions and Models

Art teachers can present documentation of their valid decision making that follows recommendations for effective art curriculum planning. These recommendations become a checklist for the teacher's self-evaluation purposes as well as conveying the validity of the art curriculum plan.

Orientation

The curriculum begins with statements to orient the reader. This statement should identify the purpose of the curriculum (without getting into details of a philosophic rationale). It should suggest the teacher for whom it is designed, that is, an elementary classroom teacher or certified art teacher. The grade level or course(s) and meeting schedule for which it is planned should be clear as in Table 7.1.

Table 7.1 **Schedule for a semester of a high school art course**

UNIT		WEEK	FIRST SEMESTER ENCOUNTERS
C U L T U R E S	A N D R I T U A L S	1	**Encounter One:** *Rituals and the Sacred* Chamush rock paintings, Lascaux cave paintings. Research visual arts in sacred rituals of early cultures.
		2	Grid drawing of line and shape patterns to increase technical skills. Tempera and charcoal painting of symbolic images in ritual.
			LABOR DAY
		3	
		4	**Encounter Two:** *Rituals and the Mundane* Mayan Battle Scene, The Mochi Makers, Melanesian painting. Identify why artists created visual expressions of daily rituals.
		5	Blind contour drawings of hands and shoe. Detailed cross contour drawing of classmates' faces. Series of gesture drawings of classmates in different poses.
		6	Contour and gesture charcoal drawing of ritualistic school day activity.
		7	
	E M B E L L I S H		**INSTITUTE DAY/COLUMBUS DAY**
		8	**Encounter Three:** *Sacred Images and Jewelry* Headdress of the Princess of Ur; Ashanti Soul Washers. Research patterns and supernatural motifs on early jewelry. Pen/ink renderings of design for jewelry piece using texture, pattern repeat, and positive/negative shapes.
		9	Practice cutting and incising techniques on metal foil. Metal foil and beads jewelry piece using contemporary motifs.
		10	
	A N D P E R S P E C T I V E S		**PARENT TEACHER CONFERENCES**
		11	**Encounter Four:** *Asian Attitudes and Atmospheres* Shen, Poet on Mountaintop; Durand, Kindred Spirits. Paper on the prevalence of aerial perspective in China and Japan.
		12	Pen and ink drawings and washes to create value and changes in detail. Pen and ink landscape using Asian techniques for creating aerial perspective.
		13	**Encounter Five:** *Near Eastern Eloquence* Incident in a Mosque, Eighteen Scholars. Give examples of historic and contemporary use of isometric perspective.
		14	Drawings of shaded and overlapped geometric shapes in isometric perspective. Still life drawing of objects symbolizing American life or traditions.
			THANKSGIVING BREAK
		15	
		16	**Encounter Six:** *European Elaborations* Raphael, The School Of Athens; Evergood, The Sunny Side of the Street. Report on contextual influences of Renaissance on use of linear perspective.
		17	Construct drawings using one and two-point perspective. Linear perspective drawing/collage of contemporary street scene elaborated with cutouts of populars thinkers and artists of today.
		18	

In Table 7.1, the plan of a high school semester clearly indicates the course theme, unit themes, and weeks expected to be involved with each encounter. Feasibility of the schedule shown is enhanced by the brief listing of experiences of each encounter considering the scheduled school breaks.

Basic Considerations

Art goals. Efland (1974) offers some criteria designed to set the standard for evaluation of art goals. Simply stated, the art goals should be compatible with the school district general education goals since art is part of the overall school curriculum. It is important that the art goals identify the unique contribution of the visual arts to a student's education. Goals should be further specified as subgoals or learner outcomes to make the meaning more clear. Finally, the wording of the goal should have the ability to evoke images of possible applications in the curriculum plan.

In addition, groups of art teachers may be ask to come to a consensus on the importance of each goal for determining appropriate weight in emphasis in the curriculum and assessment. Armstrong (1994) shows how a pie chart can visually communicate the relative weight of behaviors on which students are assessed. The same graphic can be used in reference to goals dealing with knowledge content. In a documentation of the goals, reference should be made to how the art goals measure up to recommendations from these objective sources as well as their alignment which will be discussed below.

Characteristics of the student. No group of students of the same age is exactly alike, but some characteristics of students are fairly predictable. It is the more predictable characteristics that can be shown to have been considered in planning a curriculum. An individual encounter plan can identify something about the student for whom it is planned that has been taken into consideration. It may have been in the selection of the subject of the production experience, exemplars, lesson opening (advance organizer), media, or generalization encompassing the extended lesson.

Curriculum theory. The preface to a curriculum plan should clarify and justify the basic consideration of a recognized purpose(s) for schooling that predominately influences the art curriculum. The fact that it is a consideration should be evident in any graphic presentations that attempts to portray foundational aspects of the art curriculum and unit titles or themes. Without identifying the platform of the curriculum, a reviewer cannot know what to look for in judging its consistency or cohesiveness. What purpose is this curriculum intending to serve by the encounters planned?

Aesthetics theory. The focus of this book, aesthetics as a foundational component of art curriculum planning, would be obvious in both verbal or graphic portrayals of the curriculum foundation. A grid for each grade level could demonstrate the variety of aesthetics theories and issues introduced to students. Several examples of encounter structures in chapters 4, 5 and 6 might be useful models.

Alignment. Alignment refers to the fit between all components of the curriculum plan and documents from outside stakeholders (national or state standards, the community, the school district). Alignment can be most immediately grasped by charts, grids, flow charts, or other graphic presentations. What could show that evidence of a goal was met by an experience of an encounter? It would be difficult for one figure to show the alignment from all the foundational components to assessment. A flowchart can be made to follow one sample path, i.e. breaking down one unit of a course into encounters, breaking down one encounter into its experiences, and breaking down one experience into the content to be assessed by a sample tool. Grids can show that all aspects expected from stakeholders are included.

Sources of the curriculum's theory base. Figure 4.1 in chapter 4 is a model for showing the basic considerations that contribute to the art program rationale. The components of art curriculum planning, the big picture, are visually evident. The curriculum theory serving as the basic foundation can be suggested as the "theme" to help show the cohesiveness of curriculum components that follow.

General education goals or school district's mission statement. The goals grid is a system that has been successfully used for deriving learner outcomes that align with art goals and general education goals of a school district. Figure 4.7 in chapter 4 demonstrates how one compatible intersection of art goals and general eduation goals results in a statement of a learner outcome in the visual arts. The wording of the learner outcome suggests this alignment to the arts and general education. It is not to be inferred that every intersection that can show a relationship must do so. It is better to have fewer but very convincing and unique-to-art-education learner outcomes than to claim to support all school district goals when some may be better served by other subject areas.

Each learner outcome that results from this grid portrayal can be adjusted in language and challenge to be appropriate for multiple grade levels. This language adjustment is demonstrated by one learner outcome on the goals grid, Figure 4.7.

Professional goals and/or national standards. To demonstrate their alignment, the visual art learner outcomes of a school district can be compared to goal recommendations of the National Art Education Association and the National Visual Arts Standards. With a separate coded list for national art goals and for the national standards, alignment can be indicated by inserting the codes for each under each learner outcome on the "goals grid". Figure 7.1 is part of a goals grid. In the lower corners of each outcome "cell" are codes to indicate alignment with the number of the National Visual Arts Standards (1994) and letter of the assessment means by which one can gather evidence of achievement of the outcome.

The art education reform movement has called art teachers' attention again to the levels of thinking and cognitive strategies (Gagne' and Briggs, 1974) that students in art are capable of achieving. It would be unfortunate to ignore the opportunity to present information about how the art curriculum encourages these intellectual skills and reflection on values, in addition to manipulative skills. A page with the skills listed and, for each one, a learner outcome statement that translates the skill or behavior to an art context would enable the reader to imagine the feasibility of the art goals to facilitate development of higher order thinking. The means of assessment of a learner outcome will be a clue to the level of thinking taught for and sought as evidence of achievement of the learner outcome.

Goals to learner outcomes to encounter or lesson objectives. A flowchart can exemplify the internal consistency, or coherence, of the art curriculum by the goal to assessment alignment. The logical progression toward specificity of learner outcomes through aesthetics generalizations, through encounter

Figure 7.1. Learner outcome alignment with goals, standards and assessment on a partial goals grid

General education goals \ State art goals	Explain art by relating facts from historical contexts	Give visual form to ideas attitudes and feelings	Interpret works of art and form ideas about art in general
Communicate	Identify types of communication by artists over time and contexts that influenced what artists communicated 2,4 D,E,T	Create works of art that carry a meaning to others 1,2,3 P,D,J	Observe, analyze, interpret and judge works of art accurately. 5,2 D,E
Solve problems		Use media and techniques to effectively solve authentic visual art problems 1,2 P,D,J	Analyze means used by artists to organize and manipulate elements of art. 2,5 E,D
Appreciate cultures and persons different from their own	Describe commonalities and differences in contexts that effect art forms, media, and styles 4 E,W,T		Synthesize information from cross cultural works of art and generalize about the nature and value of art. 5 D,E
Adapt to a world of change		Explore possibilities of technology new media, and new approaches in art 1,2 S,D,O	Reflect on relationships in art over time and reasons for theoretical change 4,5,6 D,E

KEY National Visual Arts Standards
1. media, techniques, processes
2. structures and functions
3. range of subject matter, symbols
4. relation to history and cultures
5. characteristics of their work and others
6. connections... visual arts and other disciplines

Means of Assessing
D discussion
E essay
J journal entry
O observation
P production
S sketchbook
T tests
W worksheets

106

structure, through concepts, and even to the assessment criteria could be demonstrated with a few examples. In chapter 4, Figure 4.9, Curricular scaffolding: Alignment from general to specific, demonstrates coherence except for the assessment which may depend on the specific instruction.

Structure and scaffolding

The kinds of relationships, graphically worked out in the process of curriculum planning, can be presented formally with brief explanations of what is being shown. Figure 7.2 succinctly shows the structure of a high school art fundamentals course which focused each unit on one of the institutions identified in connection with the Universal Fundamental Comprehensive Institutions curriculum theory.

Grade level or course specificity. Even if planning a K-12 art program, its implementation is the test of the feasibility and appropriateness of that curriculum. A table could convincingly show how a sample general component was appropriately addressed for each individual course or grade level. When details are associated with big ideas, claims for enhanced understanding, retention, and transfer of learning are more believable.

Comprehensiveness or scope

Content analysis. The curriculum planner in art is confronted with a massive amount of information that can be taught from each of the four art disciplines. It may be advisable to make gigantic lists such as shown in Dunn's (1995) book on curriculum, but the curriculum planner can add a coding system to indicate at which grade level each entry was introduced or developed. The point is to demonstrate reinforcement of basic categories of content without redundancy of specific concepts. Dunn's chart could even be

Figure 7.2 An art fundamentals course structure

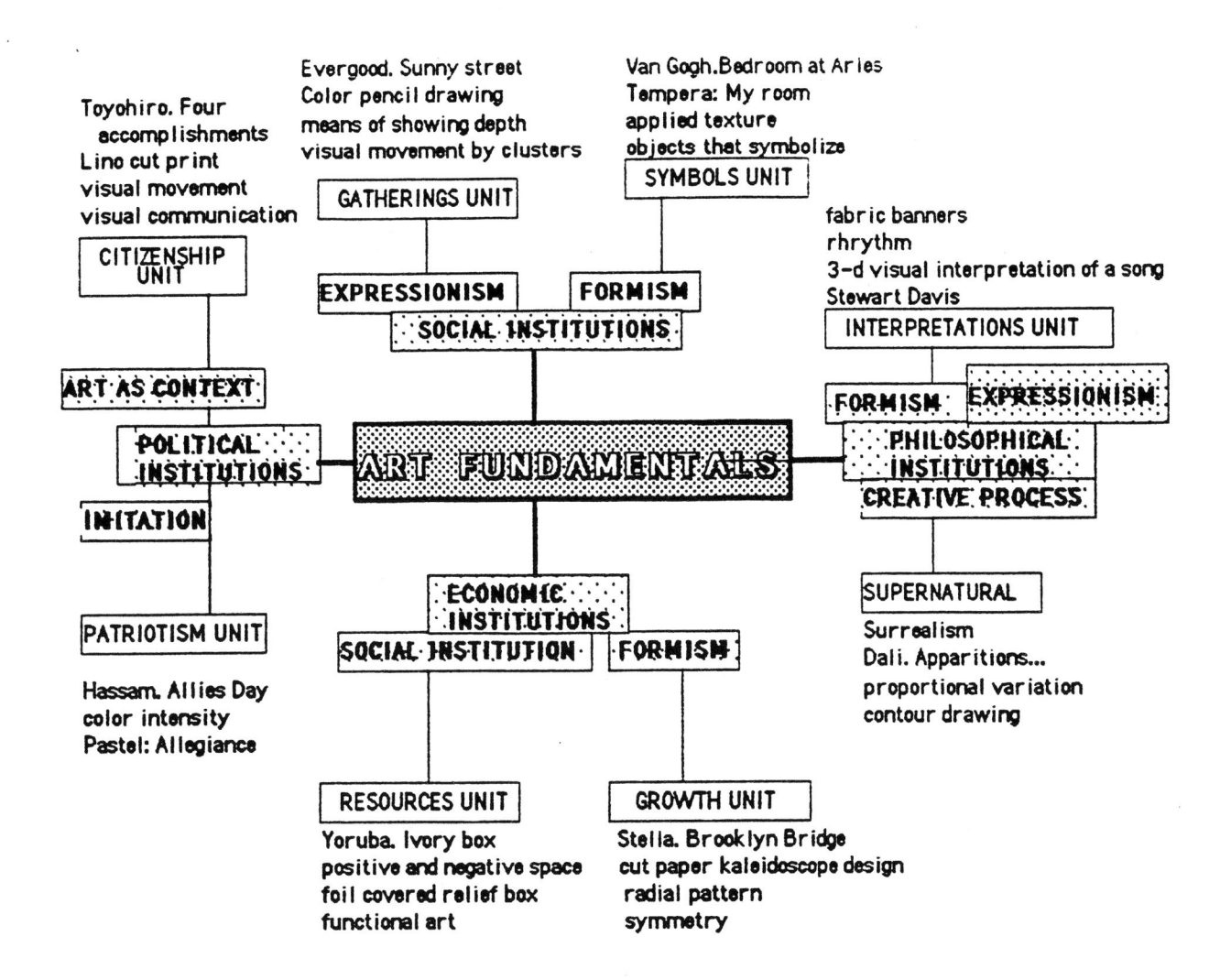

Toyohiro. Four accomplishments
Lino cut print
visual movement
visual communication

CITIZENSHIP UNIT

Evergood. Sunny street
Color pencil drawing
means of showing depth
visual movement by clusters

GATHERINGS UNIT

Van Gogh. Bedroom at Arles
Tempera: My room
applied texture
objects that symbolize

SYMBOLS UNIT

fabric banners
rhrythm
3-d visual interpretation of a song
Stewart Davis

INTERPRETATIONS UNIT

EXPRESSIONISM — FORMISM
SOCIAL INSTITUTIONS

ART AS CONTEXT
POLITICAL INSTITUTIONS ———— ART FUNDAMENTALS ———— FORMISM EXPRESSIONISM
PHILOSOPHICAL INSTITUTIONS
CREATIVE PROCESS

IMITATION

PATRIOTISM UNIT

Hassam. Allies Day
color intensity
Pastel: Allegiance

ECONOMIC INSTITUTIONS
SOCIAL INSTITUTION   FORMISM

RESOURCES UNIT

Yoruba. Ivory box
positive and negative space
foil covered relief box
functional art

GROWTH UNIT

Stella. Brooklyn Bridge
cut paper kaleidoscope design
radial pattern
symmetry

SUPERNATURAL

Surrealism
Dali. Apparitions...
proportional variation
contour drawing

expanded, or, broken into related clusters of content in order to be more specific about subsets for terms such as "form", "line", "artist", "space", or "dominance/emphasis" As students progress through the grade levels new, increasingly more sophisticated, subordinate concepts can be introduced.

As the curriculum structure takes shape, the teacher would want to keep track of the frequency with which a number of variables were incorporated at each grade level. Each major aesthetics theory (and, perhaps cultural institution) should be represented by aesthetics generalizations at each level. Quality exemplars representing a broad spectrum of time periods and cultures should be included to contribute to the education of an aesthetically and socially well-informed student.

Cohesiveness

The fit between foundational considerations is more than abstract ideas when the art curriculum planner can demonstrate the viable relationships utilized in planning encounters. Flowcharts can picture the feasibility of implementing the overall plan. They can show how foundational considerations and pedagogical recommendations can contribute to a cohesiveness in the implementation phase.

In chapter 4, the suggestion was made to develop a coding system for subsets of art goals (learner outcomes), student characteristics, a curricular theory, and aesthetics generalizations (representing the major theoretical positions). Figure 7.3 shows how art teachers could track the implementation of subsets of these basic curricular considerations as they work into the curriculum plan, encounter by encounter, for a year.

Figure 7.3. Accountability model: Inclusion of subsets of the basics

Basics	Grade 6 encounters 1	2	3	4	9 weeks 5	6	7	8	18 weeks 9	10	11	12	27 weeks 13	14	15	36 weeks 16
A	1	6	2	3	4	5	7	3	8	5	6	6	2	7	4	8
C	2	3	9	7	4	5	5	6	6	1	1	8	8	4	10	9
G	1	2,4	3,5	3,6	2,4,5	1	2,3	2,4	6,2	3,5,6	1,3	4,5	1	3,6,2	4,3	1,5
T	1	2	3	4	5	4	1	3	5	8	7	6	6	7	8	5

A: aesthetics theory   C: student characteristics   G: goal/student outcome   T: curriculum theory subsets

For demonstration purposes, imagine having selected ten characteristics of students (C1 to C10), eight aesthetics theories or issues (A1 to A8), six goals or learner objectives (G1 to G6), and eight subsets of your chosen curriculum theory (T1 to T8). With a four-part horizontal bar for one grade level, an art teacher could block off the 36 weeks of the school year. Bold vertical dividers indicate the nine week grading periods, and encounters vary in length from one to three weeks. Into this structure, insert the code for the selected subset from each basic consideration where each could complement the others in an encounter. Although this process does not need to procede from beginning to the end of the semester, logical sequence is recommended. As this accountability chart takes shape, it will become obvious if something intended has been forgotten.

In a similar manner to Figure 7.3, meaningful integration of art discipline experiences that occurs in encounters could be demonstrated.

Sequence

Vertical. As in previous criteria, the art curriculum planner can demonstrate the kind of thinking and vertical sequencing that occurred throughout the curriculum by an example. Figure 4.13 is a model of the vertical sequencing of aesthetics generalizations. Such a figure could be adapted to show the vertical sequence of subsets of a concept, art forms, media (processes and techniques) or goals. An early comprehensive art curriculum, Art Meaning, Method, and Media (Hubbard and Rouse, 1972) included a matrix of art learning tasks (essentially goals) for grade levels one through six in the beginning of each grade level book. A similar approach was used by Williams in chapter 6 who showed a four level sequence for each of ten aesthetics generalizations. The generalizations progressed from less to greater sophistication for students in Art 1 to Art 4 classes.

Horizontal. Horizontal sequence planning, and its portrayal for documentation purposes, procedes from the beginning to the end of a course or year of art as shown in Figure 4.14 in Chapter 4. By a horizontal bar representing time across a semester, art teachers can demonstrate how units of study can on the next levels of specificity be broken into sequences of encounters. Each encounter can be further delineated on a lower level into approaches and content included. While general information gives the big picture, the natural quest is to be convinced as to how learning is built across time within a course.

Graphic portrayal of curricular complexity is essential to grasping and valuing the concept. Hubbard and Zimmerman (1982) introduced "strands" of art lessons which were horizontally sequenced while allowing for individual choice of specific lessons. All art lessons developed in the book were numbered. Lesson numbers that could follow each other in a logical sequence were inserted in boxes making a horizontal flowchart. Choices of lessons that prepared students in similar concepts were stacked vertically within the generally horizontal sequence.

Practicality

The best laid plans must also have a chance for implementation. Documentation of available resources--human, community, library, organizations, reproductions, art materials, film, CD's, videos, and other teaching aids-- to implement the curriculum speaks to the realistic and thorough planning of the art teacher.

Compatibility: Assessment of Student Learning and the Curriculum
Content Validity

In Designing Assessment in Art (Armstrong, 1994), a coding bar identified the basics--art discipline, behavior, level of sophistication of that behavior, grade level, and goal--that were involved in each assessment tool. One could also note the encounters that contributed experience to enable student learning being assessed by that tool once a curriculum is planned, meeting the need for demonstrating validity.

Rating the quality of student contributions in aesthetics dialogues

Ratings of the quality of student expressions in the aesthetics dialogue is one means of assessing students' grasp of the big idea of the encounter. The statement "Artists study the real in order to imagine and invent new fantasy situations" suggests a possible and acceptable student generalization that synthesizes the experiences planned. There is is a rating scale format for recording evidence of student learning in aesthetics dialogues in <u>Designing Assessment in Art</u> (Armstrong, 1994). It is like a class list with columns for each criterion--behaviors students were encouraged to use in discussing encompassing ideas about art. Rubrics are a necessary help to maintain consistency or reliability in rating the quality of a student's participation in discussions or other performances. Rubrics are anticipated possible variations in the quality of student participation or evidence of learning. The variations are represented by a number from one to four which correspond to the quality of the student responses. Art teachers who are prepared to present their procedures for making reliable and valid assessments have completed the curriculum planning process...until revisions are warranted.

Confidence statement

Although it is impossible to be thoroughly accountable for the curriculum plan without duplicating the entire planning process, statements can also be made that affirm that because of years of experience, the art teacher can keep content in mind from, for example, art history or design that is commonly addressed in texts. Rather than teach all about educational reform and document those sources, a statement of having considered those current reform recommendations will at least indicate awareness of their existence.

Also, art teachers should include general statement about how to accommodate special needs, review plans for reteaching low achieving students, and suggest ways to accelerate and challenge students who are advanced without feeling compelled to document each detail in a curriculum presentation. A teacher can be comfortable with deviations from the planned encounter when he or she has the big picture of the curriculum plan. Changed is perceived as easier to accommodate because there are multiple ways to achieve desired ends and to modify the level of achievement of those ends.

114

8. AN AESTHETICS RESOURCE

Reference has been made to an aesthetics resource throughout this book. Chapter eight begins with an explanation of the content categories and organization of the aesthetics resource. This overview is designed to help teachers differentiate between various aesthetics theories. Reading a quotation and its generalization with the general tone of the theoretical position in mind will help to differentiate the point of the quotations. This knowledge helps guide the selection of generalizations that connect well with other components of art encounters being planned.

The overview of content and organization is followed by the aesthetics resource.

Contents of the aesthetics resource

Basic questions

Aestheticians ask two common but very thought-provoking and basic questions. They are: What is the nature of art? and What is the value of art? In other words, What makes something "art"? and What good is art? However, the answers to these simple questions vary greatly depending on the theoretical position of the one answering. These differences are acceptable if the position taken can be supported. The aesthetics resource is organized by quotations that seem to answer these two questions and a third category of issues that most aestheticians address. Table 8 shows this organization.

Theory connected quotations

Most writers about aesthetics agree on at least three or four major groups of theorists, but the groups encompass many variations. The groups of theorists whose quotations appear in the aesthetics resource answer the

Table 8. ORGANIZATION OF THE AESTHETICS RESOURCE

1. What is the Nature of Art ?
- 1.1 Art as Imitation
- 1.2 Art as Expression
- 1.3 Art as Formal Organization or Formism
- 1.4 Art as a Social Institution
- 1.5 Art as Instrumental to Pragmatic or Functional ends
- 1.6 Art as No Theory or a Combination of Theories
- 1.7 Art as Cultural Significance: Non-Western theories

2. What is the Value of Art ?
- 2.1 Art as Imitation
- 2.2 Art as Expression
- 2.3 Art as Formal Organization or Formism
- 2.4 Art as a Social Institution
- 2.5 Art as Instrumental to Pragmatic or Functional ends
- 2.6 Art as No Theory or a Combination of Theories
- 2.7 Art as Cultural Significance: Non-Western theories

3.0 **Other issues**
- 3.1 Metacriticism
- 3.2 Media-Generated issues
- 3.3 Aesthetic Attitude
- 3.4 Aesthetic Experience
- 3.5 Pleasure, Play/Therapy, Escape
- 3.6 Characteristics of the Artist, Style, Intent
- 3.7 Creative Process
- 3.8 Art and Context: Social, Political, Economic, Philosophical Institutions of Evolving Cultures

basic two questions aestheticians ask. The theory categories included follow.

Imitation. This category includes philosophies of art, descriptions of phenomenological reality and description of categorical aspection. Essentially the theorists argue that a work is art if it imitates the real or ideal.

Expression. This category of quotations includes views on intuition, the concept of a personal view of reality and imagination, a theory of emotionalism, and a position on art as communication.

Formism. This category of quotations represents philosophic positions regarding significant form, a particular description of imagination, the construct of critical or empirical naturalism, contextualism and related positions. It is the foundation for the traditionally held and now contested modernist principles of design or composition.

Social Institution. The art world can be considered one subset of social institutions in a culture. Other institutions of all evolving cultures, identified by sociologists, are political, economic, and philosophical. Each of these institutions is represented by many familiar groups. (See Figure 4.10 showing subsets of the universal institutions curriculum theory.)

Advocates of the social institution theory maintain that the question of what is art is decided by a subset of this category, the art world-- persons knowledgable about art or those who have a stake in the direction of the art world, such as gallery directors, art historians, architects, fabric designers, art teachers, etc.. Any object can be presented as a candidate for the status of art, but must be justified to the satisfaction of members of the artworld to achieve that status.

Pragmatist, Instrumentalist, Functionalist. Theorists in this category are clustered because of similar expectations that art serves an end beyond itself, for example, conveys political propaganda, sells ideas, or causes an emotive experience in the viewer.

<u>No theory</u> or <u>a combination of theories</u>. Some theorists maintain that without a definitive essence, there is no answer which allows one to draw the line between what is art and what is not art. Other theories incorporate aspects of more than one theory.

<u>Cultural significance</u> and <u>Non-western</u>. In many cultures where artistic work is valued, it is valued for its role in society rather than as a work of art as the western world conceives of an art work. Beliefs and attitudes about artistic work may never have been formalized and written. Yet admirable works are created with impressive technical quality or emotional impact recognizable by persons from different cultural backgrounds.

Issues-connected quotations

The issues identified in the aesthetics resource are among those that aestheticians frequently discuss. The quotations are comments of persons in the artworld on the issues, but are not selected for their representation of a particular aesthetics theory.

<u>Metacriticism</u>. Aestheticians attend to precise definitions of the terms used in describing art and to the explication of those definitions. In metacriticism, the meanings of basic concepts which one might use to describe, analyze and interpret art (Dickie,1971) are explored. Aestheticians examine interpretations, standards, and background information that affect the meaning of words used to describe or evaluate art.

<u>Media-generated issues</u>. Artists' employment of new materials made

possible by technological advances in society and non-traditional "fine art" media generate discussion about the legitimacy of works of art. Aestheticians ask what consideration should be given to geographic context, technology, and familiarity as opposed to similarity to works previously accepted as art.

<u>Aesthetic attitude</u>. Aestheticians' comments on observation and prehension express particular concern with the issue of how a person looks at art-- their disposition, inclination or approach to works of art.

<u>Aesthetic experience</u>. Aestheticians explore concerns related to the aesthetic experience (that is, what happens to one who is viewing art), phases of that experience, and explanations of the "sensuous surface".

<u>Pleasure, Play/Therapy, Escape</u>. Some aestheticians address the question of whether art can legitimately be an escape or release, fun or therapeutic and for whom.

<u>Characteristics of the artist, style, intent</u>. Most aestheticians address issues about the artist him/herself, the artist's style, and the artist's intent (and the ability of the viewer to know the artist's intent).

<u>Creative process.</u> A conscious intellectual activity, the creative process is frequently a topic of aesthetic inquiry. The creative process is analytically described as having behavioral stages (Armstrong, 1983) and globally described as relevant to other topics although the old question of transfer of the practice of creative behaviors to other areas is still debated.

<u>Art and Context</u>. Aestheticians examine art's involvement with the sociologial construct of institutions of all evolving cultures -- sociological, political, economic, and philosophical--and the role of the artist as

influencer, and the influenced. The logical role of these cultural institutions as part of the curricular structure is developed in Chapter 4.

Generalizations

Each generalization in the aesthetics resource is derived from the quotation or paraphrased statement listed directly below it in the text. A few generalizations are summary statements derived from several similar positions expressed by different aestheticians, or paraphrased from long passages of explanation by one aesthetician. A generalization is a simplified restatement of the quotation considering its context. It is a discussable idea which has some truth, as evidenced by some works of art, but which may be debated as not applicable to all art. Nevertheless, it may serve well as the big idea or the learning point of an encounter in art as <u>one</u> idea and in discussion, lead to some profound thinking by students of all ages.

In educational contexts, a generalization, or big idea of a lesson, encounter, or unit of art instruction, is supported by the lesson experiences but has application to life beyond the immediate art experiences. A generalization, already a summary of the direct quotation, may be further reduced in complexity to a theme or advocacy slogan. A theme is a recurring topic that is frequently applicable across time and cultures with many variations. Themes may be expressed in simple language familiar to a young student or qualified by numerous variables for the more experienced student to consider. A simple theme could be "Artists sell ideas visually."

Teacher prompt questions

Model questions are suggested to help teachers motivate dialogue, that is, to initiate open-ended group discussions about aspects of the nature and value of art or issues pertaining to the lesson experiences. These generic prompt questions pose puzzles, dissonant situations, or problem situations about aesthetics issues and **encourage students to synthesize their art experiences in supporting their responses.** So, the wording of the question, likely modified by the teacher for direct connection to the lesson experienced by the students, should prompt students to reflect on the related focus of their art history, criticism, and production components of the lesson.

The suggested questions are worded as appropriate for comprehension at four student conceptual levels (Primary, Intermediate, Junior High, and High School/Adult). They are designed to avoid the likelihood of yes or no answers. Reasons given by students for their stances taken should be supportable by experiences of the group. This last component of the aesthetics resource is compatible with recommendations for involving students in inquiry behaviors associated with the aesthetician (Clark and Zimmerman,1978; Russell, 1988; and Stewart, 1988). The teacher questions should invite the thinking approaches shown in Table 2.2 for the aesthetician. The aesthetics dialogue encouraged by openended teacher questions completes the curriculum planning cycle by enabling students to form generalizations that, in their own words, resemble the big idea of the lesson derived from an aesthetics theory or issue that guided the teacher's selection of art history, production and criticism experiences.

Each generalization-quotation-teacher questions set is numbered. This number identifies it as an answer to the question number 1 What is art?, or question number 2 What is the value of art? , or one of the Issues that aestheticians discuss, number 3. Each generalization set is further identified further identified by sub-points to indicate which theory category is the basis for the quotation. Thus, 1.3 would indicate a response to the What is art? question from a Formism theoretical position, and 3.1 would indicate a generalization set pertaining to metacriticism or definitions of terms we use. This identification would help a teacher chart the comprehensiveness of aesthetics theories introduced in the curriculum plan.

In the right margin, each generalization is numbered sequentially in bold type to help in locating the specific generalization. Feasibly, a notation on a chart might be 1.3/46 to indicate that for that encounter, generalization number 46, representing a Formalist response to the question "What is art?" is the basis for the selection of experiences--the big idea that meaningfully integrates those experiences.

IMITATION THEORY

1.1 REPRESENTATION IN ART IS EQUIVALENCE, NOT REPLICATION 1

"Representation never produces a replica of the object but its structural equivalent in a given medium." p.162

Arnheim, R.(1966). Art and Visual Perception. Berkeley, CA: University of California Press. By permission of University of California Press, Berkeley, CA.

P We look at a sculpture of a rabbit and say, "Look at the rabbit!" Is it a particular rabbit... any rabbit...every rabbit...not a rabbit?

I What is alike and different between a real object, and a painting or sculpture of that object?

J What degree of accuracy is necessary in representing action events in works of art?

H How close to photographic reality must a work of art stay to claim to be a portrayal of real life?

1.1 ARTISTS SELECTIVELY DEPICT THE ESSENCE OF THINGS IN WORKS OF ART ... BY TYPICAL OR REPRESENTATIVE DETAILS 2

"The artist sees the universal, the norm, through the particular, and the beauty of the representation is in proportion to the degree in which the artist has been able to penetrate to the universal implicit in the particular and exhibits the ideal...real character of things." p.105

Reprinted by permission of the publisher from The basis of criticism in the arts by S. Pepper, Cambridge, Mass: Harvard University Press, Copyright 1945 by the President and Fellows of Harvard College.

P What has to be present in an artist's picture of a cat for the representation to be a cat picture?

I If an artist's sculpture is to stand for people's homes everywhere, what would it include?

J If you were going to do a poster that depicts friendship to people all over the world, what would you need to show?

H How would a political cartoonist decide how to represent a _type_ of voter?

1.1 NOT A COPY OF NATURE, A WORK OF ART HAS ITS OWN LIFE 3

"But to construct something that is not a copy of 'nature' and yet possesses substance of its own is a feat which presupposes nothing less than genius." p.23

Ortega y Gasset, J., (1948,1968). The dehumanization of art. Princeton, NJ: Princeton University Press. Copyright 1968 by Princeton University Press. Reprinted by permission of Princeton University Press.

P When might it be okay to color a sky orange or to color water brown or apples, grapes, and melons all greenish?

I Why might an artist decide not to copy everything he or she sees in nature?

J Is a work of art better if it is a good copy of nature than an intensionally changed view taken from nature?

H Assuming that two works of art are comparable in quality, but one selects from nature and one is a copy of nature, is one better "art" than the other? Why?

1.1 ABSTRACTION MOVES AWAY FROM THE REPRESENTATIONAL REALITY OF ART 4

"It is not that the painter is bungling and fails to render the natural (natural=human) thing because he deviates from it, but that these deviations point in a direction opposite to that which would lead to reality." p.21

Ortega y Gasset, J., (1948,1968). The dehumanization of art. Princeton, NJ: Princeton University Press. Copyright 1968 by Princeton University Press. Reprinted by permission of Princeton University Press.

P Some people make trees that look like lollipops. Why do many artists make trees that do not look like lollipops? Why might some artists not make trees look like a photograph of a tree?

I Why would an artist make objects in realistic, photographic detail or choose not to do so?
How close must the depiction be for people to believe it is a tree?

J By what definition of art could a simplification or distortion of a tree be considered good art by comparison to accurate replication of a tree?

H How far can an artist change a realistic painting of a tree before it is no longer a representation?
What does such change ask of the viewer?

1.1 WORKS OF ART CAN DEPICT REALITY, OR AN IDEAL BASED ON REALITY 5

"'In order to paint a beautiful woman, I should have to see many beautiful women...since there are so few beautiful women and so few sound judges, I make use of a certain idea that comes into my head.'" p.6

Raphael cited in Sheppard, A.,1987. Aesthetics: An introduction to the philosophy of art. New York: Oxford University Press. By permission of Oxford University Press.

P Some real children have make-believe friends. Why might an artist want to put make-believe in art work?

I If you draw what you saw in your dream, does your drawing depict something real? Is it okay for art to lie?

J How is science fiction like some visual works of art?

H How do artists conjure up "ideals"? Is an ideal image reality? What consequences could result from portraying "ideals" as "reals"?

1.1 ART IS REPRESENTATION AND INVENTION 6

"...effective representation and description require invention. They are creative. They inform each other; and they form, relate, and distinguish objects. That nature imitates art is too timid a dictum. Nature is a product of art and discourse." p.33

Goodman, N.1976. Languages of art: An approach to a theory of symbols. Indianapolis, IN: Hackett Publishing Company. Fair use.

P When might it be important to put something in a picture that you don't always see?

I When could an art work be better if something is added that can't be seen?

J When might an exact copy of nature be less real than if the artist went beyond imitation?

H What sources are critical to artists' inventions?

1.1 ART IS BASED ON OBSERVATION OF OBJECTS, BUT GOES BEYOND COPYING 7

"And as the degree of imitation becomes less and less, that which is imitated becomes less and less the 'model' which is copied and more and more simply a stimulus to the artist or foundation from which the rest was built through his creative imagination." p.41

From Meaning and truth by John Hospers. Copyright 1946 by the University of North Carolina Press renewed 1974 by John Hospers. Used by permission of the publisher.

P If some artists were drawing trees on a winter day, and one artist drew a summertime tree, why might that be a good idea or not a good idea?

I When might it be important, or not important, to observe what is being drawn? What general guidelines do you think that artists would follow when making realistic art?

J What big ideas about art could you offer that would explain why artists' depictions of nature that they observed, e.g. Van Gogh's paintings of cypress trees, are different from tourists' photos that include cypress trees?

H When might observational drawing be "art" and when not "art" even if it is an accurate copy?

1.1 ART HAS COMPATIBILITY BETWEEN THINGS AND IDEAS AND SIGNS THAT REPRESENT THEM 8

"While the view that representation aims at illusion favours the analogy of the mirror, the view that representation is conventional tends to adopt an analogy between art and language...between art and a system of signs." p.9,10

Sheppard, A.,1987. Aesthetics: An introduction to the philosophy of art. New York: Oxford University Press. By permission of Oxford University Press.

P What makes a sculpture of a deer "art" when a road sign warning of a deer crossing is not "art"?

I Under what conditions could silhouettes of objects be "art"?

J Does good art have any common qualities with road symbols of the same subject? What makes them different in terms of being "art"?

H What, if any, essence must exist between realistic depictions and abstract symbols of the same object?

1.1 INFORMATIVE DRAWINGS OR DIAGRAMS EXPLAIN, BUT ARE NOT ART 9

"An illustration in a medical text can clarify and instruct...But these cognitive functions of pictures can never be identified with their roles as works of art." p.24

Morgan, D. Fall, 1967. Must art tell the truth? Journal of Aesthetics and Art Criticism, 26, 17-27. By permission of the editor.

P Pictures help tell a story in a book. What would make them "art" or not "art"?

I Why are detailed sculptures of horses "art" and different than a veterinarian's chart of types of horses?

J How are works of art that show detail different than drawn explanations of the structure of such objects like a skeleton, leaf, or muscles of an animal in a science or health book?

H What relationships exist between the artist's study of anatomy of an object, studies amde from nature, and the final work of art produced? Are all stages of this evolution considered "art"?

1.1 ART PORTRAYS A KIND OF TRUTH THAT MAY NOT STAND UP TO EMPIRICAL INVESTIGATION OR MAY BE A PARTIAL TRUTH 10

"...representation requires some degree of resemblance between the work of art and something in the world accessible to sense experience..." p.17

Sheppard, A.,1987. Aesthetics: An introduction to the philosophy of art. New York: Oxford University Press. By permission of Oxford University Press.

P Do artists make things the way they really are?

I Can you believe what you see in a work of art?

J If two artists portray the same event in different ways, which is believable? Of what importance is it to have a work of art show truth?

H How much of the viewer is involved in the truth "read" into a work of art? How open to interpretation should art be?

1.1 ART IS NOT A COPY OF THE REAL WORLD.   11

"...nothing is ever represented either shorn of or in the fullness of it's properties." p.9

Goodman, N.1976. Languages of art: An approach to a theory of symbols. Indianapolis, IN: Hackett Publishing Company. Fair use.

P Why would an artist draw a look-alike picture of something when it already exists <u>without</u> being drawn?

I Should art be true to the look of the world when the world is ugly as well as beautiful? Is it okay to change ugly things into beautiful things in art?

J Why would an artist, or would he or she not, realistically depict a meat cutting scene at a butcher shop, or a bomb scene, or the destruction of a nuclear plant? How could the artist's work differ from a newpaper photograph, yet document the event?

H Are there any limits of decency for artists who depict reality--horrors of war, moral issues, or results of political upheaval?

1.1 ART STARTS IN THE MIND OF THE ARTIST   12

"All art originates in the human mind, in our reactions to the world rather than in the visible world itself, and it is precisely because all art is 'conceptual' that all representations are recognizable by their style." p.76

Gombrich, E.,1963. Meditations on a hobby horse. London: Phaidon Press. Fair use.

P Why would artists show the insides of something?

I Why does some art show close-up views or upside-down views?

J Why could art made from parts of spiffy old cars be "representational art"?

H Why could a still life of kitchen tools, fruit, or a branch of an old tree be "art"?

1.1 ART IS A VISUAL LANGUAGE THAT WE LEARN   13

"... the phrase 'the language of art' is more than a metaphor, that even to describe the visible world in images we need a developed system of schemata..." p.76
Gombrich, E.,1963, Meditations on a hobby horse. London: Phaidon Press. Fair use.

P What does a flashing yellow light mean? What does a yellow sign with people's silhouettes on it mean? What "signs" might artists use in art? What do they mean? How do signs help us to "read" works of art?

I What are some different symbols that you have seen in works of art? How do people come to know what these symbols or images mean? Why might they not have meaning to everyone?

J How is short hand like Egyptian hieroglyphics? How would you learn to read Egyptian hieroglyphics? Should everyone be able to "read" all art?

H Can art be a visual language? How, for whom, and under what circumstances? Could a visual language substitute for all others?

1.1 PORTRAITS ARE MODELS OF PEOPLE   14

" It [the correct portrait] is not a faithful record of a visual experience but the faithful construction of a relational model." p.78
Gombrich, E.,1963, Meditations on a hobby horse. London: Phaidon Press. Fair use.

P Do you always look the same to your mother? Why might an artist paint a portrait of someone that doesn't look like a photograph of that person?

I An artist is painting a portrait of a great governor who is a father, plays golf, builds model planes and raises roses. How many different ways might the artist ask that person to pose? Which would be a portrait if each pose was painted? Why?

J How can a work of art be called a portrait if it looks "gross"?

H What is the role of obsrvation in painting portraits? What would be the advantage of sculpting from a live person rather than a photograph, or would it be a disadvantage?

1.1 NATURAL RULES ARE IMITATED IN THE STRUCTURES OF WORKS OF ART 15

"Art imitates them [the formative principles which operate in nature and life] by embodying them in structures made by man." p.64

Schaper, E., 1968. Prelude to Aesthetics. London: George Allen & Unwin, Ltd. By permission of Routledge.

P People plan buildings. How is a building like a tree? What would architects have to think about to make a strong and beautiful building? Why is it important to be strong? to be beautiful?

I What could be important rules for artists who want to create an effect of a windy day?

J How is a mobile sculpture like a human skeleton? How might artists imitate nature without making images of it?

H Science and art share ideas about color, light, motion, etc. How might artists use what they know from science in art? Does that make science more important than art?

1.1 WORKS OF ART REPRESENT QUALITIES OF OBJECTS 16

"...objects in art can be used to refer to things beyond themselves...does not depend upon resemblance...what Peirce calls *symbols*--conventional signs." p.60

Eaton, M. (1988). Basic issues in aesthetics. Belmont, CA: Wadsworth Publishing Company. Copyright 1988 by Wadsworth, Inc.. By permission of Wadsworth Publishing Company.

P Why would an artist make something look different than it does to you?

I Why would an artist make something look diffferent than it does naturally?

J Why would an artist change natural proportions, colors, or positions of facial features?

H How do nonrealistic modes of representation help to emphasize different aspects of reality, hence different points of view about them?

1.1 ART RECONSTRUCTS REALITY, PORTRAYING A PARTICULAR TRUTH WITH IMAGES WE RECOGNIZE   17

" It is not simple copying that we care for, but the balance that is struck between copying and convention." p.15

Sheppard, A.,1987. Aesthetics: An introduction to the philosophy of art. New York: Oxford University Press. By permission of Oxford University Press.

P Why can the same tree be painted differently by artists and each artist's work look real?

I Is a photograph more real than an artist's picture of the same place? How might an artist's picture be more real than a photograph of that place made by the same artist?

J Can a work of art done in a studio portray reality as well as a copy of the actual scene or object done at the site?

H Would a photograph or an artist's portrait be considered the "real" person"? Why? Is realistic art "real"? Why, or why not?

1.1 ART IMITATES NATURE'S ACTIVITY   18

" For Aristotle, what art imitates is 'nature's productive activity...art...imitate[s]...how nature acts.'" p.61

Schaper, E., 1968. Prelude to Aesthetics. London: George Allen & Unwin, Ltd. By permission of Routledge.

P Why could you say that art imitates nature if all you can see is wavy lines, sweeping brush strokes, or jagged lines?

I What could artists imitate about nature in works of art? What is "nature" but is not an object?

J In what ways might kinetic art be imitative of nature? of the manmade environment? How could you define imitation of nature in art?

H What conclusions are generally true about the relationship of imitation and nature in art that would accommodate works such as Nude Descending a Staircase as "art"?

1.1 ART IMITATES TO DIFFERENT DEGREES

" Imitation...is a matter of degree; in no case does it reach 100 percent."..."And as the degree of imitation becomes less...the 'model' which is copied and more and more... a stimulus to the artist...it becomes...his (secondary) material rather than his explicit subject matter..." p.41

From Meaning and truth by John Hospers. Copyright 1946 by the University of North Carolina Press renewed 1974 by John Hospers. Used by permission of the publisher.

P Why would an artist describe a work of art as " ...<u>of</u> my tree" as opposed to "<u>based on</u> my tree" ? What does that say about art?

I How can you explain differences in landscapes from the Oriental and American West painters? What idea about all art does this suggest to you?

J How can you explain the fact that three artists' paintings of the same tree at the same time result in striking differences in visual characteristics, degree of realism, mood, and amount of color?

H What statement could you make that accurately describes the role of subject matter in realistic art?

1.1 ART REPRESENTS, NOT COPIES, BUT PRESENTS A POSSIBLE REAL NATURE

"...though mimetic...the work of art is always a new fact, a fact of the productive imagination." p.62-63

Schaper, E., 1968. Prelude to Aesthetics. London: George Allen & Unwin, Ltd. By permission of Routledge.

P What makes an object more real than a sculptor's copy of it? Is the artist's sculpture real, also? Why?

I What might we conclude about copying nature in works of art that would let artists have some freedom from making a "photo" of the subject?

J How far might artists depart from copying, yet have their work considered real? What is the reason for setting the limitation you suggest?

H Planned obsolesence is a contemporary phenomena. How could that phenomena in our society impact on reaalistic art? Should it, or should it not, and why? What constitutes representative art in contemporary society?

1.1 ART DEPICTS IDEAS 21

"...what the artist imitates is not the world as we have it, but the possibilities of this world, enacted and presented in an artistic construct." p.63

Schaper, E., 1968. Prelude to Aesthetics. London: George Allen & Unwin, Ltd. By permission of Routledge.

P Smiley faces mean "good". How do works of art show that people have different moods by more than just a curved mouth?

I How would artists go about showing a party atmosphere?

J How would a work of art show "friendship" so that many people could understand it?

H How could knowing of ways that visual qualities can be varied account for a viewer's recognition of real life feelings in art?

1.1 WORKS OF ART CREATE MEANING THROUGH SELECTION AND COMPOSITION BASED ON CLUES FROM NATURE 22

"...art procedes as nature does, takes it clue for organized construction from nature, but produces that which is not a natural fact,...freely and not according to any necessity of nature." p.64

Schaper, E., 1968. Prelude to Aesthetics. London: George Allen & Unwin, Ltd. By permission of Routledge.

P How do extra objects tell about a person in a work of art?

I How would the sky or landscape around a subject help tell you what a work of art means?

J What, besides presence of meaningful objects, reveals what the artist is representing in a work of art?

H How can a viewer's life experience interfere with or contribute to recognition of the artist's view of reality?

1.1 WORKS OF ART SYMBOLIZE FEELINGS

"Art is the creation of forms symbolic of human feeling" p.40

From Langer, S.(1953). Feeling and form Copyright 1953. Published by Scribner's & Sons, New York. Fair use.

P What makes people want to have works of art around them? Is a Barbie doll a work of art?

I What is it about the Mona Lisa's smile, for example, that represents everyone's (smile)?

J What basic truth about life of a person your age could an artist depict; and how would it need to look to be true for all teenagers?

H What qualities must exist in works of art that account for their universal appeal to people?

1.1 ART MUST HAVE RELATED PARTS OR QUALITIES THAT REPRESENT SOMETHING

"An expressive form is any perceptible or imaginable whole that exhibits relationships of parts, or points, or even qualities or aspects within the whole, so that it may be taken to represent some other whole whose elements have analogous relations." p.20

From Langer, S.(1957). Problems of art. Copyright 1957. Published by Scribner's & Sons, New York. Fair use.

P If you have ten different green crayons how would you pick the crayon to best fit with ten different kinds of lines you could make?

I How could representations of objects made with recycled objects be works of art?

J Why is an oversized jack knife put in an art museum as a work of art?

H What decisions do artists make to represent something most truthfully and effectively?

1.1 THE NATURE OF AN OBJECT INFLUENCES ITS REPRESENTATION BY AN ARTIST, AND THE PROCESS OF REPRESENTING IS PART OF THE FINAL REPRESENTATION   25

"[R]epresenting ...is not a matter of passive reporting...The object itself is not ready-made but results from a way of taking the world. The making of a picture commonly participates in making what is to be pictured." p.31,32

Goodman, N.1976. Languages of art: An approach to a theory of symbols. Indianapolis, IN: Hackett Publishing Company. Fair use.

P If one artist grew up loving to ride horses and another hates horses, how do you suppose that their drawings of horses might differ?

I A camera generally photographs any object in an instant. How is that different than the way an artist would paint an object that moves fast and a quiet object?

J What might determine the decisions an artist makes about the most appropriate way to represent an object?

H What kinds of decisions are influenced by the subject an artist is addressing? At what stages of the creative process are decisions influenced by the nature of the subject?

1.1 ART REVISITS PAST IDEAS AS IT REPRESENTS LIFE TODAY   26

Representational artists can examine the art of the past for ideas grown fresh through neglect. (unknown)

P Why do you think that long ago children were pictured by artists so differently from the way they are pictured now?

I For what reasons might "realistic art" of long ago look different from "realistic art" of today?

J Why might you say that artists could depict realistic subject matter so that it is more real than life? For what reason might you say that is impossible?

H How can you explain neo-realism as an art movement that follows modern along with innovative, experimental movements? Have artists run out of ideas? Is neo-realism valid as "art"? Why or why not? Is it legitimate to return to old ways of making art and depicting life?

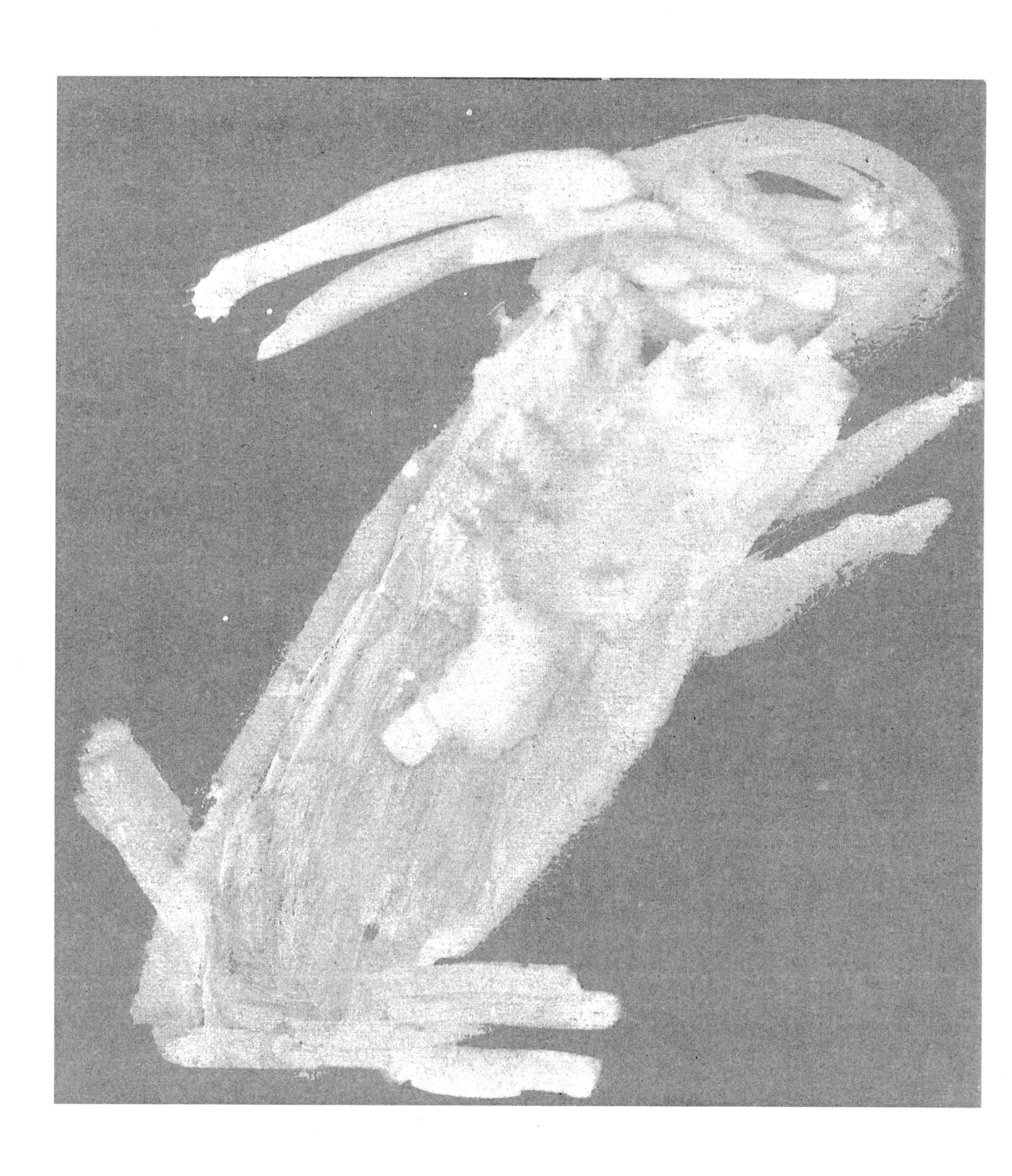

136

EXPRESSION THEORY

1.2 ART IS A DISTINCTIVE INTERPRETATION OF LIFE EXPERIENCE 27

"A work of art may accordingly be re-defined as a distinctive expression, in a distinctive medium, and by means of a distinctive type of formal organization, of a distinctive type of interpretation of man's experience and of the real world to which this experience is oriented." p.230

Greene, T.1940, The arts and the art of criticism. Princeton, NJ: Princeton University Press. Copyright 1968 by Princeton University Press. Reprinted by permission of Princeton University Press.

P If two people like the same park picture, but one shows a sunny day and the other shows a stormy day, why can they both be art?

I If two family portraits differ--stiff,frontal positions in one and relaxed positions in the other--can they both qualify as "art"?

J What about the nature of art allows us to accept works of art that interpret the same battle scene with conflicting evidence?

H What variables enter into the emergence of unique interpretations of the same life experience, all being works of art?

1.2 TO INTERPRET THE WORLD, WORKS OF ART MUST HAVE SOME SUBJECT MATTER 28

" If the true artist seeks to express in his art an interpretation of some aspect of the real world of human experience, every genuine work of art...must have *some* subject matter..not *merely* an aesthetically satisfying organization of sensuous particulars." p.231

Greene, T.1940, The arts and the art of criticism. Princeton, NJ: Princeton University Press. Copyright 1968 by Princeton University Press. Reprinted by permission of Princeton University Press.

P If a painting is just a blue spot, how would you know what the artist was saying? What would you have to see in art that tells about the town where you live?

I If an artist wants to visually explain ideas about work in a particular place, how could it be done without recognizable objects ?

J What objects are critical to themes (e.g. circus) so that viewers recognize some particular truth about them?

H What is the critical role played by subject matter in artists' interpretations of reality?

1.2 ART IS AN EXPRESSION OF THE ARTIST 29

"...with the advent of Romanticism [expression]...became one of the favorite epithets of critics...[the work of art] was valued as a symptom of the artist's state of mind, as an 'expression of personality'." p187

Gombrich, E. (1963). Meditations on a hobby horse. London: Phaidon Press. Fair use.

P If an artist shows sad people in a work of art, did the artist feel sad or want to make people sad when they saw the art, or something else ?

I Is a picture "happy" because the occasion in the picture is a happy event, because the person who posed for the painting was happy, because the artist was happy, or because the artist wanted to make people who looked at the picture happy?

J Why might works of art tell us how the artist felt?...how the subjects felt?...how society felt?

H How can the style of a period affect interpretation of the artist's work?

1.2 QUALITIES IN ART AND NATURE MAY BE ASSOCIATED WITH CERTAIN EMOTIONS FOR CERTAIN PEOPLE 30

Works of art can have properties, qualities, or characteristics that have similarity to properties in nature associated with particular emotions in particular contexts.

Summarized and paraphrased from pp. 340-344 in Hospers, J.(1955). The concept of artistic expression. Proceedings of the Aristotelian Society, 1954-1960, 55, 313-344.

P The same sun sets over the plains, mountains, and sea. Why might someone prefer one good painting of a sunset and another prefer a different good painting of a sunset?

I Artists have painted mothers and children together for many years, yet the depiction of the mother and child or children appear to differ in loving qualities in different versions of this subject. Why might this be?

J How do you account for works of art being interpreted differently as people discuss them?

H What associations can you hypothesize between interpretations of works of art and different backgrounds of people?

1.2 EMOTIONS ARE IN THE VIEWER OF WORKS OF ART UNLESS THE EMOTION IS DEPICTED AS A CHARACTERISTIC OF A PERSON IN THE WORK 31

"But if we mean that there is, for example, a woman in the painting whose face registers sadness, then, insofar as the sadness is recognized as a characteristic of her, the sadness is in the painting in the derived sense that it is a characteristic of the woman who is in the painting. Emotions occur only in sentient beings;..." p.53

From Meaning and truth by John Hospers. Copyright 1946 by the University of North Carolina Press renewed 1974 by John Hospers. Used by permission of the publisher.

P If you look at a work of art and you feel excited, why might we say that the artwork is exciting?

I If an artist depicts an emotional scene in a work of art, why would it be correct or incorrect to say the painting was an expressive painting?

J People often say art is expressive. Can a work of art be emotional? Why or why not?

H Considering the many ways of conceiving of expression in art, is emotion in art the same?

1.2 BEING EXPRESSIVE ISN'T EVERYTHING 32

"Expressiveness, then, as constituting, or even being a reliable indicator of, beauty in a work of art is a view I would reject." p.331

Hospers, J.(1955). The concept of artistic expression. Proceedings of the Aristotelian Society, 1954-1960, 55, 313-344. Fair use.

P Why could something be "art" even if it doesn't tell you a story or make you feel good or bad?

I Is it ever possible that something is "art" or not "art" depending on whether it makes you feel positive or negative toward its subject?

J Among other things, artists arrange forms in space, draw animals, paint impressions, and depict historical events in sculptural media. How would you explain the degree to which expression is involved in what we call "art"?

H What constitutes expression and to what extent does it contribute critically to "art"?

1.2 ART THAT EVOKES EXPRESSION MAY DO SO INCONSISTENTLY DEPENDING ON THE DISPOSITION OF THE VIEWER AND CONTEXT 33

"The behavioural and facial expression of emotion differs in some respects from one culture to another and cultural factors may also be responsible for the association of particular expressive properties with particular works of art." p.31

Sheppard, A.,1987. Aesthetics: An introduction to the philosophy of art. New York: Oxford University Press. By permission of Oxford University Press.

P Why could the same work of art make your friend react differently to it than you do?

I What could make a person accept a work as "art" one day, but have a different reaction to it on another day?

J Why could the same image give rise to different responses in a viewer when viewed repeatedly?

H Is it possible that legitimate "art" could be inconsistently expressive?

1.2 ART IS THE ARTIST'S VIEWPOINT OF WHAT IS REAL AND IS SHOWN IN A PARTICULAR WAY 34

"... in a work of art, (a) *reality* is (b) *interpreted,* and (c) *expressed in a distinctive way."* p.229

Greene, T.1940, The arts and the art of criticism. Princeton, NJ: Princeton University Press. Copyright 1968 by Princeton University Press. Reprinted by permission of Princeton University Press.

P Why might three artists paint the same barn and have the barn look different in each painting? Could you find the barn or is it important to be able to do so?

I For what reasons might Madonna and Child sculptures look so different and yet, all be true and good art? Are all Madonna and Child sculptures "art"?

J What contributes to the varying "realities" depicted by artists of the same event? To what extent could all interpretations be true?

H To what extent does individuality of style enter into artists distinctive, but real interpretations of the same situation? Does individual style solely account for different interpretations?

1.2 ART COMMUNICATES TO PEOPLE WHO PERCEIVE IT AT DIFFERENT LEVELS — 35

"...the language of art has become increasingly difficult. Painting must be done for and offered to everyone; not just to those who can participate only at the most superficially accessible figurative level of language, but also to those who know the world of art." p. 39

Garcia interview by M. Brenson. November, 1990. Nothing but the truth. The Journal of Art, 3 (2), 37-40. Fair use.

P   Why is it possible, or why is it not possible, to understand art from a country about which you know nothing?

I   What kinds of things could you learn from history that would help you understand art from a distant country? Why could you, or could you not, figure out the meaning of a work of art without knowing its history?

J   To what extent could one understand art from unfamiliar contexts and why?

H   What enables a person to recognize a work as "art"? What roles are played by knowledge of art and/or life experiences in perceptions of art?

1.2 ARTISTS COLLABORATE WITH AN ASSUMED AUDIENCE, AND EXPRESS EMOTIONS SHARED BY IT — 36

"...he thinks that the emotions he has tried to express are emotions not peculiar to himself, but shared by his audience" p.315 "...just as every artist stands in relation to other artists ...so he stands in relation to some audience to whom he addresses it." p.316-317

Collingwood, R. (1958). Principles of art. New York: Galaxy Press. Oxford University. By permission of Oxford University Press.

P   Think about art from all over the world that we have discussed. What might you learn about other people by looking at works of art? What might you understand easiet and why?

I   In what ways could studying a work of art be like reading a story or newspaper account of an event?

J   How is an artist's reason for creating art different from the journalists' reasons for describing an event?

H   How does the artist's intention in depicting human emotions differ from the hype of an advertising artist's TV commercial?

1.2 WORKS OF ART TRANSMIT THE ARTIST'S EXPERIENCE TO THE VIEWER 37

"...the picture [an artist's record of experience in painting a subject],when seen by someone else... produces...experiences which, when raised from impressions to ideas by the activity of the spectator's consciousness, are transmuted into a total imaginative experience identical with that of the painter." p.308

Collingwood, R. (1958). Principles of art. New York: Galaxy Press. Oxford University. By permission of Oxford University Press.

P How could art be like a magic carpet?

I What would works of art have to be like if they were to substitute for a world cruise for someone who viewed them?

J If you were to solve a mystery, which might be more helpful, a newspaper photograph or a drawing by an artist who was there at the same scene?

H What are the advantages or disadvantages of experiencing something through a work of art?

1.2 ART REPRESENTS UNIVERSALS BY THE ARTISTS' TREATMENT OF THE SUBJECT 38

"Ruskin thought that generalizing representation could never produce good art; but it can; not because it is representation, nor because it is generalizing representation, but because it can be raised to the level of art proper through being handled by a real artist." p.46

Collingwood, R. (1958). Principles of art. New York: Galaxy Press. Oxford University. By permission of Oxford University Press.

P What can artists do in the works of art that they create that tells us what is special about their subject?

I How can artists represent something so that you feel like you were there with the artist?

J To what extent can an artist speak for you in good art?

H If one artist depicts a subject which exists across time and in all cultures, but depicts his/her own experience,how can that work of art be universally representative? What criteria would make such a work "art"?

1.2 ARTISTS USE PROJECTION AND INTROJECTION OF FEELINGS IN WORKS OF ART   39

"The disowning of experiences they [psychologists] call repression; the ascription of these to other persons, projection; their consolidation into a mass of experience...,dissociation; and the building-up of a bowdlerized experience...our own, fantasy building." p.218

Collingwood, R. (1958). Principles of art. New York: Galaxy Press. Oxford University. By permission of Oxford University Press.

P How many different ways could a sculptor carve a stone dog to show the dog's diffeent feelings? What do artists change to show feelings in what they make?

I How is it possible for an artist to make objects we use to show feeling e.g. a ceramic vase's sleekness, or wiggliness, or bubbliness?

J When an artist depicts a frightening battle scene or ferocious storm at sea, does the artist have to feel frightened? Does the audience have to feel the same feeling for the work to be "art"?

H When an artist depicts apparent evil-mindedness of a figure in a sculpture or print, to what degree must the artist be involved in the emotion for the work to be "art"?

1.2 ARTISTS EXPLORE EMOTION TO UNDERSTAND IT; EXPRESSING IT FOR OTHERS IS "AFTER THE FACT"   40

"...any decision to express this emotion and not that,...represents a further process of a non-artistic kind, carried out when the work of expression proper is already complete." p.115

Collingwood, R. (1958). Principles of art. New York: Galaxy Press. Oxford University. By permission of Oxford University Press.

P Why do artists paint pictures or make sculptures?

I What might happen to artists before they decide to make a work of art? What might artists realize as they make works of art? Why do you think so?

J Why might it be acceptable for artists to set out to express a particular emotion? Why might that approach hurt or help the artist's attempt to create the effect desired?

H What does it mean to "visually express an emotion"? Why would an artist bother? How would you prioritize some reasons in a summary statement?

1.2 PSUEDO ART IS CRAFT, NOT ARTISTIC EXPRESSION FOR ITS OWN SAKE. RATHER IT IS A PRODUCTION CREATED AS A MEANS TO A PRECONCEIVED END...BUT PLANNED WORKS MAY BE WORKS OF ART 41

"But the term 'psuedo-art' means something that is not art but is mistaken for art;...characteristics which it posesses not as art but as religion are mistakenly supposed to belong to it as art." p.33

Collingwood, R. (1958). Principles of art. New York: Galaxy Press. Oxford University. By permission of Oxford University Press.

P If a furry stuffed bunny was made to sell because it was soft and huggable, could it be called art for the <u>reason</u> that it makes you feel good?

I We know that creative persons often have a good sense of humor. If an artist makes something silly that makes everyone laugh, is that reason enough, or not reason enough, to be "art"?

J If an artist designed a football pennant or some object with which you decorate your room, why is that a good enough reason, or not a good enough reason, to consider it "art"?

H What is the relationship between an artist's plan for a work of art and plans to make a marketable object having religious symbolism in terms of being "art"?

1.2 EXPRESSION IN ART DEPENDS ON RECOGNITION OF AN IMAGE AND ITS FEELING 42

" A sense impression or image becomes an expression, or intuition, when it is clearly known as an image, and when it is unified by the feeling it represents." p.745

Magill, Frank N. Masterpieces of world philosophy p.745. New York: Salem Press,Inc.1961. Copyright.©, 1961,1982, by Salem Press, Inc. By permission. (Summary of principle ideas advanced by B. Croce.)

P Is a bowl of peaches more or less easy to identify than a bowl of garbage? To be understood should art be more like the bowl peaches or more like the garbage? Why?

I What reasons can you give to explain why the same person might recognize the feeling of one painting, but not another?

J What makes a work of art expressive? Is subject matter important expression? Why or why not? Why is more needed than a facial or body expression?

H What conditions might effect recognition of expression in a work of art?

1.2 THE IDEA IS THE REAL "ART"

"Art is the idea in the artist's mind ...formulating the idea is real *art*" p.29
Eaton, M. (1988). Basic issues in aesthetics. Belmont, CA: Wadsworth Publishing Company. Copyright 1988 by Wadsworth, Inc.. By permission of Wadsworth Publishing Company.

P If an artist weaves a beautiful piece of cloth, where did the beauty of it start? If the artist thought up that "beauty", is the "art" in the artist's mind or in the cloth?

I If an architect plans an exciting new building, but many people make it, is the plan "art" or is the completed building the work of art?

J Some artists show photographs of some creative event that they planned and carried out. What reasons can you give for saying that the art work is a) the photos of the event displayed in a museum, b) the event that happened, and/or c) the artist's plan?

H How might you resolve the question of whether contemporary (or ancient) murals or the plans for them are the "art" where apprentices to the artist may actually have executed the artist's idea?

1.2 EXPRESSION OF THE WORK OF ART RELATES TO THE ARTIST AND THE OWNER

"Leo [art dealer/gallery director, Castelli] has always maintained the essential attitude that an art object is a feeling object, related to the person who made it and to the person who owns it..." p.10
From Post-to-neo: The artworld of the 1980's by Calvin Tomkins, Copyright 1988 by Calvin Tomkins. Reprinted by permission of Henry Holt and Company, Inc.

P If you want to buy an art work that you like, who else probably liked what you like about it? Why? Why do you think it would be important for that person to have liked it?

I Why is it important, or not important, that someone at an "art store" or gallery feel positive toward a work of art? Who should feel favorably toward any particular work of art? Why?

J To what extent, and why, do you think that there is a special tie between the artist who produced an art work and a person who bought it? What kind of a "tie" might that be?

H What committment toward a work of art should the person who purchases it have, and why?

1.2 "ART" IS NOT DETERMINED BY FEELINGS PRODUCED OR PYSCHOLOGICAL REACTIONS   45

"Deciding what psychological reaction a so-called work of art produces (...how a certain poem 'makes you feel') has nothing whatever to do with deciding whether it is a real work of art or not. Equally irrelevant is the question what psychological reaction it is meant to produce." p.32

Collingwood, R. (1958). Principles of art. New York: Galaxy Press. Oxford University. By permission of Oxford University Press.

P If you feel proud to be an American when looking at a sculpture of U.S.soldiers, why is that a good reason to call that sculpture "art" or not to call it "art"?

I If a photograph of a Maine seacoast or San Diego sunset over the bay makes you feel pleasant thoughts, why would, or would not, that be reason enough to declare that photo "art"?

J How would you respond with reasons to someone's statement that a work of art was "art" because "it turned me on" i.e. made one feel strongly and empathetically?

H People react emotionally--positively and negatively) to art. What considerations qualify an emotional reaction as a criterion for calling something "art"?

FORMALISM THEORY

1.3 NOT USUALLY CONSIDERED ART, SOME DESCRIPTIVE PAINTINGS MAY HAVE FORMAL SIGNIFICANCE AND, THEREFORE, QUALIFY AS WORKS OF ART

"... pictures that interest us and excite our admiration, but do not move us as works of art. To this class belongs what I call 'Descriptive Painting'- that is, paintings in which forms are used not a objects of emotion, but as means of suggesting emotion or conveying information... Of course many descriptive pictures possess, amongst other qualities, formal significance, and are therefore works of art..." p.16-17

Bell, C. (1913) Art. London: Chatto & Windus. Public domain and by permission of Chatto & Windus

P Why could art rules help make a scary Halloween picture "art"? How can rules help tell visual stories? What are some rules you could make?

I If an object tells a story, why isn't it a good enough reason to call it "art"?

J How could a photographically painted illustration of a bull fight be "art"?

H How could a painting or sculpture that describes an accident scene or a horse race qualify as "art"?

1.3 "THE FORM OF A WORK OF ART IS ITS MOST ESSENTIAL QUALITY"

"Significant form stands charged with the power to provoke aesthetic emotion in anyone capable of feeling it." p.36-37

Bell, C. (1913) Art. London: Chatto & Windus. Public domain and by permission of Chatto & Windus

P How do artists make you know what is important in a picture?

I How can artists influence the meaning you "read" into a picture?

J If artists use images that are important to depict key moments in exciting events, what else would they consider to effectively portray such events in works of art?

H How could qualities or attributes of works of art simultaneously exemplify tenets of both Formalism and Emotionalism in art?

1.3 EVERY PART OF A WORK OF ART MUST PRIMARILY CONTRIBUTE TO ITS (PLASTIC ORGANIZATION) 48

"...pictures in which representation subserves poetical or dramatic ends are not simple works of art, but are in fact cases of the mixture of two distinct and separate arts...the art of illustration and the art of plastic volumes..." p.35

Fry, R. (1956). Transformations. New York: Doubleday anchor Press. Public domain.

P What are some "rules" for making art that we have learned? How are rules for art different from rules for playing a game? Why do we have rules in art?

I Why do rules contribute to a story picture being "art"?

J What makes works of art that depict great historical events "art" or not art?

H What role does formal organization have in art that illustrates?

1.3 WORKS OF ART HAVE UNITY, COMPLEXITY AND INTENSITY 49

"...three general critical standards, unity, complexity, and intensity, can be meaningfully appealed to in the judgment of aesthetic objects,..." p. 469

Beardsley, M. (1958). Aesthetics: Problems in the art of criticism. New York: Harcourt Brace. Fair use.

P Is _what_ an object is a good reason to call it "art"? What makes it good art?

I What rules help pictures of any subject that an artist chooses to qualify as "art"?

J What makes the difference between offensive novelty and unique "art"?

H How would the critical standards by which art is judged apply when the artist considers the entire process from conception to completion to be the work of art?

1.3 WORKS OF ART ALL HAVE SIGNIFICANT FORM — 50

"...'Significant Form' [relation and combination of elements that "move" us] is the one quality common to all works of visual art." p.8
Bell, C. (1913) Art. London: Chatto & Windus. Public domain and by permission of Chatto & Windus.

P When you see art that looks so neat that you say "Wow!", what is it about the way it looks that makes it special?

I If you got a stomach ache from eating chocolates, pizza, pumpkin pie, and pineapple juice together, how could that be like bad art? Why?

J If a group of friends have different personalities, but they get along together well, how might that be like good art? Why might artists be able to make different objects fit in the same work?

H To what extent might the process of making art involve shaping some unformed matter so as to impose a form on it? Why?

1.3 THE EMOTION OF ART RESULTS FROM ATTENTION TO FORM — 51

[good artists] "...are concerned only with lines and colours, their relations and quantities and qualities; but from these they win an emotion more profound and far more sublime than any that can be given by the description of facts and ideas." p. 30
Bell, C. (1913) Art. London: Chatto & Windus. Public domain and by permission of Chatto & Windus.

P What could artists change to make you feel the importance of certain parts of a picture?

I In a gallery of art that has no titles nor pictures of objects, what might account for your inside feelings that change when looking at each different work of art?

J What comes first -- the form or the emotion in a work of art? Are they both inevitable?

H How could a work of art be considered "art" by both Formalists and Emotionalists? Are the theoretical positions mutually exclusive?

1.3 ORGANIZATION IS MORE IMPORTANT THAN REPLICATION

"Formal significance loses itself in preoccupation with exact representation and ostentatious cunning." p. 23.

Bell, C. (1913). Art. London: Chatto & Windus. Public domain and by permission of Chatto & Windus.

P When you clean up your room, why do you decide to put each object in a certain place? Why do artists decide where to put objects in works of art? Why are the reasons different or the same?

I If you were to make a good rule for making art, what would you say about the arrangement of the objects or elements? Why?

J To what extent can innovation or exact replication of actual objects contribute to an entire work of art? When might these practices interfere with good art and why, or why not?

H With recent trends toward originality and extremes in art, innovation has challenged artists. What recommendations would you make to a clever artist-friend who wants to create unique "art", but not just novelty?

1.3 RECOGNIZABLE OBJECTS IN ART ARE IMPORTANT AS ORGANIZED ELEMENTS

"...if a representative form has value, it is as form, not as representation." p. 25

Bell, C. (1913).Art. London: Chatto & Windus. Public domain and by permission of Chatto & Windus.

P Birds flutter and also sit still like kings or queens. Why would or would an artist not put birds of both shapes in the same artwork?

I It is easy to se that circular lines fit a spherical form; but what would guide sculptors who want to put all different kinds of wild animals in the same work of art? What changes could sculptors make in the animals and why? Is it okay to change an animal?

J What would be a good rule regarding the role of any kind of sculpture on buildings?

H How can artists help an assumed audience to overcome subject matter associations and to focus on aesthetics qualities of art works? Should artists avoid subject matter that calls attention to itself? Why or why not?

1.3 FORM IS BOUND TOGETHER WITH EMOTION IN ART 54
"...emotion can be expressed only in pure form." p.54

Bell, C. (1913) Art. London: Chatto & Windus. Public domain and by permission of Chatto & Windus.

P If you wanted to draw a picture of the teacher whose jewelry fascinated you, would you choose to show her with all the students in a school room or to draw her closeup? Why?

I If an artist wanted to show the quick movements of a playful cat, which material and arrangements of lines and other elements would work best to show that in a sculpture? Why?

J Which kind(s) of sculpture might artists choose to show the gentle vibration of fall leaves? Why?

H How does the effect desired by artists influence choices of media and organization of the elements? Why?

1.3 IN SUCCESSFUL ART, SMALL AND OVERALL MOVEMENTS FIT 55
" The dynamics of a composition will be successful only when the movement of each detail fits logically in the movement of the whole." p.416

Arnheim, R. (1966). Art and visual perception. By permission of University of California Press, Berkeley, California.

P Does a sneeze in the middle of a song fit? Why not? What would do a similar thing to an artwork?

I What kind of rule about movement in art would be like saying "Do not put oranges in the vegtable soup!"? Why?

J Imagine a sculpture of a stiff looking cowboy on a bucking horse. Why might that sculpture not look convincing? What would make the sculpture more successful?

H Compositions should have repetition and variation as well as movement. What is the relationship between them ? Why is this relationship important, necessary, and/or sufficient as a criterion for asserting that something is art?

1.3 ART IS HOW SOMETHING LOOKS NOT WHAT THE OBJECT IS   56

"...formalists emphasize intrinsic properties of the object...... we should not attend to *what it*[work of art] *represents*, but to *how it presents*" p.79

Eaton, M. (1988). Basic issues in aesthetics. Belmont, CA: Wadsworth Publishing Company. Copyright 1988 by Wadsworth, Inc.. By permission of Wadsworth Publishing Company.

P Peacocks are so beautiful! Is <u>any</u> picture or object of a peacock beautiful art? What else is important to be "art"? Why?

I Barbie dolls and statues of goddesses represent beauty of girls to someone. Does representing beauty make something art? What is beautiful about girls in works of art?

J Why would an artist make pottery that cannot be used, or construct a quilt to hang on a wall, or paint a painting of an "ugly" person?

H What relationship exists between what is represented and how it is presented in good art?

1.3 SUBJECT MATTER ALONE IS INSUFFICIENT FOR CREATING INTEREST   57

" There is... an 'evaporation' in *illustrational* painting;...subject-matter of the painting loses its interest... since the interest of the painting depends upon the interest in the subject-matter, the painting automatically loses its excuse for being." p.112

From Meaning and truth by John Hospers.Copyright 1946 by the University of North Carolina Press renewed 1974 by John Hospers. Used by permission of the publisher

P If an artist tells about a family in a work of art, why would it be enough, or not enough, to have each member placed side by side?

I If artists depict a sports scene, would they show it like it is, or would they make changes in the way it was? Why might they do so? What changes might be made? Why?

J Can you imagine an artwork deicting an active scene that looks boring? How do artists change the way things really looked? Why is it ok at to do so ?

H How could subject matter detract from the quality of a work of art? Is there some subject matter that would inevitably do so? Why or why not? What idea would summarize the ideal situation in regard to using realistic, illustrative subject matter in art?

1.3 FORM ENABLES EXPRESSION OF EMOTION 58

"...formalists ...seem wholly blind to the fact that form is important in esthetic objects for the very reason that it itself...is the source of certain esthetic <u>emotions</u> which nothing else can objectify..." p.198

Ducasse, C. (1929). The philosophy of art. New York: Dial Press Division of Bantam, Doubleday, Dell Publishing Group, Inc. Fair use.

P If an artist wants to show gracefullness of a seal, would it be better to show the seal gliding and turning through gentle waves or clapping its flippers on the beach? Why?

I Why do diagonal lines seem more active than horizontal lines in works of art? Why might artists need to think about how lines seem to be when making art?

J How can artists arrange shapes and lines to make a viewer "fel" a force e.g. to be jumy, to be laid back, or to crouch and spring? Why is, or is it not, important for artists to plan this?

H What is the role of principles of composition or design in expressive art, or do those principles have a role? Why might "rules" be broken or should there be no exceptions to good rules for making art? Why or why not?

1.3. BEAUTY IN ART IS SIMPLICITY, HARMONY, AND CLARITY, PLUS, PLEASURE PRODUCED IN SOMEONE BY THOSE QUALTIES IN A FORM 59

"He [St. Thomas Aquinas] concludes that the conditions of beauty are three: perfection or unimpairedness, proportion or harmony, and brightness or clarity...the cognitive (knowing) aspect of the experience of beauty... and there is the subjective factor of being pleased by what is seen or known." p.7-8

Dickie, G. (1971a). Aesthetics. New York: Bobbs-Merrill Pegusus Division of Prentice-Hall,Inc. Fair use.

P Could a beautiful picture be "art" if no-one saw it?

I Why, or why not could a painting that had everyone's favorite flower in it, be sure to be art?

J What qualities of life in a high-tech society could also be art qualities?

H If culture influences conceptions of beauty, is "beauty" a sufficient descriptor for art? Does beauty exist independently of culture?

1.3 ART IS MORE THAN MERE ILLUSTRATION: FORMAL ORGANIZATION HAS PRIORITY OVER ILLUSTRATION

"And since the art of illustration is really 'literary' and quite extraneous to the plastic medium, wherever literary values interfere with the plastic, it is the former that must go." p.104 " A painting which has no artistic merit of its own but merely illustrates some theme from history or literature, and interests people because of the things it represents or the life sentiments it evokes rather than by its merits as art, is,...an illustrational painting. Yet no one admits this to be art;..." p.108

From Meaning and truth by John Hospers. Copyright 1946 by the University of North Carolina Press renewed 1974 by John Hospers. Used by permission of the publisher

P If a picture of a tearful child makes you think of a sad time you felt, why is that a good, or not a good, reason to call the picture "art"?

I If a picture shows a war scene that shows the meanness of war, is that a good enough reason or not a good reason to call it "art"? Why?

J If a film documents a social problem and serves a good cause, is that all it must be to be valued as "art"? Why or why not?

H In what ways can illustrative subject matter get in the way of objectively judging the artistic merit of a production? Can most viewers discern art quality in spite of subject matter? Why or why not?

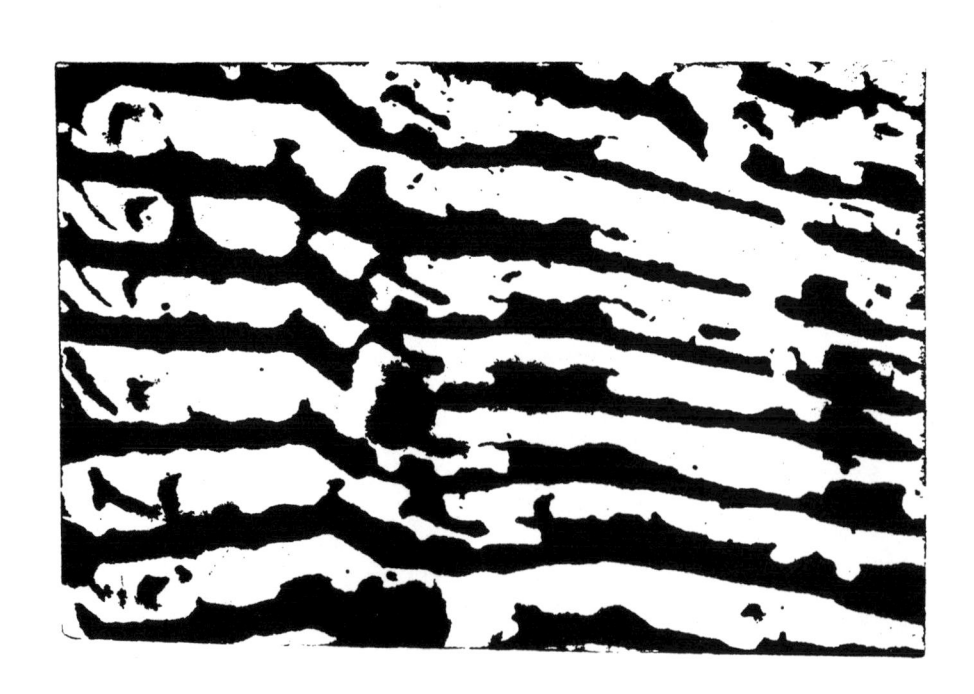

SOCIAL INSTITUTION THEORY

1.4 THE ARTWORLD AND THE ARTIST AGREE ON REASONS FOR A WORK TO BE "ART" 61

(In reference to Danto's position)"...to be an artwork, the artworld and the artist presenting something for candidacy for appreciation must share a *theory* about what art is." p.93

Eaton, M. (1988). Basic issues in aesthetics. Belmont, CA: Wadsworth Publishing Company. Copyright 1988 by Wadsworth, Inc., By permission of Wadsworth Publishing Company.

P Whose ideas about art would let an artist put a clothespin in an art show? Who might not like calling a clothes pin "art"? Why?

I What would allow artists to show paintings of blue cats, staring animals, or upside down cows? Would everyone have to agree that such strange art ideas are "art"? Why or why not?

J Is it okay for a gallery director to refuse to show the public the work of an artist who asks that his/her work be shown?

H To what extent must artists conform to standards set by persons who promote art? Why?

1.4 ART IS NOT BOUND BY PRECEDENTS, BUT BREAKS THEM AND CREATES NEW ONES 62

"Artists today are not easily intimidated, and they regard art genres as loose guidelines rather than as rigid specification." p.107

Dickie, G. (1971). Aesthetics. New York: Pegasus Division of Bobbs-Merrill. Fair use.

P Some people always observe certain customs on holidays or do things exactly the same way. Would habits help or hurt artists to think in new ways? Why?

I How do both change and custom affect what we see as art?

J How well does the idea of flexibility in thinking fit with artists' expectations of the art they and others create?

H What role could the "artworld" have in an artist's perceived license or limitation in regard to art forms, imagery, dimensions, scale, approach, media, themes, or even appropriate training?

1.4 CALLING SOMETHING A WORK OF ART REQUIRES BEING RESPONSIBLE FOR SUPPORTING THAT DECISION 63

"In conferring the status of art on an object one assumes a certain kind of responsibility for the object in its new status; presenting a candidate for appreciation always faces the possibility that no one will appreciate it and that the person who did the conferring will thereby lose face." p.108

Dickie, G. (1971a). Aesthetics. New York: Bobbs-Merrill Pegasus Division of Prentice-Hall Inc. Fair use.

P If you like something, does that make it "art" or what would make it "art"? What would make one stuffed elephant toy for a princess look so special that it could be called "art"?

I Suppose we have a plastic spoon and a very old one stolen from a museum. What reasons would be good ones to use to defend that one of these is "art"?

J How can preference be different from recognizing that something one has never seen before is "art"? Undr what conditions might a tourist buying a painting on black velvet be buying "art"?

H What are the criteria that you would consider in deciding whether something you prefer is "art"? Is a dinner place setting on a matching table more or less "art" than a silver spoon in a case in an art museum? To what degree could concensus be important?

1.4 A WORK OF ART IS AN ARTIFACT THAT ACHIEVES ACCEPTANCE BY PEOPLE WHO ARE INFORMED ABOUT ART 64

"A work of art is an artifact of a kind created to be presented to an artworld public." p.63.

Dickie. G. The new institutional theory of art.In R. Haller. Ed. (1964). Aesthetics: Proceedings of the Eighth International Wittgenstein Symposium, Part 1. pp57-64. Vienna,Austria:Holder-Pichler-Tempsky. Fair use

P Would it be possible for a child to make art so well that it could be put in art history books? Why might the age of an artist be important or not?

I When an artifact is proclaimed as "art", of what importance is the original purpose? Why?

J Of what significance is information like function, rarity, age, and/or artists' intents regarding the status of an artifact as "art"? Why?

H Should the status of an object as "art" be determined by individuals, theories, the maker of the object, art museum or gallery directors, art historians who live 100 years later, committees of upstanding citizens, or some one else? Why?

1.4 "WORKS OF ART" MEET COMPLEX CONDITIONS INCLUDING PUBLIC ACCEPTANCE 65

[institution]"...an established practice, law or custom...what makes a work of art a work of art is the network of behavioral patterns by which its status as an artwork has been conferred upon it, beginning with criticism and (sometimes) ending in exhibition in a public place, where an audience may repair to appreciate it, even to judge whether a mistake had been made by the initial conferral of status...another example of artistic criticism, as informed or uninformed as it might be." p.58-59

Kaelin, E.F.(1989). An aesthetics for art educators. New York: Teachers College Press. By permission.

P Looking at everything around you, why would you choose to call some things and not other things "art"?

I Does calling something "art" mean that you like it? Does it mean that it is good?

J If you recognize that an object is intended to be a sculpture, does that confer the status of "art" it automatically? What conditions would need to exist to do so?

H Does identifying something as art also confer permanent status to that object because of that classification?

1.4 ART THEORIES SUGGEST PARAMETERS FOR ACCEPTING NEW CREATIVE PRODUCTIONS AS "ART" 66

"... telling artworks from other things is not so simple a matter...without an artistic theory...terrain is constituted artistic in virtue of artistic theories, so that one use of theories,..., consists in making art possible." p. 572

Danto. A. (1964). The artworld. Journal of Philosophy, 61(19), 571-584. By permission.

P What is helpful about talking about art we make? Why do we learn from thinking through why others make art? Why should we talk about how important art is?

I For what reasons do people talk about art if they can't agree on what art is?

J When art is always changing, what point is there in trying to define it by old theories?

H Why can or cannot each individual decide what is art? Where do theories fit in? Is anything art? Is everything art? Why or why not?

1.4 ART IS AN OBJECT WHICH SOMEONE IN THE ARTWORLD HAS IDENTIFIED AS "ART" 67

"A work of art in the classificatory sense is 1) an artifact 2) upon which some person or persons acting on behalf of a certain social institution (the artworld) has conferred the status of candidate for appreciation." p.101
Dickie, G. (1971a). Aesthetics. New York: Bobbs-Merrill Pegasus Division of Prentice-Hall. Inc. Fair use.

P An art teacher found a wooden spoon with a carved handle in an attic. The teacher hung it on the wall like a painting. Could an old spoon be "art"? Why? Why not?

I A peacock made its foot prints in an artist's freshly poured concrete walk. The artist decided not to smooth them out. Does this decision make the footprints "art"? Can happy accidents be "art"? Why or why not?

J An artist arranges pieces of wood on a porch and enjoys varying the arrangement. Why might that be considered a work of art or not? Is it a different art work each time the wood pieces are rearranged? Is it a new kind of art? Why or why not?

H To what extent can some once-functional object be given the status of art? Is it of greater or lesser value as art depending on whether it is in an art museum? Why or why or not?

1.4 AN "ART WORLD PERSON" DEFENDING AN OBJECT THAT OCCURRED BY CHANCE AS "ART", MAKES THAT OBJECT THE WORK OF THE PERSON WHO GAVE IT THE STATUS OF "WORK OF ART" 68

"Despite the fact that Betsy [a chimpanzee] did the painting, the resulting works of art would not be Betsy's but the work of the person who does the conferring...[since Betsy]...cannot see herself as an agent of the artworld-- she is unable to participate (fully) in our culture" p.106
Dickie, G. (1971a). Aesthetics. New York: Bobbs-Merrill Pegasus Division of Prentice-Hall. Inc. Fair use.

P If you pick up ten beautiful stones that look special stacked on your table, is that stack of stones "art"? Who is the artist?

I If stones which accumulated and made a wall is described as a work of art, who is the artist?

J If an artist picks up several pieces of driftwood to arrange so they look nice together, is that "sculpture" his art? nature's? not art?

H An arrangement of wood by an artist is changed thoughtfully by the artist. The visiting dog bumps the pieces around, and the artist did not change the arrangement. Which of these arrangements can be defended as "art" and why?

PRAGMATIST, INSTRUMENTALIST, FUNCTIONALIST THEORIES

1.5 FINE ART CAN BE USEFUL; USEFUL ART CAN BE FINE 69

"To institute a difference of kind between useful and fine arts is, therefore, absurd, since art involves a peculiar interpenetration of means and ends." p.377

Dewey, J. (1958). Experience and nature. New York: Dover Publications. By permission of the publisher.

P Rugs are usually made to walk on. Why would someone hang an Oriental or Two Grey Hills Navajo rug on the wall?

I If a woven Native American basket was very special, why would you use it in your home? Why not? How might you, or when might you use it? Why?

J Suppose a potter makes beautiful pottery and uses it. A secretary buys mass produced, but very pretty and expensive china and displays it as art. For what reasons could either be "art"?

H If some artist-designed clothing ws really "art", what good qualities might the clothing have? What is the broader implication of "wearable art"? Is that implication applicable to all forms of art? Why or why not?

1.5 AESTHETIC OBJECTS HAVE UNITY, COMPLEXITY, AND INTENSITY 70

"...three general critical standards, unity, complexity, and intensity, can be meaningfully appealed to in the judgment of aesthetic objects... Objective reasons that have any logical relevance at all depend upon a direct or an indirect appeal to these three basic standards." p. 469-470.

Beardsley, M. (1958). Aesthetics: Problems in the philosophy of criticism. New York: Harcourt, Brace. Fair use.

P If you find two sculptures of a mother and child--a subject you like--, why might one be more pleasing because of decisions the artist made?

I Why do good works of art "capture" and hold the viewers' interest? What is true about the way they are thought out? Why do you say so?

J How would conceptual (the idea) complexity differ from object complexity in art works? Why is either important? Why might both be important?

H Artists' decisions should meet some basic criteria in order to have aesthetic quality according to Beardsley. Could you explain the acceptance of Inuit sculpture or minimalist art as "art" by Beardsley's criteria? Why or why not?

1.5 ART CALLS FOR NO ACTION, JUST AN AESTHETIC EXPERIENCE 71

"...the object in the painting is not a material object, but only the appearance of one." "...aesthetic objects are make-believe objects; and upon this depends their capacity to call forth from us the kind of admiring contemplation, without any necessary committment to practical action, that is characteristic of aesthetic experience." p.529

Beardsley, M. (1958). Aesthetics: Problems in the philosophy of criticism. New York: Harcourt, Brace. Fair use.

P Some people say "If I like it, it is art". Why can you agree or disagree with this reason?

I Why is it necessary or not necessary to like a production called "art"? Should art make people stop and think, or, should it just cause enjoyment? Why?

J How can you explain the difference between preference and judgment in regard to deciding if something is "art"?

H Why could someone engage in "admirable contemplation" of works of art that they would not buy for their home? Is that patronizing or insincere? Why or why not?

1.5 A WORK OF ART EXISTS IF IT CREATES AESTHETIC EXPERIENCE 72

" 'X is a good aesthetic object' means 'X is capable of producing good aesthetic experiences (that is, aesthetic experience of a fairly great magnitude).' ...I shall call these Functional definitions of 'good' in its adjunctive use as applied to aesthetic objects." p. 530-531.

Beardsley, M. (1958). Aesthetics: Problems in the philosophy of criticism. New York: Harcourt, Brace. Fair use.

P If a sculpture is placed in a shopping mall, but no one gives it more than a glance, does that mean it is not very good art? Why? Why not?

I For what reasons would you say that people should not be able to resist stopping and looking at real art? Must good art make people appreciate it? Why or why not?

J How can appreciation of a work of art be measured? Should we try to determine if a work is good art? Why?

H To what extent could one's individual personality enter into whether a work of art functions as an object capable of producing aesthetic experiences?

1.5 THE FUNCTION OF A WORK OF ART CAN BE UNDERSTOOD BY RECOGNITION OF THE STRATEGY THE ARTIST USED IN SOLVING HIS/HER PROBLEM 73

"Critical and imaginative works are answers to questions posed by the situation in which they arose. They are not merely answers, they are <u>strategic</u> answers, stylized answers" p.1.

Burke, K. (1941) <u>The philosophy of literary forms: Studies in symbolic action</u>. Baton Rouge, LA: Louisianna State University Press. By permission of M.Burke, Co-trustee, Kenneth Burke Literary Trust.

P What can someone find out by stopping to examine a work of art? Why might it be important?

I How can looking for decisions the artist might have made help in understanding art? Why do artists' decisions influence what the work of art means?

J How can looking for and mentally playing out the different routes an artist might have taken, contribute to a viewer's understanding of why something is art?

H Why are there different styles in art? What relationship might exist between function or meaning of a work of art, and the artist's style?

1.5 THE PRODUCT IS NOT THE WORK OF ART 74

"The <u>product</u> of art--temple, painting, statue, poem--is not the <u>work</u> of art. The work takes place when a human being cooperates with the product so that the outcome is an experience that is enjoyed because of its liberating and ordered properties." p.214.

From <u>Art as experience</u> by John Dewey. Copyright 1934 by John Dewey, renewed 1973 by The John Dewey Foundation. Used by permission of G.P. Putnam's Sons, a division of Penguin Putnam Inc.

P Why would someone make art and want to show it to someone else? Would it make it better art? Why or why not?

I If art must be experienced by someone, why might some art never be recognized as "art"?

J Is the product of an artist a work of art if no one sees it? What part should recognition of the worth of an artwork play? Who might need to recognize its worth? Why?

H Products of artists are frequently not recognized as worthy until long after the artists' deaths. How could you defend these works as "art" before the artists die? Why would the work have to be enjoyed by others or would that not be necessary? Why?

1.5 ARTISTIC CREATION IS NOTHING MORE THAN PRODUCTION OF A SELF-CREATIVE OBJECT 75

"...the artist can,... manipulate the elements of the medium so that they will make the quality emerge...The powers...are...those of nature...a miracle that celebrates the creative potentialities inherent in nature itself." p. 303.
Beardsley, M.(Spring,1965). On the creation of art. The Journal of Aesthetics and Art Criticism, 23(3), 291-304. By permission of the editor.

P What does it take to make art? Can paint make a painting? Can an artist "think" a painting into being here? Can colors and lines arrange themselves? How does something get to be art?

I We can see a beautiful color in the sky, so why do we say an artist created it when that color is on a canvas?

J How can you explain art as a work of an artist if all the artist did was select and arrange colors that existed... like stocking grocery shelves...or is it? Why or why not?

H Is the artist just a manipulator of elements and media using tools with the artwork being what is creative; or, is the artist a creative person who gives life to otherwise unimportant elements and media? Are there other explanations?

1.5 WORKS OF ART EMERGE AS ARTISTS AND MEDIA INTERACT 76

"The act of expression that constitutes a work of art is a construction in time....a prolonged interaction of something issuing from the self with objective conditions, a process in which both of them [artist's self and medium] acquire a form and order they did not at first possess." p.65.
From Art as experience by John Dewey. Copyright 1934 by John Dewey, renewed 1973 by The John Dewey Foundation. Used by permission of G.P. Putnam's Sons, a division of Penguin Putnam Inc.

P Have you ever imagined creatures in the clouds? Artists' media can be for artists what clouds are for you. Why could that be true? Is it art when you see pictures in the clouds? Why?

I What is it about watercolor...or clay...or the natural form of a rock or a kind of yarn that could effect what an artist made? Why? Would those same objects have the same effect on non-artists? Why or why not?

J What comes first in art, the idea or the medium in which the idea is portrayed? Could media inspire ideas? Do artists look for media which fit an idea or ideas to go with media? Why?

H Why do artists act on their response to objects, effects, media or phenemena that are visible to all people?

163

1.5 ART MUST HAVE UNITY--COOPERATIVE INTERACTION OF OPPOSING ENERGIES

"There is no art without the composure that corresponds to design and composition in the object. But there is also none without resistance, tension, and excitement; otherwise the calm induced is not one of fulfillment. In conception, things are distinguished that in perception and emotion belong together." p.160.

From <u>Art as experience</u> by John Dewey. Copyright 1934 by John Dewey, renewed 1973 by The John Dewey Foundation. Used by permission of G.P. Putnam's Sons, a division of Penguin Putnam Inc.

P People rest after jumping rope. How is that similar to quiet, empty spots in a busy art work? Why might that be a good thing to plan in an art work?

I When can a person know what it is like to be restful? How could artists help people looking at a work of art to experience a restful feeling? Why would a feeling of jumpiness require that the artist use tools, media, and techniques that are different?

J How can tension and resolution of a sports event have parrallels in the visual arts of sculpture, drawing, painting, etc.?

H Why can tension and compositional fit both exist as components of a unified work of art?

NO THEORY/COMBINATION OF THEORIES

1.6 ART IS A FUSION OF PSYCHOLOGICAL ASPECTS AND THE FORMAL QUALITIES 78

"One does not need to know the original story in order to appreciate the delightful expressiveness of the forms, though doubtless knowledge of the story assimilated into the aesthetic experience would enrich it." p.322.

Reid, L. A criticism of art as form. In L.Reid, Ed. (1954) A study in aesthetics. New York: The MacMillan Company. Fair use.

P How does the title of a picture help or get in the way of your enjoyment of the picture? What else helps people enjoy pictures?

I If a work of art is like a murder mystery, what things can give clues to its meaning?

J How do "read" a work of art without its title to guide your interpretation?

H What is the relative importance of the title and of the formal qualities for enabling a viewer's response to the expressiveness of a work of art?

1.6 THE DEFINITION OF ART SHOULD BE CLEAR, NON-CIRCULAR, COMPREHENSIVE, AND EXCLUDE THINGS THAT ARE NOT ART 79

The minimal criteria required to establish the true definition of 'art' are: 1) clear...testable terms, 2) no circularity, 3) covers all cases and all properties of works of art, and 4) things clearly not art are not included...but there is no sufficient statement of the function, significance or value of art.

p. 53-54. Paraphrase of Weitz, M. In E. Eisner & D. Ecker. (1966) Readings in art education. Waltham, MA: Blaisdell Publishing Company.

P Does art have to be made by a person? ... by a self-trained artist? ...by a trained artist? Why?

I What tests can be applied to determine if something should be called "art"? What is not art?

J Why might pieces of clothing from one culture be viewed as works of art in another culture where they are not worn as clothing? Should they be considered art? Why or Why not?

H Why must a definition of art satisfy all objects regarded as art across time and cultures? Is one definition possible? Are several definitions appropriate? Why or why not?

1.6 IF "ART" IS DETERMINED BY GOOD EXAMPLES, COMMON QUALITIES, AND MUST ALLOW NEW IDEAS, THERE IS NO SUFFICIENT THEORY OF ART 80

Meaningful talk about or defining art involves conditions of having paradigm cases, strands of similarities among properties, and allowance for new examples of works of art with their new properties...the last of which disallows defining work of art..it makes it an open concept because the properties of new art cannot be predetermined. p. 53-54

Paraphrase of Weitz, M. In E. Eisner & D. Ecker. (1966) Readings in art education. Waltham, MA: Blaisdell Publishing Company.

P If an artist's painting of one egg is a work of art, what other objects might be made as "art"? Why might such common things become the subject of a work of art? Does the object make it "art"? Is it something that the artist does in showing the object, and if so, what?

I Scientists and artists invent. Invention in art may show us what we have never seen before or dreamed of. If it is called "art" by the artist, how else could we know that it is really "art"?

J Is a jungle gym enough like artists' constructions that it could stand as an art work? Why or why not?

H What conditions must innovative work meet in order to be viewed as "art"? Why? Who must view the work and decide that it is art? Why?

1.6 "GREAT WORKS OF ART TEND TO DEAL IN UNIVERSAL VALUES" 81
p.69-70

Booth, W. (1961). The rhetoric of fiction. Chicago: University of Chicago Press. Copyright 1961 by the University of Chicago. By permission.

P If you wanted to make something in art that would be important to everyone, what would it be about? Why?

I What is it that makes art important to people of all ages, all times, or in all places?

J About what subject would you make a work of art that would be important to people in all cultures?

H What relationship is there between universally perceived importance of a work of art and values?

1.6 ART IS NEITHER FRILL NOR FACT   82

"So long as we continue to accept the absurd alternative which offers art as only a specious choice between art as a diversion or decoration, on the one hand, or as a peculiar second-rate substitute for true-blue empirical knowledge, on the other, we shall block every hop of understanding ourselves or our culture." p.21.

Morgan, D. (Fall, 1967). Must art tell the truth? Journal of Aesthetics and Art Criticism, 26, 17-27. By permission of the editor.

P If there are many ways that artists can show a mother loving her child, is this kind of picture always "art"?

I What variations can exist in works of art showing a mother and child and still be showing essentially the same truth about their relationship? When is such a depiction not "art"?

J What criteria must be met or what must remain constant in works of art showing varying, but effective, interpretations of "motherly love"? What is "serious art"?

H How much universal truth is critical to accepting individual interpretations of the theme such as "motherly love" in a work of art? Is that enough or what else is needed?

1.6 ART SHOULD HAVE THE SAME COMPELLING FORCE AS REAL LIFE EXPERIENCE   83

Whereas "culture has never kept the real realities of life away... we must extract from what is called culture, the idea whose compelling force is identical to that of the life phenomena" (unknown)

P Why could an artist's painting of your funny friend be more like your friend's expression than a smiley face symbol?

I What qualities of the elements of art and their arrangement would help the viewer "experience" a horse race, Christmas shopping, or summertime?

J How is it possible for art to depict an object or situation so effectively that a viewer can have the same experience as being there?

H Why would totalitarian entities choose to use art as an effective means of spreading doctrines or ideologies.

1.6 DEFINITIONS OF MODERN ART ARE TENTATIVE   84

" Modern art came out of the art of earlier periods"..."Modern art is neither a hoax nor a religion, and it has neither a beginning nor an end." p.106-107.

From Post.-to-neo: The artworld of the 1980's by Calvin Tomkins, Copyright 1988 by Calvin Tomkins. Reprinted by permission of Henry Holt and Company, Inc.

P If your neighbor who is an artist makes a new painting, is it "modern" art? What reasons could be given to call it modern or not call it modern?

I Why should modern art stop being called "modern" or should it <u>not</u>? If "modern" was no longer used, then what would the artworks that <u>were</u> called "modern" be renamed? Why?

J If 80 years is old for a person, is it old for a work of art? When does "modern" become old? Why?

H If an art museum was running out of space in a very productive period, would it be best to store or give away art that didn't last very long, old art, or stop acquiring new works of art? Why?

1.6 WORKS OF ART ARE INTENDED AS SUCH BY THE ARTIST   85

"Intentionalists claim that art cannot be distinguished from non-art unless one knows that ...an artist...intended to make a work of art....intentions are necessary, but not sufficient, for something to be a work of art." p.19.

Eaton, M. (1988). Basic issues in aesthetics. Belmont, CA: Wadsworth Publishing Company. Copyright 1988 by Wadsworth, Inc.. By permission of Wadsworth Publishing Company.

P Can art be a happy accident? Is it necessary that persons try to make something "art" if, when it is finished, they expect others to call it "art"?

I If a sculpture made out of inclined planes is shown in a public place and attracts skateboarders for play, is it no longer "art"? Does the artist's intent count? What might the artist think?

J If an artist doodles while talking on the telephone, what reasons could you offer for defending them as "art" or not "art"? What would you consider in order to decide?

H Considering sketches of renown artists that are shown in major art museums, how could you debate their recognition as "art" if there is no information abut the artists' intent?

1.6 ART IS A SOCIAL PHENOMENA 86

"...a general sociology of art is implicit in the existing empirical studies of social and cultural conditions of artistic expression." p.1.

Kavolis, V. (1968). Artistic expression: A sociological analysis. Ithaca, NY: Cornell University Press. By permission and fair use.

P What might happen in all cultures about which artists could make art? How might they differ? Would the art show the same things as being important in those events? Why or why not?

I If art is about people, their lives, and living and working together, what are some common things that people do to live that could be common subjects for artists in different countries and at different times? What might this say about art and people?

J What questions do you ask about life that might be asked by young people growing up in other times and places? What role has art played relative to these questions? Can art that is functional be fine art? Why?

H What sorts of objects become the status symbols of groups of people in our culture, that parallel cros-cultural roles of art? Should art be used to these ends or should it not? Why?

1.6 ART IS UNDERSTOOD WITHIN ITS SOCIAL CONTEXT 87

"Structuralism is an attempt to *reconstruct* the form and content of a work according to general, repeatable social phenomena...Deconstructionists believe that the access to contexts...are not available...for we are never in all ways like the creator." p.97.

Eaton, M. (1988). Basic issues in aesthetics. Belmont, CA: Wadsworth Publishing Company. Copyright 1988 by Wadsworth, Inc.. By permission of Wadsworth Publishing Company.

P If people believe that girls should be treated differently than boys, how and why might that effect the clothing designed for girls, their toys, and how artists showed them in artworks?

I What experiences made the artists of long ago, like three thousand years ago, create the kind of art that they did? Can we know how they lived and how they thought? Why or why not?

J How can you explain the creation of art for religious purposes in contrast to creation of art that seems to contradict basic values of most religions? Can we know how values effect art? Why?

H Within documented historical periods, why can we, or can we not, understand the social context that explains the source of the original idea and nature for a work of art?

1.6 QUALITY IS VARIABLE AND QUESTIONABLE AS A CRITERION FOR "ART" 88

"In view of the art world's increasing multiculturalism, the scales of quality are becoming...sliding scales. The problem with invoking quality is that it creates an artificial sense of security for everybody concerned." p.25.
Storr, R. (1990). Raiding the icebox at MOMA. The Journal of Art, 3 (2), 25-26. Fair use.

P If artists like something about children's pictures and use similar things in creating their artwork, is their art worth the same amount of money as the children's pictures or not? Why?

I If a very old cross is found that was exquisitely detailed and well-crafted, and it is placed next to a very simplified, graceful and unadorned cross, why could you say that one was better art or not?

J Does using images that characterizes art from an underdeveloped country indicate or alter the quality of the artwork? If so, how and why? If not, why?

H What differences in backgrounds of people could account for different definitions of quality in art? What examples can you give to support your reasoning?

1.6 "ART" IS PARTICULAR TO THE ENCOUNTER OF OBJECT, PERSON, AND TIME 89

"...there is something that happens in front of a particular work of art, at a particular time in space, with a particular individual that is completely unlike anything else." p.25.
Storr, R.(1990). Raiding the icebox at MOMA. The Journal of Art, 3(2), 25-26. Fair use.

P Why might looking at some art make you forget where you are?

I Have you ever not heard your mother call you because you were totally interested in watching TV? Why might someone claim that a person can look at art and "become part of it"? What does that mean? Do you agree or not and for what reason?

J To what extent is the response to a work of art predictable? Why or why not?

H What influences differing reactions to art? Which of the reasons ought to contribute to decisions about whether an object is art? Why?

1.6 DESIGN PRINCIPLES ARE COOPERATIVELY EMPLOYED IN WORKS OF ART 90

[art as logical empiricism] "Contrast, gradation [relatedness], theme [or pattern] -and- variation, and restraint [suspence and balance] are, then, the four principles of design... not mutually exclusive...are mutually cooperative, and any considerable work of art employs all of them together." p. 57.

Excerpt from Principles of art appreciation by Stephen C. Pepper, copyright 1949 by Harcourt Brace & Company and renewed 1977 by Frances P. Tarson and Elizabeth P. Wood, reprinted by permission of the publisher.

P At night, could you see a black or a white cat easier? How would that help an artist to know how to make important parts of a picture show up? Does that make a good picture? Why or why not?

I Do artists have to follow rules of art to have good works of art? Can artists be individual and creative and also make art that follows rules?

J We've observed rules that artists seem to follow in making art. To be "art" do <u>all</u> the rules need to have been followed? Why or why not?

H Can a work of art be succesful if the artist employs fewer than <u>all</u> of the principles of good composition? Why or why not? Why might artists in some culture disregard what we know as principles of composition?

1.6 BEAUTY IN ART IS SIMPLICITY, HARMONY, AND CLARITY, PLUS PLEASURE PRODUCED IN SOMEONE BY THOSE QUALITIES IN A FORM 91

"He [St.Thomas Aquinas] concludes that...the conditions of beauty are three: perfection or unimpairedness, proportion or harmony, and brightness or clarity...the cognitive(knowing) aspect of the experience of beauty...and there is the subjective factor of being pleased by what is seen or known." pp.7-8.

Dickie, G. (1971). Art and the aesthetic: An institutional analysis. Ithaca, NY: Cornell University Press. By permission and fair use.

P Could a beautiful picture be art if no one saw it? Why? Why not?

I Does making art that follows the general rules of beauty assure that people will like an artist's work? Why is it likely to please, and why might a good art work not please?

J What qualities of life in a high tech society could also be qualities of new art forms ? Why?

H If culture influences conceptions of beauty, is "beauty" a sufficient descriptor for art? Does beauty exist independent of a viewer? Why or why not?

1.6 A WORK OF ART IS "ART" IF IT IS SIMILAR TO ANOTHER WORK THAT IS "ART"

(Concerning Ziff's and Weitz's views) "According to the new view, an object becomes a work of art by sufficiently resembling a prior-established work of art" p.57 "The closest they can come to theorizing about art is to say that there is a class of objects to which the terms "art" and "work of art" meaningfully apply and that this class cannot be theoretically characterized further." p.58.

Dickie, G. The new institutional theory of art. In R. Haller (1984). Aesthetics: Proceedings of the Eighth International Wittgenstein Symposium, Part 1 pp 57-64. Vienna, Austria: Holder-Pichler-Tempsky. Fair use.

P Would it be a good reason to call a plastic toy horse "art" if it is the same color and size of one that looks like it in an art museum? Why or why not?

I Does being in an art museum make a fancy dish "art"? If your mother has a fancy dish at home like the one in the museum, why might it be an art object? Why not?

J Some artists make huge comic strip frames and they are hung in art museums. does the size make them "art" whereas the dily comic strips are not? ...or are they also "art"?

H If a political cartoonist exhibits excellance in technique and insight about the country's political institutions, could those works qualify as "art" along with time-honored paintings in art museums? Are all cartooons "art"? Where would you draw the line? Why?

NON-WESTERN THEORIES

1.7 ART IS SKILLFUL, SENSUOUS PRESENTATION OF MEANING   93

"Art is culturally significant meaning, skillfully encoded in an affecting, sensuous medium." p.238.

Anderson, R. (1990). Calliope's sisters: A comparative study of philosophies of art. Englewood Cliffs, NJ: Prentice-Hall. By permission of Prentice-Hall Division of Simon & Schuster.

P   How could you try to understand art from a very different country? Why might you not understand the art without help?

I   Why might groups of people need artists to tell stories visually when they can pass them on by telling?

J   Judging from the look of Japanese art and the look of Inuit art, what is common about the nature of art in these cultures although the art looks very different? Why do you think that they treat things that are common to both cultures so differently?

H   What could be necessary and sufficient criteria for calling something art that would apply across time and across cultures?

1.7 ART REPRESENTS THE PAST AS PRESENT IMAGES   94

[Australian Aboriginal art works] "...are tangible representations of the sacred mythological past in the present, the bridge that links man with his gods." p.7.

Berndt, R. (1964).The world of the first Australians. Chicago: University of Chicago Press.Copyright 1964 by the University of Chicago. By permission.

P   Have you ever seen someone in a dream who doesn't really exist? Why might artists put such a person into their art?

I   How many ways do artists today make people of the past more memorable in forms of art? Can this form be accurate ? Should it be accurately depicted as in the past? Why or why not?

J   What is the nature of art that portrays sculptures of Civil War heros, gods , and other non-present personages?

H   What roles might art play in belief systems, giving honor, or cultural traditions? Is this nature of all art? Why or why not?

1.7 ART CHARACTERIZES AND SIMPLIFIES WHAT THE MIND KNOWS 95

[Australian art] "Its makers use a 'subjective vision' representing things not as they briefly appear to the eye but as the mind knows them eternally to be...allowing a few characteristic features to represent the whole subject." p.62.

Anderson, R. (1990). Calliope's sisters: A comparative study of philosophies of art. Englewood Cliffs, NJ: Prentice-Hall. By permission of Prentice-Hall Division of Simon & Schuster.

P How much of a cat do you have to see to know that it is a cat? Why might artists show just enough to suggest what an object is?

I If artists want to make objects more simple than they really are, yet suggest them clearly enough, what aspects of objects would be important to show? Why?

J Why are images of animals in some cultures so simple and not in realistic settings or positions? Do you think this reflects the artists' capability to draw? Why or why not?

H What principles could explain the practice of various cultures of the past to extremely simplify images? Do the same principles apply to contemporary simplification of images? Why or why not?

1.7 ART IS WHAT IS REAL 96

"...true art comes from the gods and is manifest in the artist's mystical revelation of sacred truth." [Aztec] p.152.

Anderson, R. (1990). Calliope's sisters: A comparative study of philosophies of art. Englewood Cliffs, NJ: Prentice-Hall. By permission of Prentice-Hall Division of Simon & Schuster

P A pretty sunset disappears in minutes. Is the sunset real? Can a paintng of a sunset be real? Why might someone say that a painting of a sunset is real?

I Why could people believe that art shows truth?

J Why would you say that artists have revolutionary powers that other people do not have or is that not true?

H Where a culture doesn't accept the idea that truth from the gods is revealed in art, why is there a lingering expectation that artists are at least more perceptive and show truth?

1.7 WORKS OF ART MAY IDEALIZE HUMAN FORM BY CLARITY, HIGH POLISH, PROPORTIONS, FINENESS, MODERATE ROUNDNESS, CORRECT DIGNITY; SKILL; AND PHYSICALITY   97

[Yoruba art reflects a concern with maintaining social equilibrium] "...midpoint mimesis." "...the figure should be generalized to the degree that it represents the finest and best in the human form...[and]the highest ethical standards." p.130.

Anderson, R. (1990). Calliope's sisters: A comparative study of philosophies of art. Englewood Cliffs, NJ: Prentice-Hall. By permission of Prentice-Hall Division of Simon & Schuster.

P How might you stand when you wasnt to look perfect and calm? Why would or wouldn't a sculptor show you like that?

I Why might a sculptor omit some details in showing how you look?

J "Art portrays the ideal form of any object." Why is this a satisfactory, incomplete, or inaccurate statement?

H How can art contribute to a lasting cultural cohesion? Why is that or is it not a distortion of true art?

1.7 ART IS THE LINK BETWEEN HUMANS, THE NATURAL WORLD AND THE SUPERNATURAL   98

"Eskimos recognize the frightening chasms that separate humans from...the cold, unresponsive material world...and...the supernatural and eternal...beyond us....The Inuit answer to the dilemna is that a link does indeed exist, and that it is art." p.54.

Anderson, R. (1990). Calliope's sisters: A comparative study of philosophies of art. Englewood Cliffs, NJ: Prentice-Hall. By permission of Prentice-Hall Division of Simon & Schuster.

P Why do you think that churches use so much art...in windows, murals, fabrics?

I Halloween recognizes that people fear the unknown. How have people turned to art to help explain some unknowns?

J Why might at be thought of as an escape for viewers? If so, ...escape <u>from</u> what, <u>to</u> what, and why?

H What vestiges of seeking connections between humans, nature, and the unknown do you think remain in art of modern societies? Why?

176

IMITATION THEORY

2.1 ART THAT IMITATES NATURE INCREASES THE VIEWER'S KNOWLEDGE OF THE SUBJECT   99

"Hamlet...reflecting surfaces...show us what we could not otherwise perceive...and so art, insofar as it is mirrorlike, reveals us to ourselves, and is, even by socratic criteria, of some cognitive utility afterall." p.571

Danto, A. (1964). The artworld. Journal of Philosophy, 61(19), 571-584. By permission.

P Electric lights help us see better at night. Why could looking at works of art be like turning on the lights at night?

I Magnifying glasses reveal more detail and truth about objects. What truths could be revealed by looking at artists' pictures, sculptures, drawings, etc. of people?

J How would you explain the statement "Art is like a mirror"?

H What purposes might be served by the truth that artists reveal in works of art that imitate life?

2.1 ART HAS MEANING AND IT IS RECOGNIZED IN DIFFERENT WAYS   100

" Gombrich [favors]...a substitution theory, where items substitute for or stand for things depending on our needs and purposes." p.61

Eaton, M. (1988). Basic issues in aesthetics. Belmont, CA: Wadsworth Publishing Company. Copyright 1988 by Wadsworth, Inc., By permission of Wadsworth Publishing Company.

P Smiley faces mean "good". How do works of art show meaning by more than just a curved mouth?

I How would artists go about showing a party atmosphere?

J How would a work of art show "friendship" so that many people could understand it?

H What rules could you formulate about the use of symbols in art that would contribute to viewer's <u>recognition</u> of real life meanings in art?

2.1 ARTISTS' REPRESENTATIONS REVEAL CHARACTERISTICS AND RELATIONSHIPS THAT MAY HAVE GONE UNNOTICED   101

"Representation or description is apt, effective, illuminating, subtle, intriguing to the extent that the artist ...grasps fresh and significant relationships and devises means for making them manifest." p.32-33

Goodman, N.1976. Languages of art: An approach to a theory of symbols. Indianapolis, IN: Hackett Publishing Company. Fair use

P How could many artists' portraits of the same child be different from each other yet be good?

I If you know that a good artist is not conceited, why might he or she make many self portraits?

J Why might artists depict a greatly magnified view of an object or natural occurrence like a raindrop on a leaf, the center of a flower, the point of an icicle, or a dew-covered spiderweb?

H Why might study of artists' realistic works enhance truth that is not revealed through one's own close visual observation?

2.1 WORKS OF ART CREATE MEANING BY COMPOSING SYMBOLIC OBJECTS OR ELEMENTS TO PORTRAY THE ARTIST'S INSIGHT   102

"A work of art is far more symbolic than a word...and presents its import directly to any beholder who is sensitive at all to articulated forms..."" ...importance of abstracting the form, banning all relevancies that might obscure its logic, and especially divesting it of all its usual meanings so it may be open to new ones." p. 59-60

From Langer, S.(1953). Feeling and form Copyright 1953. Published by Scribner's & Sons, New York. Fair use

P How do extra objects tell about a person in a portrait? ...in other works of art?

I How would the sky or landscape around a subject help tell you what a work of art means?

J What, besides presence of meaningful objects, reveals what the artist is representing in a work of art? Will those things insure a single meaning?

H How can a viewer's life experience interfere with or contribute to recognition of the artist's insight into reality?

2.1 WORKS OF ART CAN CONVEY MEANING

(In reference to Goodman's position) "Successful representation is denotative or referential in painting...stand for something beyond...the sign to what it signifies." p.63

Eaton, M. (1988). Basic issues in aesthetics. Belmont, CA: Wadsworth Publishing Company. Copyright 1988 by Wadsworth, Inc. By permission of Wadsworth Publishing Company

P What makes young girls want Barbie dolls? What could an artist's painting of Barbie dolls tell people and who or what other things would need to be added?

I What is it about Mona Lisa's smile that represents everyone's smile, or does it?

J What basic truth about life of a person your age could an artist depict; and, how would it need to look to convey what is true for all junior high age students?

H What qualities are necessary and sufficient for work of art to convey meaning?

2.1 THE VISUAL IMAGES OF WORKS OF ART SHOW EXPERIENCES

"...language... articulates the world of our experience. The images of art...do the same." p.78

Gombrich, E.,1963. Meditations on a hobby horse. London: Phaidon Press. Fair use.

P How do artists tell us how things look or "are" without using words? Is that way as good as using words? Why or why not?

I Can you imagine a world where all description was in words? What would it be like? Is art important for providing information and depicting experiences? Why or why not?

J What reasons can you give to support or refute the idea that the visual arts are an adequate language through which to show experience? Do all the arts equally depict reality? Which arts depict what kind of thing best? Why?

H Which conditions might influence the effectiveness of the visual arts to portray the reality of life experiences. Why?

2.1 ART REPRESENTS, BUT MAY NOT BE FACTUAL KNOWLEDGE   105

"...the artist knows nothing worth mentioning about the subjects he represents, and that art is a form of play, not to be taken seriously." p.333

Plato. (1941). How representation in art is related to truth. The republic of Plato. Translated by Francis Cornford. New York: Oxford University Press. By permission of Oxford University Press.

P Telling someone a secret may be the truth, but somehow it seems different than reading the same thing in a book. How might telling a secret be like what an artist does in art? Why?

I For what reasons would you or would you not "count on" what you see in an artwork? Should art be exactly correct? Why or why not?

J Is an artist's photograph of a situation factual reality? Why could it be so? Why might it not be?

H To what extent can an artist depict totally accurate representations of objects, yet fall short of providing factual knowledge of those same objects? Why?

2.1 IMITATIVE WORKS OF ART CAN CONTRIBUTE TO UNDERSTANDING   106

"...art works can be assessed...as being more or less adequate imitations... convincing representations..." [forms that contribute to understanding by their structure] p. 66-67

Schaper, E., 1968. Prelude to Aesthetics. London: George Allen & Unwin, Ltd. By permission of Routledge

P How could observing the shape of a cat's eye or mouth, or the direction in which its hair grows, help you make more accurate pictures?

I Many young people like to draw horses. What do artists learn by drawing horses while looking at them? Would artists look at drawings or sculptures of horses? Would all artists' horses help? Why?

J What have you noticed is true about an object in real life... after you saw an artist's interpretation of it? How can good representations help us?

H What could be the "times and places" for art that is convincingly realistic? What contribution is made by such art?

2.1 ART MAY ALTER OR EXPAND ONE'S UNDERSTANDING OF NATURAL SUBJECTS 107

"All that art can do in the way of imitation of a given natural subject is, first, to negative a spectator's own preconceptions...and secondly, to impregnate him with this fresh, this alien understanding." p.95

Morgan, C. In Langer, S. (1958). Reflections on art. Baltimore, MD: Johns Hopkins University Press. By permission of the publisher.

P Someone said you could bring luck by putting salt on the tail of a bird. How close can you get to a bird? Why can artists help you see what you cannot get close enough to see yourself? How can you learn to see like an artist?

I Artists draw or paint objects from many views. How can artists change what we thought we knew about an object?

J Why might some artist paint the same subject many times at every hour of the day?

H What sorts of subject matter, viewpoint, media, conceptions of art forms changes can artworks bring about? What is the value of each change?

2.1 ART REPRESENTS NATURE AS BEAUTIFUL AND IDEAL 108

"Assuming that the purpose of painting was to produce something beautiful, various schemes were worked out which told the artist how he could be both faithful to Nature and yet represent her in an idealized manner." p.75 in Boas, G. & Wrenn, W.W. (1966).

Boas, George & Wrenn, Harold Holmes . What is a picture? Pittsburgh: University of Pittsburgh Press. Copyright 1964, University of Pittsburgh Press. By permission.

P If you could, would you change anything about the way you look? What things might an artist change in a portrait?

I Is it acceptable for artists to change the way people look in portraits? What should, or should not, be changed in your opinion?

J Flattery will get you anywhere, some say. Why is that a good or poor thing to believe as the reason why artists make changes in portraits of people?

H What should be considered when you try to decide whether art should idealize reality? What are possible positive and negative outcomes of promoting an ideal?

2.1 REPRESENTATION DOESN'T EXPLAIN THE VALUE OF ALL ART 109

"Representation does play a part in our valuing of representational art but since not all art is representational it cannot be representation which explains the value of all art." p.17

Sheppard, A.,1987. Aesthetics: An introduction to the philosophy of art. New York: Oxford University Press. By permission of Oxford University Press.

P Can art be important even if it does not look like something we know? Why or why not?

I We admire a portrait that looks like the person intended, or a realistic landscape. Why could some ideas be hard to show with a realistic picture?

J Have you ever thought about what proportion of art (of all times) is representational? Would you include abstract symbols, decorative motifs, or woven art as representational?

H To what extent can one ascertain the value of representational art in a cross-cultural context? Why could value be mistakenly assigned to objects from unfamiliar cultures on formalistic grounds?

2.1 THE BALANCE IN ART BETWEEN COPYING AND SYMBOLIZING CHALLENGES THE VIEWER'S IMAGINATION 110

"It is not simple copying that we care for but the balance that is struck between copying and convention. Works which achieve that balance are valued because of the imaginative effort they demand from us." p.15

Sheppard, A.,1987. Aesthetics: An introduction to the philosophy of art. New York: Oxford University Press. By permission of Oxford University Press.

P Computers have little pictures that you can select and use. Why is this not art, or could it be?

I Businessmen give talks and use stick figures or symbols to help get a message across. Why don't they claim to be artists?

J If smiley faces are too simple to be art, yet scientific illustration may be argued as not having artistic priority, what possible suggestions do you have regarding art that interests and
challenges viewers?

H If an artist creates his/her own conventions, how could that effect the imaginative experience of viewers positively and/or negatively?

2.1 ARTWORKS SHARE AN ARTIST'S IMITATION OF A NATURE OF SOMETHING

"...what the artist imitates or is true-to is an essence... true-to his own vision... that...can be the vision of others..." p.194

From Meaning and truth by John Hospers. Copyright 1946 by the University of North Carolina Press and renewed 1974 by John Hospers. Used by permission of the publisher.

P Why might one artist make a drawing of a bird on a nest while another artist draws birds diving for insects in flight?

I Why might a 1980's sculptor travel to Spain to sketch the original type of mustang for a Texas Mustang sculpture? Is it okay if the sculpture doesn't look like mustangs do now?

J If an artist painted all-black night time pictures of town and country scenes with only the lights to reveal edges of the forms, would that be just weird or what might be the reason? Do other artists do basically the same? Why do you think so or think not?

H If artists use subject matter or a style that is not "cool", what could that indicate? Why? Some artists works closely resemble that of their teacher. If you were the art historian observing this, what value would you give the former's work?

EXPRESSION THEORY

2.2 ARTISTS ASSIMILATE LIFE EXPERIENCES AND GIVE FORM TO THEIR INTERPRETATION — 112

"... even the doctrine of art as self-expression implies that the subject matter of art is...as much of the objective world as the artist has assimilated in the development of his own personality... artistic form as a vehicle not for mere self-expression but for what he has felt to be a true and revealing interpretation of some aspect of his environment." p. 232-233

Greene, T.(1940). The arts and the art of criticism. Princeton, NJ: Princeton University Press. Copyright 1968 by Princeton University Press. Reprinted by permission of Princeton University Press.

P Artists have painted Mother and Child pictures in many different ways. Why is it okay to have such very different pictures of one idea?

I Why do eye witnesses to the same accident give different reports of what happened? How would an artist depict the same scene?

J Why would you say that an artists' self-expression is a revelation of deep-seated psychological conditions or just a personal interpretaion of the observable world?

H Why might something an artist makes be considered "art" if it depicts a scene that has special **personal** meaning to the artist?

2.2 ART SELECTS FEELINGS TO EXPRESS THAT CONTRIBUTE TO "GOOD" IN PEOPLE — 113

"...feelings less kind...replaced by others kinder and more needful for that end [the well-being of mankind]. That is the purpose of art." p.231

Tolstoy, L. (1962). What is art? And essays on art. New York: Oxford University Press. A Hesperides Book. By permission of Oxford University Press.

P Why is it important that artists show kindness of people from all countries?

I Why might art do good by showing the way people worked or played long ago? Why is it good now?

J If artists all over the world make art about their country's heroes, and we have our heroes, how could that give art international importance?

H Art portrays ideal standards of behavior in all cultures. Why could the study of multi-cultural artworks be a positive influence on young people looking to a future in a shrinking world?

2.2 ART EXPRESSES FEELINGS BY COMPOSITION OF ITS ELEMENTS 114

"...the expressive content of a work is embodied in its very forms; ...the way ...elements are combined are not mere technical differences... but mark differences in expression and feeling." p.77

Taylor, J. (1981). Learning to look:A handbook for the visual arts. Chicago: University of Chicago Press. Copyright 1957, 1981 by The University of Chicago. By permission.

P American family portraits show friendly, loving, relaxed, and unfriendly looking families. why do you suppose that difference exists? How did artists arrange family members to fit the ideas about families?

I An artist is painting a landscape but wants to show how it looked when there was a 60m.p.h. wind. What combinations of changes would need to be made and why?

J Ten artists draw the same house, but the "moods" of the houses were all different. Can you explain **how** this could be so, and whether that is **good**?

H How can art embody the spirit of expression in matter?

2.2 FORMAL ANALYSIS OF A WORK OF ART REVEALS ITS EXPRESSIVE CONTENT 115

"In describing the difference in effect...in expressive content...terms... which seemed inseparable from our experience: *color,...line,...light and dark... volume and mass, ...plane*...necessary in discussing organization of space" p.63

Taylor, J. (1981). Learning to look:A handbook for the visual arts. Chicago: University of Chicago Press. Copyright 1957, 1981 by The University of Chicago. By permission.

P What do we find out when we look at a work of art for answers to our questions about how an artist put it together?

I A recipe tells a cook how to put together the designated amount of ingredients to get a particular flavor. How might that be like an artist creating a work of art?

J How would you defend the statement: "Any variation of an element of art has some kind of expression." Is that true? If so, what would be necessary if a whole artwork was to have one expression? Is that possible?

H Why is a white on white painting "expressive" and how might its expressiveness be discovered?

2.2 THE FUNCTION OF ART IS TO SHARE FEELINGS   116

" The stronger the infection the better is the art....the degree of infectiousness of art depends on ..."[individuality of the feeling transmitted, clarity of the expression, sincerity or force of the artist's feeling of the emotion he transmits] p.228

Tolstoy, L. (1962). What is art? And essays on art. New York: Oxford University Press. A Hesperides Book. By permission of Oxford University Press.

P Have you ever seen art that made you feel jittery? How do you know whether that is what the artist felt? What might make you think it is or not?

I When is an artist trying to help people feel like the artist does: in art with recognizable subject matter, or non-objective matter?

J How is art showing expressive faces the same or different from physiognomics? Does "expressive faces" mean smiling or frowning, etc. Why or why not?

H What would be factors that enter into deciding whether a viewer was having a feeling transmitted to him/her through an artwork? Does art have supernatural powers?

2.2 ARTISTS EXPLORE THEIR EMOTIONS WHICH ALLOWS OTHERS TO UNDERSTAND   117

"Until a man has expressed his emotion, he does not yet know what emotion it is. The act of expressing it is therefore an exploration...trying to find out what these emotions are...but the end is not something foreseen and preconceived..." p.111

Collingwood, R. (1958). Principles of art. New York: Galaxy Press. Oxford University. By permission of Oxford University Press.

P What makes children play with wooly worms? What do they learn by playing with them? How might artists learn more about things they think they would like or dislike?

I Do you ever not know for sure how you feel about something? Why would this uncertainty make an artist curious enough to look and study something?

J Why could focus on interpretation of works of art provide insight into one's own struggle with emotional feelings?

H How would you explain the idea that artists understand their emotions by exploration in their work of art? When might this statement not apply?

2.2 ART LIBERATES SELF-EXPRESSION   118

"Whatever value is created in the arts may or may not become an enduring part of the social structure (depending upon the related institution of criticism), but the institution within which it is created--art--nevertheless functions to liberate the human impulse to self-expression." p.194

Kaelin, E.F.(1989). An aesthetics for art educators. New York: Teachers College Press. By permission.

P Sometimes it is important to be quiet and not blurt out a thought. How can artist **quietly** say whatever comes to their minds?

I America is known as a free country. Why are artists usually thought of as the **most** "free" or individualistic?

J Where does social responsibility mesh with self-expression? Would curtailing an artist's self-expression be destructive or constructive to society? How would it affect art?

H If art is important to society, why does it change so quickly now and what meaning does that have for society?

2.2 UNLIKE ART PROPER, MAGICAL PRACTICES FUNCTION TO AROUSE EMOTION   119

"When magical art reaches a high aesthetic level, this is because the society ...(...artists and audience alike) demands of it an aesthetic excellance quite other than the very modest degree of competence which would enable it to fulfill its magical function...it remains at a high level only so long as the two motives are felt as absolutely coincident." p.69

Collingwood, R. (1958). Principles of art. New York: Galaxy Press. Oxford University. By permission of Oxford University Press.

P If we went on an art hunt in our local churches, how might we decide what was art? Do objects have to be gold or fancy to be art? How might you tell "art"?

I Why is an expressive work of art different than the images, colors, etc in a Halloween spookhouse?

J Common people scratched visual symbols in sand (as if they were doodling) to identify themselves as Christian. Today those symbols are incorporated into church art. How could the reason for making a symbol be a factor in deciding whether the use of the symbol was art?

H Is art used in religious contexts "art proper"?

2.2 THE PURPOSE OF ART IS TO TRANSMIT AN INDIVIDUAL'S FEELINGS TO OTHER PERSONS OR CULTURES 120

"... the purpose of art...is to widen the province of personality, so that feelings, emotions, attitudes, and values,...in one particular person, in one particular culture, can be transmitted with all their force and meaning to other persons or to other cultures." p.16

Mumford, Lewis. (1952). Art and techniques. Copyright 1952 by Columbia University Press. Reprinted with permission of the publisher.

P What kinds of feelings of an artist-weaver could be shown by the yarns chosen for a fabric? Which yarns would give which feelings?

I People say, "A picture is worth a thousand words." When is this saying true and why? Could all art forms give off feelings?

J How can art communicate as a visual language to share feelings? To what extent can it be effective or in what aspect of the total communication process?

H For what reasons might you expect some art forms (sculpture) of representative subject matter to more effectively communicate cross-culturally? Why not or why equally well?

2.2 ART INFLUENCES IDEAS, ATTITUDES, AND FEELINGS 121

"Readers, listeners, and lookers often articulate claims about the world that are suggested to them by the art works." p.72

Eaton, M. (1988). Basic issues in aesthetics. Belmont, CA: Wadsworth Publishing Company. Copyright 1988 by Wadsworth, Inc.. By permission of Wadsworth Publishing Company.

P How can artists teach us by the artworks they make?

I How have artists pictured the American Indian in ways that gave people ideas about them? Which different feelings did artists portray? What do you think about this? Is it fair for artists to influence people?

J How could it be true that artists are educators? Why might artists deny this? Are artists necessarily unbiased educators?

H What examples could you give to support the idea that artists portray a personal view of reality that is shared by someone, somewhere, sometime --an assumed audience--who might be brought to share that viewpoint? How would you counter or qualify this?

2.2 IS GOOD ART CONTAGIOUS?

" The feelings with which the artist infects others may be most various...If only the spectators or auditors are infected by the feelings which the author has felt, it is art." p.122-123 "There's one indubitable sign distinguishing real art from its counterfeit - namely the infectiousness of art. (The artist's individuality, clarity and sincerity determine the degree of infectiousness.)" p.227

Tolstoy, L. (1962). <u>What is art? And essays on art</u>. New York: Oxford University Press. A Hesperides Book. By permission of Oxford University Press.

P People catch measles from someone who has them. What could people catch from looking at art?If as boys or girls pass a certain work of art, each one smiles, grins or chuckles, what do you suppose the artist did for each person to "catch" the humor? Why should good art be catching, or should'nt it?

I For what reasons could the **way** an artist portrayed an historical event make you feel a certain way about the people or event depicted in the artwork? Can a work of art be good if people viewing that art work do not show that they feel like the artist must have felt?

J What effect does an artist's feeling **when creating** a work of art have on its ability to make viewers feel the same? Some people don't catch on to jokes. Is it the same in art, or, if it is a good work of art, should the artist's feelings be transmitted to any viewer?

H What might be the relationship between an artist's intent for the viewer to feel, the work of art, and the viewer of that work ?To what extent can good works of art overpower ignorance or resistance and effect viewer's feelings?

2.2 THE ELEMENTS OF ART ARE EXPRESSIVE IN THEMSELVES 123

"Colors, sounds and shapes ...can be expressive of other things not merely by association with them, but also because of their own intrinsic natures." p.71

From Meaning and truth by John Hospers. Copyright 1946 by the University of North Carolina Press and renewed 1974 by John Hospers. Used by permission of the publisher.

P   What shape is your body when you're curled up sleeping?... when you wake up and stretch? What does a stretching line look like? ...a curled one? What could you say about how just shapes, textures and lines can make you feel?

I   Why can a line "say" so many different things? Why might one "hear" a texture, or a color or a shape?

J   Expression makes us think of smiles or frowns, but how can artists be expressive without using images that we recognize?

H   For what reasons might you say that non-representational art can be universally expresssive or not?

A boy got into the bathtub and the water was too hot. He said "Oh!"

FORMALISM THEORY

2.3 ORGANIZATION OF VISUAL QUALITIES IN A WORK OF ART CAN BE EXCITING TO AN INFORMED VIEWER 124

" A good work of visual art carries a person who is capable of appreciating it out of life into ecstacy ... they talk about the shapes of forms and quantities of colors...quality of a single line...lines and colors, their relations and quantities..." p.29-30

Bell, C. (1913).Art. London: Chatto & Windus. Public domain and by permission of Chatto & Windus.

P Can we appreciate a beautiful sky without recognizing objects in it? How can looking at some art be like admiring a beautiful sunset or rolling clouds?

I How does learning to work with art materials help you appreciate artists' works?

J Why should some works of art be purchased for lots of money? What makes them valuable?

H What combinations of viewers and works of art create the value of art?

2.3 MEETING THE CRITERIA OF GOOD FORM IS MORE REWARDING THAN SHALLOW PLEASURES AS SUBJECT MATTER OR EXPRESSIVENESS 125

"And let no one imagine, because he has made merry in the warm tilth and quaint nooks of romance, that he can even guess at the austere and thrilling raptures of those who have climbed the cold, white peaks of art." p.32-33

Bell, C. (1913).Art. London: Chatto & Windus. Public domain and by permission of Chatto & Windus.

P How does what we do in art class help you see and understand more?

I What is the purpose of learning rules in art? How do rules help you show your idea?

J How could examining works of art be like the job of a detective? What can be uncovered in a work of art even if there are no images?

H Why does an art class have specific assignments rather than just allowing students to make what they like?

2.3 ORGANIZATIONAL PRINCIPLES CONTRIBUTE LONG-LASTING SATISFACTION VALUE TO WORKS OF ART 126

"...supposing the picture to envisage plastic expression, that the moment anything in it ceases to serve towards edification of the whole plastic volume, the moment it depends on reference to something outside the picture...it becomes part of an actual, and not a spiritual reality." p.56
Fry, R. (1956). Transformations. New York: Doubleday Anchor Press. Public domain.

P If you like all kinds of dogs, is it enough that paintings contain dogs? Why might some be worth more than others?

I A cartoon makes a point and usually uses several elements of art. What could make an artist's cartoon valuable for many years?

J Does an arrangement of art elements serve the message or does the message emerge out of the arrangement in visual art forms?

H Under what conditions could illustrations of life-values be "art"?

2.3 ART IS SEPARATE FROM THE ART OF ILLUSTRATION WHICH SERVES DIFFERENT ENDS 127

"Co-operation...between the two experiences derived from the psychological and plastic aspects of a picture does not appear to be inevitable." p. 27
Fry, R. (1956). Transformations. New York: Doubleday Anchor Press. Public domain.

P Picture book pictures help tell a story. Can artists' work tell stories? How is the picture in picture books different than an art work?

I Are picture book illustrations "art"... Why, why not, or when

J Science fiction pictures might be drawn by artists. Does that make science fiction illustrations "art"? Why or why not?

H What is the critical difference between illustration that is not art, and "art"? What could make such a differentiation debatable?

2.3 GREATNESS OF ART EXCLUDES SUBJECT MATTER   128

"*Artistic* greatness...is measured by what is *in* the work of art; and subject matter is pre-artistic, outside the work of art." p.138

From Meaning and truth by John Hospers. Copyright 1946 by the University of North Carolina Press and renewed 1974 by John Hospers. Used by permission of the publisher.

P   When you look at oil making colorful swirly lines in a puddle of water, it is beautiful. If an artist put those colors on a canvas that way, but had no faces, things or scenery to see, cold that artwork be good "art"?

I   Imagine an ocean sunset painting. A viewer raves about the great sunset, ship on the water and cumulus clouds while the artist said what mattered was the color relationships, value variations and shapes of the clouds. Why?

J   Why is there value to non-objective art? Why might artists have started making non-objective art?

H   What could be a justification for excluding consideration of subject matter in determining quality of artworks? Why should subject matter be a factor?

2.3 ART PORTRAYS THE IDEAL UNIVERSALS IN A CULTURE   129

"...for the formist aesthetic value is found in (1) the ideal representation of the norm; (2) conformity to a norm; and (3) conformity to or expression of a culture." p.106

Pepper, S. (1945). The basis of criticism in the arts. Cambridge, MA: Harvard University Press. Copyright 1945 by the President and fellows of Harvard College. Reprinted by permission of the publisher.

P   What could an artist show in art work that everyone in your family would appreciate? in your town? Should artists make what everyone likes or not?

I   Why might artists make art for just themselves, another person or many people? If many, how might that determine what the art work is about or how it looks?

J   Should artists portray what a culture considers ideal? Should artists depict females as Barbies or the latest movie actress?

H   To what degree is representation of ideals in a diverse culture possible in art? What are cultural commonalities that produce cohesiveness.... or is representation necessary?

2.3 ART INTEGRATES SENSATIONS, IMAGES, THOUGHTS AND EMOTIONS 130

"An object of 'great aesthetic value' in the *organicist's* view, is one that achieves or closely approaches an 'organic integration of feeling;', that is, an 'integration of the ways in which ...come together of their own accord about a perceptive center such as a physical work of art." p.9

Pepper, S. (1945). The basis of criticism in the arts. Cambridge, MA: Harvard University Press. Copyright 1945 by the President and fellows of Harvard College. Reprinted by permission of the publisher.

P What would make a gingerbread house beautiful to look at? If any candy was available, which kinds would you chose and why would these make it look good?

I What could an artist do to make a ceramic vase special? Would it need lots of decorations or not? Why would an artist choose to make it fancy or plain?

J Under what circumstances might visual complexity be "clutter"? When not?

H In what kinds of situations could embellishment be false beauty?

2.3 BEAUTY MAY BE SIMPLE OR COMPLEX 131

"There are beautiful things which are simple...beautiful things which are complex. The simple things have unity in common and the complex things have measure and proportion of parts in common...Unity is an *always accompanying* characteristic rather than a *defining* characteristic" p.4-5

Dickie, G. (1971a). Aesthetics. New York: Bobbs-Merril Pegasus Division of Prentice-Hall. Inc. Fair use.

P What would make a gingerbread house beautiful to look at? If any candy was available, which kinds would you chose and why would these make it look good?

I What could an artist do to make a ceramic vase special? Would it need lots of decorations or not? Why would an artist choose to make it fancy or plain?

J Under what circumstances might visual complexity be "clutter"? When not?

H In what kinds of situations could embellishment be false beauty?

2.3 BEAUTY IN ART IS RECOGNITION OF ITS PERFECT STRENGTH, PROPORTION OR HARMONY, AND BRIGHTNESS OR CLARITY 132

"...the conditions of beauty are three: perfection or unimpairedness, proportion or harmony, and brightness or clarity." "...and there is the subjective factor of being pleased by what is seen or known." p.7-8

Dickie, G. (1971a). Aesthetics. New York: Bobbs-Merril Pegasus Division of Prentice-Hall, Inc. Fair use.

P   Could a beautiful picture be "art" if no one ever saw it?

I   If an artist painted the perfect paintinf, but threw it away, thinking she/he could do a better one, was that a work of art? If someone saved it from the trash and displayed it because it was good, whose art word is it? Who is the real artist?

J   A king's treasure chest is deep in the ocean. Practically, it does not exist. How is this like a work of art destroyed in a war? ....like an artwork stored in someones's attic and its value unrecognized? ....like a good work of art rejected by galleries? ...like a painting thought out, but never painted?

H   How beautiful is a work of art that is seen by naive viewers who are aesethetically illiterate?

2.3 MEANING IN ART DEPENDS ON INTERRELATIONSHIPS BETWEEN THE ELEMENTS 133

The artist's vision, when communicated to us through his painting, can make us see anew not only light and space and volumn, but also form...particularly form... the most important 'essence' that painting can reveal to us..." p.190-191

From Meaning and truth by John Hospers. Copyright 1946 by the University of North Carolina Press and renewed 1974 by John Hospers. Used by permission of the publisher.

P   Why might a flower in a painting look like it was growing right out of the canvas? Is that an art trick? Is it a good idea? Why?

I   How does an artist show what a place is like so that those who see that art get the idea of being there? Would that artist need to draw realistically? How could an artist show the place without realism?

J   Imagine two paintings with exactly the same amount of each color, lines, etc., but one has a clearly recognizable subject and the subject of the other is totally obscure. Why might there be this difference? Is one more valuable than the other? Why?

H   Is it enough that the elements in a work of art are interrelated to create meaning? Does meaning depend **only** on compositional factors?

2.3 ART REVEALS LIGHT, SPACE, VOLUMN AND FORM IN NEW WAYS 134

The artist's vision, when communicated to us through his painting, can make us see anew not only light and space and volumn, but also form...particularly form ...the most important 'essence' that painting can reveal to us..." p.190-191

From Meaning and truth by John Hospers. Copyright 1946 by the University of North Carolina Press and renewed 1974 by John Hospers. Used by permission of the publisher.

P How and why do things look different on sunny days from on cloudy days or at night? How can an artist help people see the same things in different ways?

I Someone said an artist was like a magician. A magician can make one believe that something is true that isn't. Why might this statement be true or not true?

J Why is it possible or not for four artists to paint the same scene resulting in four paintings that are are so different that the likenesses of the scene cannot be discerned, and yet all four paintings are judged accurate?

H To what extent could "accuracy" serve as a criterion for judging the effective visual communication of works of art?

2.3 ORGANIZATION AIDS RETRIEVAL AND EFFECTIVE COMMUNICATION OF IDEAS ABOUT ART 135

...it is not enough to accumulate vast amounts of information about, and a rich experience of, the art you are interested in; you must be able to organize those data in a fruitful way, and you must formulate them so that they can be understood. (unknown)

P Why do we spend time talking about art instead of just making things?

I Why do we spend time thinking of reasons for what we say when we talk about art we've made or that artists have made?

J Have you ever tried to match dark blues in clothing? How might an artist who weaves, organize shelves of yarns? Why? Why would the weaver make a colored pencil plan of the weaving to be made?

H What would an artist, like a jeweler, have to know and recall to create works of art and why? How much would an artist have to commit to memory or what alternatives are there?

ART AS DEFINED BY A SOCIAL INSTITUTION

2.4 ART MAKES THE FAMILIAR STRANGE SO THAT IT CAN BE SCRUTINIZED 136

"Conventions may pervade a whole artistic tradition....or they may be peculiar to an individual and part of his or her personal style, as Chagall's cows and violins are." p.11,12

Sheppard, A.,1987. Aesthetics: An introduction to the philosophy of art. New York: Oxford University Press. By permission of Oxford University Press.

P Why might an artist make something look different than it does to you?

I Why might an artist make something different than it looks naturally?

J Why might an artist change natural proportions, colors, or positions of facial features?

H How do nonrealistic modes of representation help to emphasize different aspects of reality, and what might be the purpose of doing so?

2.4 ART INFLUENCES BY MAKING ARTWORLD VALUES VISIBLE 137

"The cash culture consists of ideas, art forms, and social institutions created, maintained, and promulgated by the educated elite"..."perpetuating these art forms and the value system they represent." p.217, 220.

Hamblen, K. (1990). Beyond the aesthetic of the cash-culture literacy. Studies in Art Education, 31 (4), 216-225. By permission of NAEA.

P Who do you think decides what artworks are shown in your school? Who should decide? Why? Does it matter as long as it is art?

I Why do you suppose that some art becomes part of art museums? Is art found in other places? Where?

J A mural on the side of a building expertly creates the illusion of variations in depth. Below it, in less sophisticated media and technique is a wall painting showing life of the poor in the city. By what criteria could one decide each is art?

H To what extent should there be concensus about the purpose of art? To what common values could one look across cultures, sub-cultures and time to find such concensus, or should it be left to those trained in art to decide?

2.4 ART PUBLICLY SHOWS THE AESTHETIC MOTIVATION OF AN ARTIST 138

"...the work of art is viewed [in the Social Institution theory] as the vehicle by which the aesthetic motivation of individuals come to be expressed in a social context." p.59.

Kaelin, E. F. (1989). An aesthetics for art educators. New York: Teachers College Press. By permission.

P Is it okay for artists to show in artwork what **they** find interesting, or not okay? Should artist show what **you** find interesting? Why or why not?

I What good might come from art showing what turns the artist on, rather than what he/she thinks viewers like to look at?

J What might an artist be trying to say by showing ready-made objects as art? Why?

H Why should the individual thoughts of an artist be given a public forum and recognition over **any**one's individual thoughts? What is special about the artist's mode of communication?

2.4 "WORKS OF ART ARE A KIND OF A THING CREATED FOR PRESENTATION" 139

"In some cases they are actually presented, and some cases they are not...Someone might create a work of art intending to present it, but be prevented from doing so...[or] an intention to create a kind of thing to be presented and an intention not to present it." p.215

Dickie, G. A reply to Stecker. In Dickie, G., Sclafani, R., & Roblin, R. (1989). Aesthetics: A critical analysis. Copyright 1977 by St. Martin's Press, Inc. Reprinted with permission of St. Martin's Press, Inc.

P Why do you show your friend a picture you made? Why do artists show art that they make?

I If an artist didn't care if anyone saw the art that he/she had in mind, would the artist paint that picture, or weave that fabric, or form that piece of jewelry? Why? Why not?

J Do artist expect to become famous from creating their art? Could they have other reasons? If other reasons, would other people be shown the artwork? Why or Why not?

H What could be the purpose for creating art if an artist never hoped to financially gain from it?

2.4 ART COMMUNICATES WITH THE SUPPORT OF THE ARTWORLD 140

(in reference to Danto's theory) "...work of art to make a statement...requires a series of roles...that allow individuals to enter into the social fabric of human institutions where their behavior becomes mutually communicative and significant." p.59

Kaelin, E.F. (1989) An aesthetics for art educators. New York: Teachers College Press. By permission.

P Artists make art in their homes or studios. Why do they take their work to galleries and museums?

I It is a big world. How can artists get people to see their art?

J What might an artist need to do in order to become "discovered"? How might he/she survive until sales from artworks provide an adequate living? Why don't all good artists achieve this level?

H Why should the artworld decide what artworks get public viewing? Does this fit the individuality of the artist? Why? What are alternatives?

2.4 ART IS VALUABLE BECAUSE OF MANY DIFFERENT PROPERTIES IT HAS THAT WE VALUE 141

"...critics...talk about the valuable properties of works...compare works informally...and when they do go on to issue specific evaluations...estimating where a work of art they are talking about falls in a comparison matrix that they somewhat baguely but not necessarily inaccurately have in mind." p.181

"...the value of works of art derives from valuable properties of art <u>and</u> that there are many different valuable properties." p.163

Dickie, G. (1988). Evaluating art. Philadelphia. Temple University Press. By permission.

P Think of something that is good... food, fields, fan, traffic, action, bright colors? Which of these have artists shown in works of art? Why **do** we like art?

I Why isn't art valuable because of the cost of the materials that the artist used or the time it took to make the artwork? Why is art valuable?

J Value is measured by money, but also by a sense of pleasure. What kinds of art works satisfy each of these ways of measuring value? What other ways can art be valued? How could you summarize your thoughts about why art is valuable?

H To what extent can art be valued for certain common properties?

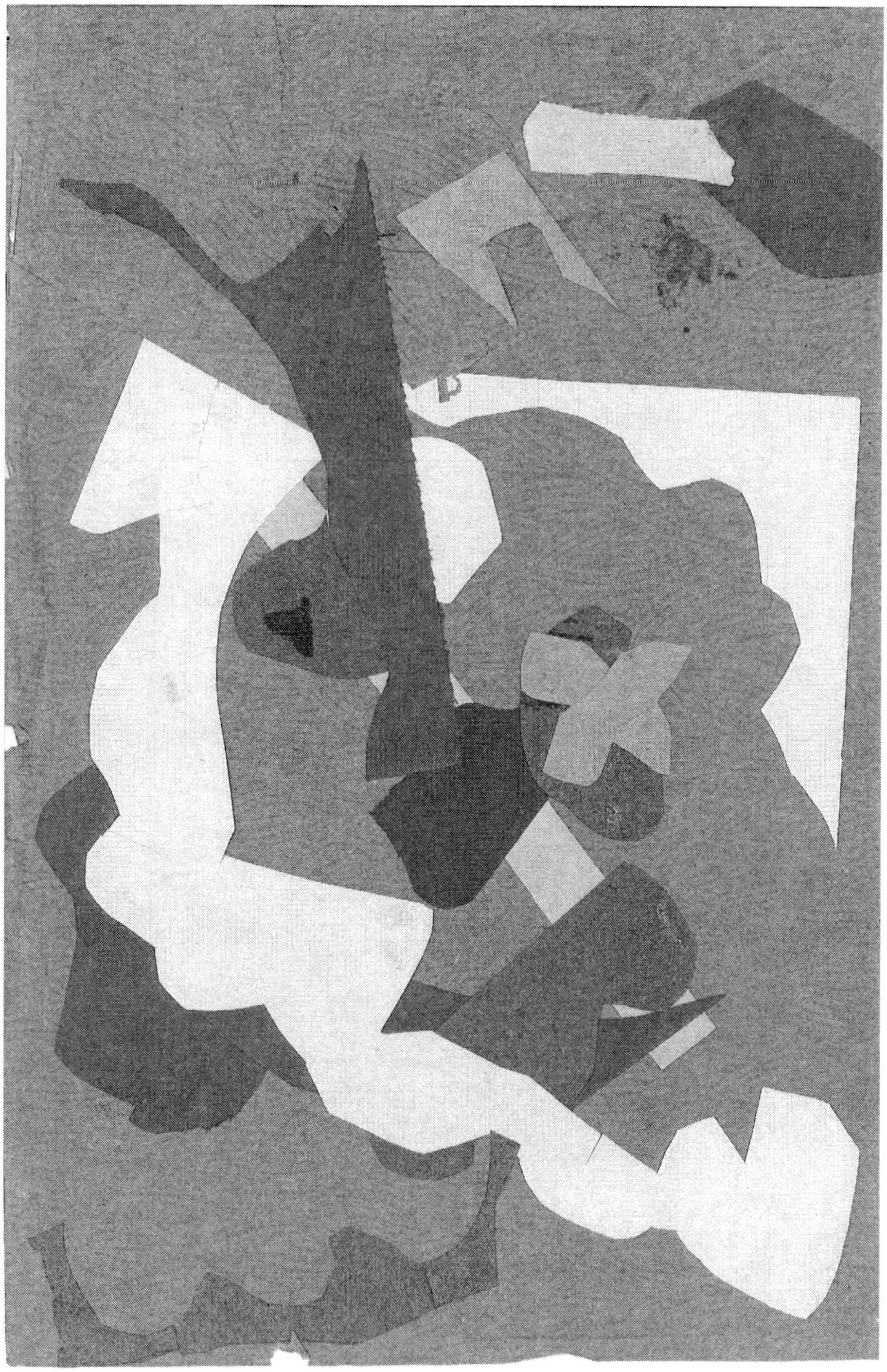

PRAGMATIST, INSTRUMENTALIST, FUNCTIONALIST THEORIES

2.5　ART IS USED TO BRING ABOUT SOCIAL CHANGE　　　142

" Art serves as an instrument for facilitating social change, as art is a tool for advancing social causes." [Theory of instrumentalism] p. 232-233

Adams, R. L. Alain Locke revisited: The reconsideraation of an aesthetic. In B. Young, Ed. (1990). Art culture,and ethnicity, pp.231-240. Reston, VA: National Art Education Association. By permission.

P　How do "Be kind to animals" posters or the Bambi film make people feel about animals? How does art help people to appreciate nature?

I　Political cartoonists use art to call attention to politics or other issues that concern people. Is this a proper use of art? Is it art? Why or Why not?

J　Art has often served other ends than personal expression or to give pleasure. Is it "using" art to that it should be a means to some end in a culture? Why? Why not?

H　Some people feel that art ought to be good for some cause. Why do you concur or disagree?

2.5　ART IS AESTHETICALLY GRATIFYING　　　143

"Gratification is aesthetic when it is obtained primarily from attention to the formal unity and/or the regional qualities of a complex whole, and when its magnitude is a function of the degree of formal unity and/or the intensity of regional quality." p.225

Beardsley, M. (1970). The aesthetic oint of view. In H. Kiefer & M. Munitz (Eds.) Perspectives in education. religion. and the arts. pp.219-237.Albany, NY: State University of New York Press. Fair use.

P　Why might you get "lost" in a painting? Is that a good place to get lost for a while? What does it mean to get lost in a painting?

I　Do artists pay attention to rules of composition? What result can they expect from all parts of their artwork fitting together well?

J　Can art be good and not follow the rules? Which came first, analysis of art to find the rules or rules by which art is defined and promoted?

H　For what reasons might people expect to be gradified by art that attends to Western ideas of formal unity? Do those reasons serve adequately to accept these criteria for all art?

2.5 THE VALUE OF WORKS OF ART MAY BE IN THE EXPERIENCE PRODUCED 144

" 'X has greater aesthetic value than Y' means 'X has the capacity to produce an aesthetic experience of greater magnitude ...than ...Y...defines 'aesthetic value' in terms of consequences, an object's utility or instrumentality to a certain sort of experience, I shall call it an Instrumentalist definition of 'aesthetic value'." p.531

Beardsley,M.(1958). Aesthetics:Problems in the philosophy of criticism.New York:Harcourt,Brace. Fair use.

P If a certain work of art really is wonderful to look at for you, but a different one is most exciting to your friend and only a little to you, do you think that the one you like is better? What if your friend also liked your choice almost as much as her first choice?

I If one work of art easily won the "most popular picture" award from an art museum survey of all visitors, should that affect how much money it is worth?

J Does shock effect make an art work better than a non-arousing one? Why or Why not?

H How can one measure the magnitude of aesthetic response across time? Why is this or is this not a good measure of quality?

2.5 ART ENABLES OTHERS TO UNDERSTAND A CULTURE 145

"...the art characteristic of a civilization is the means for entering sympathetically into the deepest elements in the experience of remote and foreign civilizations. By this fact is explained also the human import of their arts for ourselves. " p.332

From Art as experience by John Dewey. Copyright 1934 by John Dewey, renewed 1973 by The John Dewey Foundation. Used by permission of G.P. Putnam's Sons, a division of Penguin Putnam Inc.

P Japanese art work uses graceful strokes. How does this fit with the way people are taught to be in Japan?

I American Indian weavings and pottery show symmetry and contrasting, somber hues. Why would you expect art like this rather than curliness and flamboyant lines?

J As technology "shrinks" the world, what effects might be observed on art of cultures that traditionally have been very homogeneous?

H What is the relative importance of visual art forms and historical writings as sources of information about the values and beliefs of a culture? Why?

2.5 ART UNITES PEOPLE   146

"Art is the extension of the power of rites and ceremonies to unite men, through a shared celebration, to all incidents and scenes of life....Art also renders men aware of their union with one another in origin and destiny." p.271

From Art as experience by John Dewey. Copyright 1934 by John Dewey, renewed 1973 by The John Dewey Foundation. Used by permission of G.P. Putnam's Sons, a division of Penguin Putnam Inc.

P What is true about people all over the world? What events happen in lives of most people but possibly in different ways? Why does art help us to know this about other people and help understand our differences?

I Why might it be good to study Kachinas and the meanings of the dress and symbols of these art works? To what degree would that help understand persons of Hopi descent in 1991?

J Must art be associated with rites or ceremonies to unite people? Why is, or is not, the uniting effect of art limited to culturally significant events? What possible parallels exist in oursociety that are tied to social phenomena rather that religious events?

H To what extent is art universal? What **is** universal to which art might contribute and how?

2.5 ART PUTS THE PAST AND FUTURE INTO PERSPECTIVE   147

"Only when the past ceases to trouble and anticipations of the future are not perturbing is a being wholly united with his environment and therefore fully alive. Art celebrates with particular intensity the moments in which the past ...[reinforces] the present and in which the future is a quickening of what now is." p.18

From Art as experience by John Dewey. Copyright 1934 by John Dewey, renewed 1973 by The John Dewey Foundation. Used by permission of G.P. Putnam's Sons, a division of Penguin Putnam Inc.

P What does art help us to remember? Why?

I Newspaper headlines soon become second page news. Why might artworks give us some distance from which to view events? What good might result?

J Does art thrive under peaceful or troubled conditions? Why? Why not? What purpose does art serve under any condition?

H What is it about life conditions that stimulates creative activity? Does competition, consolation, threat, celebration or other pervasive moods affect creative artistic work?

2.5 ART CREATES "WHOLE" EXPERIENCES BY RELATING AND ORGANIZING PARTS 148

[In reference to John Dewey on expressionism] "Artists provide us with experiences by producing structured objects...that bring together...disjoint perceptions and organize them into coherent wholes." p. 29

Eaton, M. (1988). Basic issues in aesthetics. Belmont, CA: Wadsworth Publishing Company. Copyright 1988 by Wadsworth, Inc.. By permission of Wadsworth Publishing Company.

P How do you know when people are bored, tired, or excited (without telling you in words)? How do artists help you to understand what it is like in a scene they paint?

I How might artists create art that clearly has one message, even using objects that are different?

J Of what importance do you think "knowing about art" is in order to experience it fully? Is the experience inevitable with well organized art.?..for everyone?...for trained viewers?...for other artists?

H If a society is diverse, how can art that represents it be "coherent" i.e. fit together as a related whole? Why is that important or not?

2.5 COMMUNICATION THROUGH ART CONTRIBUTES TO COMMON UNDERSTANDING AND VALUING 149

"...communication... may or may not be followed by agreement, or what is called 'communion'- a community of feeling which expresses itself in identical value judgements." p. 336

Isenberg, A. (July,1949). Critical communication. The Philosophical Review,58 , 330-344. By permission.

P An artist painted a make-believe picture of animals who are natural enemies just sitting together peacefully. Why would this be painted? What good might come from artworks?

I Which comic strips often have a message about life? Why can artworks help people understand about life and get along better?

J How would a verbal confrontation and a visual confrontation in an artwork differ in their effect? Why might the visual artwork lead to valuing as a result fo understanding?

H Art is not universally understood to the same degree everywhere, but why can it contribute to understanding and to valuing?

NO THEORY OR A COMBINATION OF THEORIES

2.6 TRADITIONAL ARRANGEMENTS OF THE ELEMENTS OF ART BECOME THE CONSTANT FORM OR STYLE BY WHICH A GROUP OR ERA IS CHARACTERIZED 150

"By style is meant the constant form--and sometimes the constant elements, qualities, and expression-- in art of an individual or a group." p.287.
Schapiro, M. In A. L. Kroeber, Ed. (1953) Anthropology. Chicago: University of Chicago Press. Copyright 1953 by The University of Chicago. By permission.

P Many product designs are make to look like Mondrians paintings. Is it good to have art styles copied by package designers? Why?

I What seems similar in Eskimo art, African masks, Pointillism, etc. How does that help one recognize it?

J Does style emerge naturally or by design? If by design, who guides what becomes style?

H What are general characteristics of something called "style" and does style have merit?

2.6 ART CAN MAKE US CONSCIOUS 151

"Art is the community's medicine for the worst disease of mind, the corruption of consciousness." p.336
Collingwood, R. (1956). Principles of art. New York. Galaxy Press. Oxford University. By permission of Oxford University Press.

P How could artists' pictures of war, or other unpleasant events, be a good thing?

I Who has shrugged an "I don't care "? Why can art make us care about things for which we should take responsibility?

J Why might an artist make a work of art based on a disgusting situation or one of which society should not be proud?

H What is inferred by letting art works serve as the vehicle for keeping people aware? Why is that an appropriate function of art? Why is it a sufficient function or not?

2.6 THE ARTS REFLECT AND/OR HELP SOLVE PROBLEMS OF A SOCIETY 152

The arts must adapt to a society which has undergone massive changes in mode of life and thought...help solve problems of society. (unknown)

P Artists can make jewelry out of plastic cheaper than out of silver. Should jewelry be kept expensive and for people who can afford it? Why or Why not?

I If art of a group of people was valued as art for its intricate handwork and if machines are invented to help those people sell more of their designs and improve their lives, are the machine-made items a good thing to happen?

J What about a home is worth restoring? What makes preservation of historic sites worth the land that could be income-producing?

H To what extent do artists **lead** society by expression of what they perceive; and what extent do artists solve... or do they find (identify)... problems in reponse to societal changes? Why? In other words, are artists leaders or followers or problem solvers or problem identifiers or none of these?

2.6 "...FEELINGS ARE REGARDED AS FACTS..." IN JUDGING ART 153

Mechanism is a view that the worth of a work of art...consists in its being an object of men's preferences, likings, satisfactions, pleasures. (unknown)

P Why is "If I like it, it is art" a good or not good reason to judge something to be good art?

I If a work of art is considered important by one person because it gives a jittery feeling, and by another person because it gives a happy, joyful feeling, can such different reactions be reasons to say it's good art? Why or Why not?

J Can a work of art retain its status as "art" if people who know nothing about art like it and consider it art for the "wrong" reasons?

H Is the quip, "Say it three times and it becomes a fact" applicable in relation to gerneral opinion about art? How does the newsmedia coverage of a disputed work of art or artist's work enter this debate?

2.6 ART PLAYS A ROLE IN BALANCING THE EFFECTS OF THE MACHINE AGE AND PASSIVITY 154

"...The great problem...is ...to command the machines...to bring back...that respect for the essential attributes of personality, its creativity and autonomy..." p.11.

Mumford, Lewis. (1952). Art and techniques. Copyright 1952 by Columbia University Press. Reprinted with permission of the publisher

P The camera is a machine that records scenes quickly. Drawing the scene takes time. Which of these is art or are they both art? What might change about art in today's modern world?

I If video is used as an artistic medium, how might an artist use that medium to create art as opposed to documentation that any person might make of a family reunion, for example.

J If modern technology is used to make sculptures in the U.S., should hand woven rugs, hand-printed fabrics or the ancient pyramids be valued higher as art because they did not have machines?

H Does high tech necessitate a new conception of what art is? How adjusted to change can art become before art cannot be recognized or is that not the question? What dangers exist?

2.6 ART EMPHASIZES IDEAS, VIEWPOINTS OR VISUAL CHARACTERISTICS 155

Art develops visual perceptual awareness in contexts where reacting analytically to visual qualities and relationships in art is encouraged. (unknown)

P Why would an artist show the insides or backside of an object or draw something upside down ?

I What purpose might an artist have in exaggerating the scale of an object?

J Why might artists confront viewers with works of art that are not "pretty"?

H What role is played by distortion, exaggeration, and confrontation of subject matter in art? Is there a possible relationship between emphasis and "good taste" in art?

2.6 LEARNING TO UNDERSTAND ART CAN ENHANCE US AS HUMAN BEINGS 156

"We must indeed learn and know in order to become ready to participate in art, but our participation alone can turn all our learning and knowing into human being." p.27.

Morgan, D. (Fall, 1967). Must art tell the truth? *Journal of Aesthetics and Art Criticism*, 26, 17-27. By permission of the editor

P How might creating art make someone a better person?

I Why is learning about art different from learning from art?

J Would subject matter that the artist is concerned with possibly interfere with becoming a better person? Why or Why not?

H What in the nature of art might contribute to the artist becoming a better human being, or does it?

2.6 ART DOES MANY THINGS, BUT NONE ARE SUFFICIENT TO EXPLAIN ALL ABOUT ART 157

"...art...has various social functions, and that, as a consequence, no single one of them can reasonably explain art in all of its manifestations." p.5.

Kavolis, V. (1968). *Artistic expression: A sociological analysis*. Ithaca, NY: Cornell University Press. By permission and fair use

P Can you tell all the things that are good about your favorite person in a minute? How can art be like that?

I If a work of art shows how love can exist in a family without physical contact, is that worth showing in art? Is that enough for that work to call it "art"?

J What good is art? Is "good" in one situation good in all? Is there one good, many? How much good must be represented in one work of art to qualify as art.. somewhere, or anywhere?

H How can you expand on the general statement, or qualify it, that art serves social functions that establish its value.

2.6   ART TAKES US OUT OF THE USUAL   158

"Art distances for us...creates a context in which we are removed from our ordinary interests..." p.40.

Eaton, M. (1988). Basic issues in aesthetics. Belmont, CA. Wadsworth Publishing Company. Copyright 1988 by Wadsworth, Inc.. By permission of Wadsworth Publishing Company.

P   Why are dreams often fun? How can art be like a dream?

I   Why would you agree or not agree that art can take you to places and experiences that you cannot go to or experience yourself?

J   Why do artists fantasize places and events? Is that kid stuff? Why or Why not?

H   Does fantasy in art serve a purpose... for the artist... for the viewer? Is all art fantasy of a kind? Why? Why not?

2.6   ART PROVIDES ADVENTURE...NOT DECORATION NOR SCIENTIFIC TRUTH   159

"...so long as we continue to accept the absurd alternative which offers us only a specious choice between art as diversion or decoration...or as a peculiar second-rate substitute for true-blue empirical knowledge...we shall block every hope of understanding ourselves and our culture." p.21.

Morgan, D. (Fall, 1967). Must art tell the truth? Journal of Aesthetics and Art Criticism, 26, 17-27. By permission of the editor

P   It isn't necessary to ask you to choose beween a friend you like to skate with and a friend you like to talk to. What are different reasons why you might like two very different works of art?

I   What's the difference between saying you, "like all art if it has lots of color" and saying you, "like all art but not for the same reason"?

J   How is art like exploring a new cave, going on a new carnival ride, or galloping a horse across a field? Why?

H   When do art theories facilitate understanding about art; when could adherence to one theory facilitate understanding; and when would art theory adherence inhibit understanding art?

2.6 WORKS OF ART BRINGS UNDERSTANDING BETWEEN VIEWS OF THE ARTIST AND THE VIEWERS OF THE WORK   160

"The work of art mediates between the subjective world view of the author and the subjective world views of the perceivers of the work." p.164.

Streb, J. (1984). Thoughts on phenomenology, education and art. Studies in Art Education, 25 (3),164 By permission of National Art Education Association

P How could sculptures of "family" explain different kinds of family ties to you?

I What kinds of better understandings could someone gain by looking at works of art with gaining an understanding mind?

J What would "understandings about people" from looking at art mean? What kind of looking and thinking would be needed?

H Individuality in art is valued, but can artists' individuality and subjectivity contribute to a cohesive society? Why, or why not? When, or when not?

2.6 STATUS IS ASSOCIATED WITH PERSONS WHO OWN WORKS OF ART   161

"One influential (though not universal) tendency has been to assume that the main [sociological] function of art for its consumers is status enhancement." "...a partially valid, but generally superficial interpretation of art." p.4

Kavolis, V. (1968). Artistic expression. A sociological analysis. Ithaca, NY. Cornell University Press. By permission and fair use

P Some people buy art to brag or be better than someone else. Do artists make art to allow this?

I Why would artist cooperate with gallery directors who sell art to people who buy it as a status symbol like a fancy car?

J If persons who have lots of money buy their favorite artist's work and the price goes up because others think it must be good, then what determines the worth of artists' works that don't fine a "patron"?

H What is the relative merit of a state or other objective "board of ar" to determine worth of works of art as opposed to letting the market place decide which art gets attention and recorded in history?

2.6 ART REINFORCES VALUES BY USING SYMBOLS THAT ARE UNDERSTOOD 162

"...one of the crucial social functions of art style may be the subconscious assertion of value orientations by filling the visible world with shapes emotionally suggestive of the value orientations held." p.160.
Kavolis, V. (1968). Artistic expression: A sociological analysis. Ithaca, NY: Cornell University Press. By permission and fair use.

P If a heart shape is in a work of art, what would most people think of and why?

I How could sleek and shiny works of art reinforce what people expect in a modern day society?

J What is the same about multi-colored, luminous colors of clothing and some art of today, in more ways than color?

H To what degree could the incorporation of suggestions of social values in art serve the role of art in a society? What would that role be?

2.6 ART CAN INSTRUCT 163

"...all these people intend for their work to...be a reform vehicle, and so I think that this work is instructive." p.15.
Dialogue with Richard Armstrong In French, C. (November, 1990). A taste for narration at the Whitney. Conceptual sculpture for the 90's. The Journal of Art, 3 (2), 15. Fair use.

P Why can art help you see and know more?

I Do teachers help you find ways to change, just give you the idea, or make you change? How does artwork teach?

J What kind of an artist (or teacher) would expect to influence reform by the artwork (or instruction)? Why might an artist perceive his/her role as arousing viewers to societal needs?

H In what ways might the artist expecting to change people, be like a dictator, a salesperson, a parent, or a teacher?... or unlike them?

2.6 ART SERVES OUR NEED FOR IDENTITY, KNOWLEDGE, AND STIMULATION   164

"Three related roles for art, then, may have shaped our biological propensities toward art making, helped select for it: art as the material manifestation of human identities,...art as the representation of human knowledge; art as s(t)imulation." p.168.

McCorduck, P. (1991) Aaron's code: Meta-art, artificial intelligence, and the work of Harold Cohen NewYork: W. H. Freeman. By permission of the author

P   We eat to live and to satisfy hunger. There are reasons for doing anything. Why would someone want to make art? What good does art do the people who make art? Why does it make them feel satisfied?

I   What kinds of things could an artist make that would show how much was known or understood by the artist? Why might art be a better way of showing what one knows than telling or writing it?

J   Why might it be true that art, "helps people know themselves", "shows what people know" and "acts out what life is about"?

H   What basic urges drive people to make art? What purpose does art serve for the artist? Why is art a fulfilling profession or pastime?

2.6   ART GENERATES MEANING   165

"...magic of art lies in its powers of evocation...art is a meaning generator, not a meaning communicator." p.167.

McCorduck, P. (1991). Aaron's code: Meta-art, artificial intelligence, and the work of Harold Cohen NewYork: W. H. Freeman. By permission of the author

P   How can art be like the beginning of a story that you finish in your own mind?

I   Why does art **tell you what to think** or why does it **ask you to think** about what it means?

J   How does art tease?

H   What role could the viewer of art have in the meaning of an art work?

2.6 ART PERIODS REVISE RATHER THAN REVOLUTIONIZE ART THAT WENT BEFORE 166

[Modern architects]"...bring symbolism, message,and meaning back into the built world without sacrificing the rationality and techniogical progressiveness of early modern architects..." p.17.

Bonenti, C. (June,1987). Symbolism, message, and meaning. Art New England, 8 (6), 16-17. Printed with permission from Art New England magazine.

P Porches and railings on houses are new and old. How could you explain that statement?

I What do big porches on houses say differently now than what they said when people had large families, and porch gatherings at harvesting time?

J When artists come up with a new style, how new is "new"? How original can an artist be? Why?

H Why do architectural features that were originally functional, seem to resurface under different social conditions?

2.6 ART CONVEYS MEANING BECAUSE OF STRUCTURAL SIMILARITIES IN PEOPLE 167

"Forms signify space-cross culturally because they reflect the universal cognitive structures of the human mind." p.107

McCorduck, P. (1991). Aaron's code: Meta-art, artificial intelligence, and the work of Harold Cohen. NewYork: W. H. Freeman. By permission of the author.

P Why might you understand family, city or country art works from any country?

I What would be the same in the way artists go about making art in any country as they make any kind of art? (media, think, experiment, decide, close)

J Given different languages, how could the way people think and solve problems be the same all over the world? What differences could exist and why?

H To what extent could you defend the universality of art across cultures and across time? Is it a myth or truth, and why?

2.6 ART ALERTS US TO SOCIAL CHANGE 168

"Visual art remains an early warning system for deep-rooted shifts in a culture's means of understanding itself and its place in the world." p.9.

Narrett, E. (June, 1987). Art consulting and the new patronage. Art New England, 8 (6), 8-9. Printed with permission from Art New England magazine.

P Artist like to examine things and imagine. Why might they be good fortune tellers about the way the world is going?

I Artists look closely and analytically at their visual world. Why do you think that this fact would help them predict changes in the way people live and think? Would there be **no** carry over?

J People have long debated whether artists respond to cultural change by their sensitive perception or whether artists actually influence change. What evidence from art would seem to support either position?

H How does the newest art being shown suggest a perceptive nature of the artist or the role of the artist in influencing change?

2.6 PRINCIPLES OF ART MAY NOT BE UNIVERSAL 169

"...aesthetic principles--though they may to some extent transcend a particular culture, class, or period in time-- are largely culturally based and fall short of universal appreciation by peoples of all cultures." p.238.

Adams, R. L. Alain Locke revisited: The reconsideraation of an aesthetic. In B. Young, Ed. (1990). Art culture, and ethnicity, pp.231-240. Reston, VA: National Art Education Association. By permission.

P People in the U.S. dress differently than people do in other countries where rules for dress or fashion differ. Why might rules for arranging lines and colors well in art also be different?

I If rules for organizing art in other countries differ from our principles of compostion, is one set of rules right and one not? On what might the answer depend? Can anyone make up his/her own set of art rules?

J Are principles of organizing the elements of art physiologically and universally determined or determined by cultural expectations? Why? What good are rules in art?

H What general consistency might exit between cultural rules for art that appear to be different specifically?

2.6 ART ENLARGES WHAT WE KNOW ABOUT THE WORLD   170

"Minor art...nostalgic art...reinforces the grasp we have on the world. But radical art, the masterpiece, enlarges that grasp." p.167.

McCorduck, P. (1991). Aaron's code: Meta-art, artificial intelligence, and the work of Harold Cohen. NewYork: W. H. Freeman. By permission of the author.

P Some art is nice. Some makes you notice. Why is each important?

I Some art reminds us of what we've experienced. What good is art that we have to study to understand? Why is that good or not?

J Some art lulls us into our cosy comfort zone. Others jolt us and create discomfort. Should art be one or the other? Why or Why not?

H What positve ends are served by radical art that is disturbing?... by art that maintains the status quo?

2.6 ART ENLARGES OUR EXPERIENCE   171

"...artistic content has the function of helping man to develop an emotional involvment with the objects of his social and cultural environment and that the creation of art, by providing new symbolic voci of sociocultural integration, contributes to the reintegration of society after disturbance of a relative equilibrium."p.5.

Kavolis, V. (1968). Artistic expression: A sociological analysis. Ithaca, NY: Cornell University Press. By permission and fair use.

P Could someone who always lived in the desert draw a good picture of cornfields? Why, or why not?

I What rule or rules might help a city artist draw farm scenes "well"?

J What would need to be considered by artists depicting situations that they had never experienced? Could the artist adequately portray them?

H To what extent can vicarious experiences or other substitutes for direct experience inform people?

2.6 ART INFLUENCES CORPORATE PERSONNEL   172

[regarding corporate art-buying] "Art on the walls of the workplace is said to foster innovative thinking and 'creativity' among employees...boost morale, impress clients, and attract top quality personnel." p.213.

From Post-to-neo: The artworld of the 1980's by Calvin Tomkins, Copyright 1988 by Calvin Tomkins. Reprinted by permission of Henry Holt and Company, Inc.

P What good reasons can you think of for showing art on the walls of schools or other public places?

I Why is it okay to hang art in a bank or lawyers' office, or should art be hung in art museums?

J Why would it, or why would it not, be just as important to hang art in a factory as in a lawyers office or bank?

H What are the pros and cons of art in public places, and is there any reason for limiting what public places are appropriate?

2.6 ART HELPS US SEE ANEW   173

"Appreciation of painting gives us new 'ways of seeing' but no knowledge, no facts, no propositions..." p.206.

From Meaning and truth by John Hospers. Copyright 1946 by the University of North Carolina Press and renewed 1974 by John Hospers. Used by permission of the publisher.

P Why might art be good to look at even if it exaggerates what is real?

I If an artist's tree made with wire coils helps you notice some curliness in trees, why might the artist's wire coil sculpture not be the truth? Why can that sculpture be good for us?

J To what extent can one count on art to be fact?

H How could the **purpose** of art be explained in terms of a continuum from fantasy to fact?

NON-WESTERN THEORIES

2.7 ART CAN HAVE A POWERFUL EFFECT AND CONVEY MEANING THAT TRANSCENDS NORMAL DISCOURSE 174

"...a distinctive property of art is its capacity to ineffably convey meanings in a way that transcends the rational, the explicit, the unambiguous." p.243.

Anderson, R. (1990). Calliope's sisters: A comparative study of philosophies of art. Englewood Cliffs, NJ: Prentice-Hall. By permission of Prentice-Hall Division of Simon & Schuster

P What makes jumping rope fun? Is it the jumping? Is it the singing? Is it the rhythm? Is it the friends? What is it that makes a work of art like jumping rope?

I Why might objects used in celebration be considered art? When not?

J If an object served a communication purpose in a culture, why might it be considered a work of art in another culture?

H What criteria would need to come together in a ceremonial object for a Western art museum to consider it art? Why isn't or is, it's function part of the criteria for establishing its quality?

2.7 ART CONVEYS RELIGIOUS MEANINGS 175

"First, art plays a crucial role in several influential religious traditions. Shintoism...creation myth; Buddhism...unity and intuitive development...art's efficacy for spiritual development." p.197.

Anderson, R. (1990). Calliope's sisters: A comparative study of philosophies of art. Englewood Cliffs, NJ: Prentice-Hall. By permission of Prentice-Hall Division of Simon & Schuster.

P Why might an artist be asked to make a religious object, like a cross or candle holder for a church.

I How do religions use art? What do objects mean? Why do you think churches don't just <u>talk</u> about religion? Why have art works?

J What roles do art objects play in religions? What purposes do they serve?

H Are art objects used in religious traditions "art" or "religious symbols"? Under what conditions might they be both or neither?

2.7 ART CONVEYS MESSAGES THAT ARE DEEP AND OBSCURE 176

"When religious concepts are so abstract that even initiates grasp them only with difficulty, art can serve as a means whereby the people at large can gain some grasp of religious principles." p.251.

Anderson, R. (1990). Calliope's sisters: A comparative study of philosophies of art. Englewood Cliffs, NJ: Prentice-Hall. By permission of Prentice-Hall Division of Simon & Schuster.

P Why would people want artists to make pictures on walls of churches or public buildings when the ideas are written in books already?

I How could a work of art be like the key to a secret hiding place?

J Why are people able to "read" pictures or sculptures? Is having a readable meaning in a work sufficient reason for calling it "art"?

H How could art be compared to a riddle? a metaphor? a parable?

2.7 "...CONSCIOUS USE OF ART TO OBTAIN PLEASURE AND MORAL BETTERMENT SHOULD NOT BE NECESSARY.." p.167. 177

"Artist and audience members alike tap the powerful energy of art only insofar as they engage the emotions that are systematized in the theory of raza [sensuously and spiritually gratifying state of pleasure]." p.170.

Anderson, R. (1990). Calliope's sisters: A comparative study of philosophies of art. Englewood Cliffs, NJ: Prentice-Hall. By permission of Prentice-Hall Division of Simon & Schuster.

P How should good art make you feel and why should it do so?

I Why are artists supposed to make people better by their art, or is that not their purpose?

J What is the point of works of art: to detect the artist's intent or to subject oneself to being influenced by the power of the work of the art? Why? Is there another point?

H If objects that the Western art world calls "art" were created for their magical function, what aspect about the object would apply cross-culturally, i.e. be a necessary component of a definition of value of the object? Would man-made objects be of special importance?

2.7 IMPORTANT MESSAGES MOTIVATE CREATING GREAT ART 178

" The relationship between art and value is reciprocal in that an important message necessitates important art." p.247. [Navajo]

Anderson, R. (1990). Calliope's sisters: A comparative study of philosophies of art. Englewood Cliffs, NJ: Prentice-Hall. By permission of Prentice-Hall Division of Simon & Schuster.

P When you want to be heard, you might shout. Why might art "shout"?

I When people make important speeches, they stand above the crowd and use a microphone. How might artists make their messages more visible?

J What kinds of things might artists do to have an important idea noticed? Why might the approach you suggest work?

H Which would come first: an important message or an effective way of creating art that communicates? Why?

2.7 ART GIVES PLEASURE AND SHOWS PEOPLE HOW TO BETTER THEMSELVES 179

"...moral betterment implies ...pursuit...of righteousness and spiritual emancipation...material prosperity and...refined, worldly pleasures." " So when Indian writers say that art exists to help a person progress along the path to Brahman, they are thinking of individual improvement...both sacred and the secular dimension of life." p.162

Anderson, R. (1990). Calliope's sisters: A comparative study of philosophies of art. Englewood Cliffs, NJ: Prentice-Hall. By permission of Prentice-Hall Division of Simon & Schuster.

P Why could an artist's work make you a better person?

I Why might someone say that art teaches people to be good? When might that not be true?

J What ways can people seek to improve themselves? How can art influence people relative to each of these ways of improvement?

H To what extent can artist shape world views? Why could they have an influence on persons' striving for a good life ? On the community and personal levels? Why is it likely or not?

2.7 ART ENHANCES LIFE TODAY AND IMPROVES TOMORROW 180

"...Eskimos appreciated the immediate pleasure that artist's production can give. ...know that through art mortals can influence events in the otherwise indifferent realm of nature, and that art touches the spirits that stand above both humans and the natural world." p.54.

Anderson, R. (1990). Calliope's sisters: A comparative study of philosophies of art. Englewood Cliffs, NJ: Prentice-Hall. By permission of Prentice-Hall Division of Simon & Schuster.

P Someone might find a pretty stone and keep it just to hold. Why might an art work be the "something special to keep" for some persons?

I Why might some art be like a good luck charm?

J What good is art that you think is special for some reason felt by you alone?

H How is the pleasure gained from a work of art different form and similar to the natural world?

2.7 WORKS OF ART CONTACT AND INFLUENCE SUPERNATURALS 181

" But the greatest significance of Aboriginal art is...the cultural integration of the aesthetic system from which art derives...through art mortals come into immediate, intimate and genuine contact with all-important spirits of the Eternal Dreamtime." p.71.

Anderson, R. (1990). Calliope's sisters: A comparative study of philosophies of art. Englewood Cliffs, NJ: Prentice-Hall. By permission of Prentice-Hall Division of Simon & Schuster.

P People make art of things that are real and things that are make-believe. Why is art important for making believe?

I Puppets may stand for real or make-believe creatures. How might puppets be a functional art form?

J Masks are functional art forms in many cultures. How might masks function in different cultures you can name?

H Why might art objects that are functional for belief systems have qualities that other cultures can appreciate for their beauty?

2.7 ART OF A CULTURE GIVES MEANING TO A SUBJECT THROUGH STYLE, SKILL, AND A SENSUOUS MEDIUM 182

"Art generally embodies culturally significant meaning that is encoded in a traditional style and sensuous medium, and this is accomplished with uncommon skill." p. 282.

Anderson, R. (1990). Calliope's sisters: A comparative study of philosophies of art. Englewood Cliffs, NJ: Prentice-Hall. By permission of Prentice-Hall Division of Simon & Schuster.

P Why does the way artist hold or move a brush help tell about the kind of hair style or action of the person in a painting?

I If an artist wanted a subject to suggest "confusion", what media and technique or approach would help to do so and why?

J What kinds of "fits" can you imagine between media, style and subject to convey a particular meaning and why would this combination work well?

H What is the basis for artists' decisions about media - style - subject combinations in order to affect viewers' interpretations? How do you defend such a generalization?

2.7 ART EMBODIES UNSEEN FORCES OR ESSENCES AND REPRESENTS EMOTIONS 183

"In his art, a good spirit embodied in a reproduction would assure good fortune. Contemporary artists...graphically...represent emotions, spiritual essence, or unseen forces hidden behind a subject's physical facade." p.18.

Dockstader. (1962). Indian art in America. Greenwich, CT: New York Graphic Society. Published by Little, Brown and Company. Fair use.

P Why might a work of art be like telling what a dream was _about_ without revealing, at first, what made it most exciting?

I Why would you recommend slow visits to an art exhibit?

J Why might an artist choose not to be obvious in a work of art?

H What might be an artist's purpose in having subtle, hidden messages in art work?

2.7 FOLLOWING CRITERIA OF BEAUTY, ART CONVEYS RULES OF GOODNESS AND ENERGY 184

"The identification of sensuous beauty with sociocultural goodness is found again and again in Yoruba life." p.131 "...art makes a crucial contribution to Yoruba culture by conveying the fundamental theme of harmonious energy." p.136.

Anderson, R. (1990). Calliope's sisters: A comparative study of philosophies of art. Englewood Cliffs, NJ: Prentice-Hall. By permission of Prentice-Hall Division of Simon & Schuster.

P What makes art good? Is beauty good? What is beautiful?

I What things do we call both beautiful and good?

J What kinds of things that we associate with "art" are considered beautiful in any culture?

H Even though recognition of "art" for its own sake varies from culture to culture, how does Western "art" embody cross-cultural criteria of beauty? Does it do so without exception?

2.7 ART ENHANCES ONESELF BY DECORATION 185

"...a desire to improve one's looks and enhance one's beauty is the chief motivation for the San's making and wearing jewelry, tatooing and painting their bodies, decorating their clothes, and cutting their hair." p.23.

Anderson, R. (1990). Calliope's sisters: A comparative study of philosophies of art. Englewood Cliffs, NJ: Prentice-Hall. By permission of Prentice-Hall Division of Simon & Schuster.

P Artists make large and small art. Why would someone want to wear small sculptures, i.e. jewelry?

I When is a hair style "art" or not? Why?

J When a person chooses a designer-made shirt, a jeweler-made bolo tie, and a fancy decorated pair of cowboy boots that go well together and with the person's character, is there one, or more artists involved? How many and why?

H What reasons support or reject the notion that a cross-cultural art form is the way a person dresses?

2.7 ART MAY CARRY SPIRITUAL MESSAGES 186

"... [Australian Aboriginal] art may carry a sacred or idealized message by mere affiliaton with religious affairs." p.241-242.

Anderson, R. (1990). Calliope's sisters: A comparative study of philosophies of art. Englewood Cliffs, NJ: Prentice-Hall. By permission of Prentice-Hall Division of Simon & Schuster.

P Why does seeing a candle in a church mean something different than on a dinner table? How would you know what a candle means in art?

I How could you know what is meant in an art work of people dancing?

J Why are symbols in art insufficient by themselves to communicate sacred messages accurately, or are they?

H How does context enter into the message of a work of visual art?

2.7 SOME ART ASSERTS MASCULINITY FOR MEN 187

"...Art is a manifestation of phallic aggression, expressing... masculinity by conveying messages of male fierceness and pride, to friends as well as to enemies." p241 *"Through their art, Sepik men assert their masculinity and dominance over their adversaries, be the enemy their own women or men of hostile villages."p. 87.*

Anderson, R. (1990). Calliope's sisters: A comparative study of philosophies of art. Englewood Cliffs, NJ: Prentice-Hall. By permission of Prentice-Hall Division of Simon & Schuster.

P Why might artists show muscles on men, or glasses on scholars, farmers with overalls, or women in long dresses?

I Why would an American artist paint a wrestling match? a baseball game? a wood chopper?

J Why might art vary from culture to culture in the way males or females ar depicted?

H How might art contribute to cultural cohesion through visual image making? Why would it do so?

2.7 ACROSS CULTURES, ART OF VARYING QUALITY AROUSES EMOTIONAL RESPONSES 188

"The basic role of the artist is the same in any culture: to arouse an emotional response in his audience." p.17.

Dockstader. (1962). Indian art in America. Greenwich, CT: New York Graphic Society. Published by Little, Brown and Company. Fair use.

P Imagine two works of art of the same place: one by an artist and one by a friend who is not an artist. Why might you have more feeling from viewing one than the other?

I What effect could a thousand copies of the same artifact have on your initial response to it? Is a copy necessarily less effective emotionally, in all cultures?

J If a copy is dictated by a cultural tradition, what effect might it have on viewers responses, or would it not?

H To what extent does technical quality of a cultural symbol enter into the anticipated viewer response in that culture? Would your answer differ if the viewer was from another culture?

2.7 ART EMBODIES SPIRITS OF THE SUPERNATURAL, OF THE MAKER, OF THE USER 189

"...art works provide residences for members of the spirit world upon whom present and future life depends." "Sepik art serves not only as a vessel for the powerful spirits...but also for the souls of the men who make and use the art." p.84

Anderson, R. (1990). Calliope's sisters: A comparative study of philosophies of art. Englewood Cliffs, NJ: Prentice-Hall. By permission of Prentice-Hall Division of Simon & Schuster.

P If you put on a bear mask at Halloween, you'd probably act and sound like a bear, too. Why might a good bear mask artist be "bear-like"

I An actor "becomes" the character portrayed. What parallel could exist in visual art forms? Why?

J Why might some culture using art in a ceremony, choose to create a mask rather that a symbol like a candle, cross or heart?

H What purposes can be served by art that is given priority for its spiritual powers?

2.7 ART IS ETERNAL AND PROTECTING   190

"...art is everlasting...its essence will...last forever." p.150. "...it [art] can protect humans from the inevitable destruction of our fragile and temporary world." p.153

Anderson, R. (1990). Calliope's sisters: A comparative study of philosophies of art. Englewood Cliffs, NJ: Prentice-Hall. By permission of Prentice-Hall Division of Simon & Schuster.

P Sometimes we make pictures of make-believe events. What good could come from artists' make-believe art?

I Why might someone create an artwork af an imaginary situation or place unlike this world?

J What purposes can be served by art that depicts out-of-this-world religious ideas... today in the U.S.? ....in third world nations?...in hunting and fishing societies?

H If art conveys truth, how can one resolve apparently conflicting conceptions of our world and life emerging from different cultures?

2.7 ART SUSTAINS AND RESTORES THE WORLD'S BEAUTY AND HARMONY   191

"The world was created in beauty and harmony..mortals should sustain and restore the world's primal beauty...through the production of art...singing chants and sandpainting, as well as...artful living..." [Navajo] p.103.

Anderson, R. (1990). Calliope's sisters: A comparative study of philosophies of art. Englewood Cliffs, NJ: Prentice-Hall. By permission of Prentice-Hall Division of Simon & Schuster.

P Why is it important to take care of our environment? Why is that like creating a work of art?

I What reasons for creating art apply to maintaining a beautiful environment in our world? Why is that important?

J How could principles for making harmony in art apply to environmental concerns? Why could those principles apply to harmony among people?

H Line and color are elements of art. What elements need to be brought into harmony for artful, harmonious living? Does art fit in? How? Why?

228

METACRITICISM
WHAT DO WE MEAN BY THE WORDS WE USE TO DESCRIBE ART?

3.1 ARTISTS EXPRESS FEELING, BUT DO NOT PLAN AROUSAL OF FEELING   192

"...expression of feeling is to be distinguished sharply from the deliberate arousal of it;" "...he [the artist] cannot *calculate* in advance what effects he wants to produce and then proceed to produce them." "...expression is the activity of an artist, while arousal is the activity of a clever craftsman or a trained technician." p.315.

Hospers. J.(1955). The concept of artistic expression. Proceedings of the Aristotelian Society, 1954-1960, 55, 313-344. Fair use.

P Do artists plan how you should feel, or, plan to paint something about the artists had feelings, or what?

I If an image arouses feelings in people, does **that** make it "art", or, does it make it "not art"? Why?

J If art is "expression", are emotions expressed, ideas expressed, ideas intended to arouse emotions a subject that shows expressiveness, or what?

H How do we know whether an artist was *expressing feelings* about the subject of a work of art? Whose feelings?

3.1 ART COMMUNICATES BY SENSORY QUALITIES AND SYMBOLS   193

[Communication is a] "process by which a mental content is transmitted by symbols from one person to another..." p.336.

Isenberg, A. (July, 1949). Critical communication. The Philosophical Review, 58, 330-344. By permission.

P What can you learn by looking carefully at art and hearing how others "read" a work of art?

I Why is sharing your observations about art verbally with others important?

J Some persons "know what they like about art" and are reluctant to even discuss what doesn't fit that idea. Why is this an issue to anyone?

H People say something is learned when they need to teach it. Why could that relate to consciously recognizing the approach to, and group discussions about, interpretations of works of art?

3.1 EXPRESS HAS VARIABLE MEANINGS: an *artist's emotion*, emotion an artist evokes through his/her work, emotion *depicted in* the subject of the work of art, and an artist's communication to a viewer by his/her work. 194

"Ultimately, the meaning of 'express' will depend upon the context of its utterance." p.31

Eaton, M. (1988). Basic issues in aesthetics. Belmont, CA: Wadsworth Publishing Company. Copyright 1988 by Wadsworth, Inc.. By permission of Wadsworth Publishing Company.

"To use 'express' in this sense without saying to whom is to make an incomplete statement." p.65.

From Meaning and truth by John Hospers. Copyright 1946 by the University of North Carolina Press and renewed 1974 by John Hospers. Used by permission of the publisher.

P A baby is expressing feelings when it cries. Do just **people** express or can **things** express? Why?

I If an artist paints a crying person, is the artist sad? Would everyone looking at the painting be sad?

J What kinds of things or persons express feelings? Does a "thing" have feelings?

H How many ways can you explain that a work of art expresses emotion?

3.1 UNITY MAY BE SACRIFICED BY TOO MUCH CONCERN FOR EFFECT 195

"...Intensity of the quality is acheived at too great a sacrifice of unity ... too much concern for effect." p.463.

Beardsley, M. (1958). Aesthetics: Problems in the philosophy of criticism. New York: Harcourt, Brace. Fair use.

P When you scream for joy, you are likely smiling big with arms up high. What else might an artist do in a work fo art to help that happy scream along?

I In a midnight horror story, why might quiet periods be important rather than all action. How would a visual artist show this?

J Of what importance is the background to a work of art that is meant to shock the viewer if
"shock " is an immediate condition?

H Which is more important in a work of art...unity or effect.. and why? With deconstructionist ideas, is unity and appropriate criterion to expect in artworks?

3.1 CRITICISM HELPS ART COMMUNICATE BY NOTING VISUAL QUALITIES AND RELATIONSHIPS THAT CREATE MEANING 196

[Communication]...it is a function of criticism to bring about communication at the level of the senses; that is to induce a sameness of vision, of experienced content." p. 336.

Isenberg, A. (July,1949). Critical communication. The Philosophical Review, 58, 330-344. By permission.

P When two people talk, we say that they communicate. Why does looking carefully at a work of art help the work to communicate with the person looking at it?

I In art criticism, we ask questions about and look for answers in a work of art. What reasons can you give for calling art criticism "communication"? Who or what is talking to whom?

J Why is or why is not an art criticism experience a two-way communication? Who or what is involved in the communication?

H How many levels of communication are involved as an artwork is initiated, emerges and stands completed? How many communicative interactions take place? What or who communicates with what or whom in the whole process?

3.1 "WORK OF ART" IMPLIES SOME STRANDS OF SIMILARITIES AMONG PROPERTIES 197

(unknown)

P What makes a painting of a horse and a sculpture of a horse "art", but not a plastic model of a horse "art"?

I Three bouquets (silk flowers, real daffodils, and metal sculptured flowers) sat on a table in front of a painting of flowers. Which of these is art and why?

J Imagine a tall street light and a sculpture of a straight, tall human. Are they enough alike to both be "art"? Why or why not?

H Which or what kind of similarities must two objects have to be works of art? Why? If one has a painting of a horse, a stone sculpture of a horse, a real horse, and a plastic model of a famous horse, which of their differences would make any one or all of these "art"?

3.1 EXPRESSIVE CONTENT IS A FUSION OF SUBJECT MATTER AND FORM 198

"To keep from confusing what we normally call the subject matter...with the more complete aspect ... adopt the term 'expressive content' to describe that unique fusion of subject matter and specific visual form which characterizes the particular work of art." p. 51.

Taylor, J. (1981). Learning to look:A handbook for the visual arts. Chicago: University of Chicago Press. Copyright 1957, 1981 by The University of Chicago. By permission.

P When frightened, you might raise your eyebrows, straighten your fingers and a cat's hair would stand on end. Why would an artist use straight upward or jagged lines to make a landscape look frightening?

I Why might artists use what they know about body movement and reacting to emotions to make art?

J When the subject matter of an ad and a work of art is the same, what makes one a work of art? Why?

H Why do we say art is expressive? Is it automatically so when an artist manipulates art tools? Is it the nature of the subject? What might arrangement and choices about varying elements contrbute to expressive content.

3.1 RELATED PARTS IN ART MAKE "FORM". FORM IS THE RELATIONSHIP BETWEEN PERCEPTIBLE ELEMENTS. 199

" The term 'perceptible elements' refers to what can be...seen. To speak of the relations of perceptible elements to one another is to refer to what artists and critics sometimes call 'form'." p. 15.

Arnstine, D. (1966). The aesthetic as a context for general education. Studies in Art Education 8 (1), 13-22. By permission of National Art Education Association.

P An artist doesn't like everything thrown together like garbage. How could an artist change a square to fit with wiggly lines and shapes and not look like garbage? Why would this be
important to do?

I What colors would an artist use in a "rustic" picture? Why?

J Why would a collage artist end up with "art" not street trash even if actual street trash was used?

H Why would artists use throw-aways in making new art?

3.1 SIGNIFICANT FORM MEANS EFFECTIVE ARRANGEMENT 200

"When I speak of significant form, I mean a combination of lines and colours (counting white and black as colours) that moves me aesthetically." p.12.

Bell, C. (1913).Art. London: Chatto & Windus. Public domain and by permission of Chatto & Windus.

P Why do you notice a work of art more than an object that is not art?

I What is the reason that works by artists take on a special quality that we respond to?

J What does it take to impress you? Why has a work of art that is non-objective impress you?

H What qualities or combinations of qualities in art works are critical to effecting an aesthetic response regardless of subject matter?

3.1 JUDGMENT OF BEAUTY DEMANDS AGREEMENT WITHOUT CONSIDERING CONTEXT. 201

Judgments of beauty are "disinterested"; that is they are indifferent to the real existence of their objects...[and demands agreement] concerning the pleasure which everyone ought to derive from the experience of form." p. 27,29

Dickie, G. (1971). Art and the aesthetic: An institutional analysis. Ithaca, NY: Cornell University Press. By permission and fair use.

P Can some art be beautiful to one person and not to another? Why?

I If everyone in a group agrees that an artwork is beautiful, is it? Why? If the group has people from all over that world, why could they still agree?

J What is absolutely necessary for any work of art to have beauty? Why?

H What does understanding the context do to judgements about beauty of works of art? How does the meaning of beauty change by considering the context? Should the context be a variable in determining beauty or not?

3.1 UNITY, COMPLEXITY AND INTENSITY ARE CRITERIA FOR JUDGING AESTHETIC OBJECTS 202

" ... unity, complexity, and intensity..." " Objective reasons that have any logical relevance at all depend upon a direct or indirect appeal to these three basic standards." p.469,470

Beardsley, M. (1958). <u>Aesthetics: Problems in the philosophy of criticism</u>. New York: Harcourt, Brace. Fair use

P Why might dill pickles on chocolate ice cream be like art that isn't very good?

I Why might a painted portrait be hung in an art gallery rather than a big picture of Peanuts?

J If accuracy and usefulness is important in math, what is important that art works have?

H How would you defend one or more criteria that all works of art must have?

3.1 ART CRITICISM INVOLVES DEBATE ABOUT AND JUSTIFICATION OF THE CRITERIA USED IN JUDGING WORKS OF ART. 203

"It is not possible to write responsible art criticism without positing at least a provisional definition of art, which in turn is dependent on art's relationship to a given culture." p.19.

Allara, P. (June,1987). The writing of art criticism. <u>Art New England</u> 8 (6), 18-19 and 28. Printed with permission of <u>Art New England</u> magazine.

P What do we mean by beauty?

I What do we mean by realism and representation?

J What do we mean by symbolism?

H What do we mean by aesthetic, aesthetic meaning, truth?

3.1 WORKS OF ART ARE DESCRIBED IN TERMS WHICH DESCRIBE AESTHETIC QUALITY 204

"...aesthetic qualities ultimately depend upon, the presence of features which, like curving or angular lines, color contrasts placing of masses, or speed of movement, are visible...without any exercise of taste or sensibility."
p.424
Sibly, F. (October,1959). Aesthetic concepts. The Philosophical Review, LXVIII, 421-450. By permission.

P   When we describe how an art work looks, why would we not need to know what's good in art? How would we describe how it looks to someone who is blind?

I   Why would looking closely at art works make one search for new or more complicated words?

J   Why would written or oral descriptions cause a person to look more closely at an art work or visa-versa?

H   What kind of a vocabulary is needed to adequately describe a work of art? Is it better to strive for sophistication or simplification?

3.1 NEITHER HABITS NOR NOVELTY GUARANTEES QUALITY 205

Expectation breeds habitual response, but does not guarantee quality nor responsibility.
(unknown)

P   If you walk home the same way each day you don't have to think about where to turn. Is that a good way to go about making art? Why or why not?

I   Is it okay for an artist to keep one style of working? Why or why not?

J   What is the chance that an artist could get in a "rut"? Why could that happen? Is artistic style being in a "rut" or not?

H   What is significant about an artist who changes styles and directions even when successful? Is change for the sake of change valid? Why or why not?

3.1 AFFECTIVE BASES FOR JUDGING ART (PLEASURE) ARE VAGUE AND NEGLECT TO RELATE THE EFFECT TO QUALITIES OF THE WORK. ART MUST BE MORE THAN AFFECTIVE 206

"...Affective reasons by themselves are inadequate, because they are uninformative in two important ways. First,...what kind of pleasure it gives...the second...features of the work on which the effect depends." p.461

Beardsley, M. (1958). Aesthetics: Problems in the philosophy of criticism. New York: Harcourt, Brace. Fair use.

P If a picture is about dogs and you like dogs, why is that a good reason or not a good reason to call a picture art?

I If a work of art makes you feel pleasant, is that enough? What might the artist have done to accomplish that result on the viewer? Which is more important?

J Why is a good feeling reponse not a good enough reason for determining quality in art works? What else can be good about art?

H How would you qualify "affective response" as a criterion for determining quality in art works and why?

3.1 MEANING IS AN INDIVIDUAL MATTER 207

"...a work of art means to us whatever effects (not necessarily emotions) it evokes in us; a work which has no effects on us means nothing to us, and whatever effects it does evoke constitute its meaning for us." p.75.

From Meaning and truth by John Hospers. Copyright 1946 by the University of North Carolina Press and renewed 1974 by John Hospers. Used by permission of the publisher.

P Why might object or color in a work of art make someone notice it?

I If art works made persons recall memories or dreams, why could everyone in the class find different art works' important to them?

J Why can the same material, like feathers used in an artwork, mean something quite different to a hunter and a naturalist, and a participant in ceremonial African dances?

H Why do different art works appeal differently to members of the same society?

3.1 FADS AND LACK OF KNOWLEDGE WOULD NOT CONSTITUTE A BASIS FOR DETERMINING "TASTE" 208

" His [Hume's] claim is then that the normative question of what...to call beautiful can be solved by a comprehensive survey of the taste of man...certain kinds of cases must be discounted...the caprices of fashion and mistakes of ignorance and envy." p.24.

Dickie, G. (1971). Art and the aesthetic: An institutional analysis. Ithaca, NY: Cornell University Press. By permission and fair use.

P Why do art museums and art classes help people to make good decisions about art and what is beautiful?

I A man said, "If art doesn't look like something I've seen, it's not art." Why is this not a good enough reason to judge art?

J A newspaper headline read, "What's in and what's not in art." Why is the person who relies on such guidance taking a **bad** chance on showing **good** "taste"?

H Is it elitist or egalitarian to insist that "taste" in art requires knowledge and independence of fads, fashion, and profit motives? Can an Australian aborigine have good taste in art? Why or why not?

3.1 DEFINITIONS MAY BE SPECIFIC TO A CULTURE OR TIME 209

"By referring the judgments of the ancients on beauty to our conception of it, as is usually done in aesthetics, we give the words of the ancients a meaning which is not theirs." p.91.

Tolstoy, L. (1962). What is art? New York: Oxford University Press. A Hesperides Book. By permission of Oxford University Press.

P A child in Thailand once bowed as the teacher passed. Do we bow to teachers to show respect? How can art show certain people's ideas of respect? Why can art show what people mean without using words?

I How would an artist in your grandmother's school days show "walking to school" differently than one would today. Why can the same topic "look" so different?

J Why don't parents and teenagers always understand each other? How is misunderstanding represented in art? Why?

H If art is a universal language, why can't people read the visual symbols of other cultures?

3.1 AETHETIC FUSION DOES NOT NEGATE EMPHASIS 210

"...even when much psychological fusion occurs, a complexity of meaning remains...but esthetic fusion does not mean the disappearance of the parts."
"...emphasis upon and attention to...is not incompatible with aesthetic fusion."
p.24
Reid, L. A criticism of art as form. In L.Reid, Ed. (1954). A study in aesthetics. New York: The MacMillan Company. Fair use.

P If lines and colors should fit well together in art, how might the artist make what is important stand out?

I A center of interest or part emphasized in art work must stand out to get the point across. Why does this contradict or fit the idea of unity in art?

J What reasons can you give for the importance of aesthetic unity in works of art?

H What relationship exists between psychological fusion, aesthetic fushion, and emphasis by contrast in works of art? Does the existence of one eliminate the possibility of another? Why or why not?

3.1 INCONOGRAPHY STUDIES THE SYMBOLISM OF IMAGES 211

"Where iconology studies the similarity between structures of images and their corresponding perceptual objects, iconography studies the symbolism of these images." p.183
Kaelin, E. F. (1989). An aesthetics for art educators. New York: Teachers College Press. By permission.

P We "read" a painting by noticing how the artist changes body positions. Why might an outstretched arm held above the head mean "hello" or "good bye"?

I Referees are dressed alike but they each use signals that mean certain things. How do artists make icons have different meaning? Why does this work?

J Body language is as old as the human race. How do artists use body language in works of art? Why do they do so?

H How does gesture of an icon depicted by an artist differ from artists depicting gestures of any human figure? How far can artists go in using their individuality to depict icons? Why?

3.1 REGIONAL QUALITIES ARE FORMAL QUALITIES WE SEE IN ART 212

"*Regional qualities* are such things as color, pitch, or rhyme--qualities *in* an object that we perceive ...that others have referred to as 'formal qualities' or 'intrinsic qualities valued for themselves alone' ..." p.47,49.
Eaton, M. (1988). Basic issues in aesthetics. Belmont, CA: Wadsworth Publishing Company. Copyright 1988 by Wadsworth, Inc.. By permission of Wadsworth Publishing Company.

P   What are little girls made of? What are little boys made of? What is art made of? Why do you think those are important things that make something "art"?

I   Sentences are made up of words in certain order. Why are works of art something like sentences. Why can't we read foreign language sentences? Is art like language? Why?Why not?

J   Each human has qualities by which one can describe another. Can you point to all qualities of people? Can you point to the things that are qualities of an art work? Why or why not?

H   Can we explain art in terms of what we see? Is there any quality that an artwork can acquire that can not be attributed to a manipulation by the artist? If so, what and why, or why not?

3.1   IMITATION OR REPRESENTATION: WHAT, WHEN, WHERE?   213

"Representation...is more non-committal about the value of the representation [than 'imitation'] and is more likely to suggest the context of art." p.8
Sheppard, A.,1987. Aesthetics: An introduction to the philosophy of art. New York: Oxford University Press. By permission of Oxford University Press.

P   How can the word "copy" mean two different things in art?

I   When might it be preferable to saay that artists "represent" something, and when, that artists "make imitations of" something?

J   If an artist were to depict"holiness", how would you visualize the difference when such a work of art imitates, represents, or symbolizes "holiness"? What word best describes how you first visualized "holiness"? later?

H   Throughout history artists have made studies of other artists' work as well as "copied" natural scenes. What is the meaning of the terms you would use to declare either of the activities creating works of art?

3.1 REPRESENT AND SYMBOLIZE MEANS TO "STAND FOR" 214

"Whenever one item in our experience stands for another, the first item is said to <u>represent</u> the other, or to be a <u>symbol</u> of the other, while the thing symbolized or represented is called the <u>referent</u> of the symbol." p.29.

From <u>Meaning and truth</u> by John Hospers. Copyright 1946 by the University of North Carolina Press and renewed 1974 by John Hospers. Used by permission of the publisher.

P If a smile means that yu would act as someone's friend, how might that be like a railroad crossing sign? a Christian cross, a candle?

I People send messages and heart symbols on Valentine's Day. Does the heart stand literally for that body part or does it refer to something else? What can be said that applies to the use of symbols in art

J How are visual symbols in art like a secretary's shorthand? Are they like a secret code? Why or why not?

H Realistic images symbolize as well as abstractions. How could many levels of representation and sybbolizations of referents exist in the same work of art?

3.1 THE ARTIST'S INTENTION IS NOT PART OF THE WORK OF ART 215

"...success in realizing intentions cannot be used as a criterion of the value of a work of art." p.112.

Dickie, G. (1971a). <u>Aesthetics</u>. New York: Bobbs-Merril Pegasus Division of Prentice-Hall. Inc. Fair use.

P How many meanings can you think of for a painting of a single rose? Why do you think the artist painted it?

I If artists play jokes on people with their art, how can you know for sure what the artist really means to show? Why or why not?

J Is it true that an artist's intention in creating a ceremonial mask is not an important consideration or part of the work? Why or why not?

H Is it wise to guess an artist's intention in appreciating an art work or is it true that all art stands regardless of knowing the intention of the artist?

MEDIA-GENERATED ISSUES

3.2 TECHNIQUE IS A MEANS TO THE END OF CREATING A WORK OF ART   216

"Technique is the means to the creation of expressive form, the symbol of sentience..." p. 40.
From Langer, S.(1953). Feeling and form Copyright 1953. Published by Scribner's & Sons, New York. Fair use

P What is important in making art, and <u>why</u>: what you make, how you make it, or something else?

I If artists work hard at making a certain media do what they want it to, is it how well they make the brush or chisel work that makes their product "art" or something else?

J How important is the time it took to make something? What role does good technical quality play in qualifying something as "art"?

H What is the relationship of technical quality and media used, to "art"?

3.2 KNOWING THE MEDIUM OR TECHNIQUE HELPS IN DESCRIBING THE ARTISTIC CHARACTER OF THE WORK   217

"As with the formal elements...to recognize the medium or technique...becomes of significance only when a knowledge of the technique helps in describing the particular artistic character of the work." p. 70.
Taylor, J. (1981). Learning to look:A handbook for the visual arts. Chicago: University of Chicago Press. Copyright 1957, 1981 by The University of Chicago. By permission.

P How would your self-portrait differ if you used colored pencils or tempera with large brushes? Why would an artist choose the colored pencils? Why the tempera paint?

I What difference does the media chosen in art make on the quality of the work of art? Why?

J How would or would not a surface on which a scene is painted e.g. black velvet, contribute to the worth of a painting? Would the same image in gold be of greater artistic value?

H What is the advantage of experience with art media, if you never intend to make art yourself, but want to be able to appreciate art? Why?

3.2 A BUILDING IS A COMPOSITION OF FORMS THAT AGREE WITH ONE ANOTHER AS AN INTERIOR WORLD AND AN EXTERIOR MASS 218

"A building is not a collection of surfaces, but an assemblage of parts in which length, width, and depth agree with one another in a certain fashion, and constitute an entirely new solid that comprises an internal volume and an external mass." p.20.

Focillon, H. (1948). The life forms in art. New York: George Wittenborn, Inc. Fair use.

P If a sculpture must look good as people walk around it, is it enough that a big sculpture--a building into which people can walk--looks good on the outside?

I If architecture is art, why would the inside of a building be part of what is considered in deciding whether or not that building is good art?

J What does the inside of architecture have to do with its outside?

H What is the importance of inside spatial relationships to exterior relationships of forms in architecture?

3.2 ARTISTS USE UNUSUAL MEDIA OR APPROACHES TO PROVOKE THOUGHT 219

"Recently, he [Julian Schnabel] started to do paintings on velvet, a surface heretofore associated with souvenir-shop art." p.92.

From Post-to-neo: The artworld of the 1980's by Calvin Tomkins, Copyright 1988 by Calvin Tomkins. Reprinted by permission of Henry Holt and Company, Inc.

P Why might one be surprised to see detailed flowers carved from stone? Why would you be surprised to see a real lollipop in an art work?

I Why would use of a toothbrush, candy, combs, toy soldiers, wood scraps and light bulbs in a sculpture cause people to stop and look?

J Why might a sculptor use pieces of automobile tire tread for creating an alligator sculpture?

H Why is the use of unusual media to make art a legitimate practice and beyond the show stopper, or shock effect?

3.2 FOLK ART, OFTEN REUSING MATERIALS THAT WERE NO LONGER FUNCTIONAL, HAS SHOWN STRENGTH OF EXPRESSION--HONESTY 220

"Mother had learned quilt-making in the free-hand piecing technique her grandmother...had taught her. The result was that Mother's tankas were an amazing and original blend: a tanka that was Tibetan and African inspired. In 1980 Mother and I collaborated on our first and only quilt...I didn't realize where my mother's free-hand design approach was coming from." p.76.

Ringgold, F. (1995). We flew over the bridge. New York: Bullfinch Press Division of Little, Brown, and Company. Fair use.

P Why did your great grandmother make rugs from stripWhy are they made by machines and still available to us? Were they "art" then? Are they now?

I To what is an artist responding when making found object collages of natural or made objects? How can the combining of objects not made by the artist become an art work?

J Why are masks made in Africa constructed differently from masks made in Thailand or by American Northwest Coast Indians?

H When is honesty in use of geographically available materials to make art, discarded and the motive of profit continues a practice? When is the product no longer art, or does it remain art always? Why?

3.2 MEDIA PLAYS AN IMPORTANT, INDEPENDENT ROLE IN THE WORK OF ART 221

"It is the medium of art, then, that determines the character of the content and obliges us to distinguish this from the subject matter, where this latter is relevant...a medium in art is not...a means to an end." p.268.

Parsons, M. The concept of medium in education. In R. Smith, Ed. (1970). Aesthetic concepts and education pp263-285. Urbana, IL: University of Illinois Press. Fair use.

P Why might an artist choose to make a water pitcher out of clay rather than tightly woven threads?

I Why might an artist choose to dribble rather than to brush paint on a canvas?

J Why would an artist tell a story with fabrics in a quilt form rather than put the same images and words in a book or on a canvas?

H What is the relative importance of the medium in a work of art? Is it more than a carrier or means to the end of the idea? Why or why not?

3.2 ORNAMENT MAY HAVE VALUE IN ITSELF AND TOGETHER WITH THE OBJECT IT ENHANCES

"Ornament shapes, straightens, and stabilizes the bare and arid field on which it is inscribed. Not only does it exist in and of itself, but it also shapes its own environment-- to which it imparts a form." p.18.
Focillon, H. (1948). The life forms in art. New York: George Wittenborn, Inc. Fair use.

P Many young girls love to play dress-up, but other people do too. Why do artists also make things very fancy, like jeweled crowns or elaborately decorated eggs (not Easter eggs!)?

I Why do houses that provide shelter have non-functional "gingerbread" decoration along the roof lines, porches, etc.?

J Why is non-functional decoration functional? What purpose is served by being fancy?

H How many ways do people create ornamentation from the personal level to the public level? How can you account for this striving to decorate?

3.2 BY STYLIZATION, THE POPULAR ARTIST CREATIVELY COMMUNICATES THROUGH SELECTING, EMPHASIZING AND STRESSING

"...conventions provide an agreed upon base from which true creative invention springs... The popular artist may use conventions...so as to delight the audience with a kind of creative surprise...Mass art uses the stereotypes... to simplify the experience... and to 'get them going.'" p.69.
Hall, S. & Whannel, P. (1964). The popular arts. New York: Pantheon Permission granted by Random House, Inc.

P When would an artist use a smily face, or wouldn't he/she?

I Why might an artist overuse typical symbols...putting an overabundance of them in a picture in ways that individually meant nothing?

J Society has simple symbols that are recognizable to many. Artists also create their own "conventions" by which their style is recognizable. Which is art and why?

H If stylizations are conventionally understood symbols, to what extent might an artist utilize them in his/her work and why? When should art be easily understood or should it not?

3.2 IN ARCHITECTURE, FUNCTION AND FORMAL QUALITIES MUST FIT
224

"...in architecture...physical use must be...so thoroughly linked to our formal experience of the building that we could no more separate that which was created by dictation of utility and that created to serve formal expression than we could separate actual structure from structure expressed." p.96.

Taylor, J. (1981). Learning to look:A handbook for the visual arts. Chicago: University of Chicago Press. Copyright 1957, 1981 by The University of Chicago. By permission.

P What is wrong when a building is easy to walk through but boring to be in?

I What good is it to have decorations on buildings? Are they always good?

J Is an architect really an artist when the product is so practical? Are all buildings art? Why or why not?

H How does architecture differ from 2-D art forms in application of formal principles? Why is some architecture more renown than other architecture... use of formal principles, social function, other?

3.2 ARTISTS MANIPULATE MEDIA AND TOOLS TO CAPTURE WHAT THEY WANT TO SHOW
225

"...the artist composes... with... the elements of his primary materials... 'in view until he gets the pattern of them that captures what he wants exhibited (content) to prehensive vision'." p.39-40.

Aldrich, V. (1963). Philosophy of art. Englewood Cliffs, NJ: Prentice-Hall. Fair use and by permission of the publisher.

P If the only art medium available was finger paint, could artists make it show any effect they wanted? How? Why or why not?

I How would what an artist wanted to weave determine the material to be used? When might a weaver want to make a basket with silk threads, or when not?

J Why would an architect planning a mall need to think about the materials being used to carry out the design?

H Why might an artist abandon a favorite medium by which the artist's career sucess is identified?

3.2 THE ARTIST CHOOSES A MEDIUM BASED ON HOW THE NATURE OF THE MEDIUM AND THE ARTISTIC FORM WILL UNITE 226

"...whether he chooses from a great range of media or works unquestioningly in traditionally prescribed material, the artist will tend to visualize the ultimate expressive form of his work in terms of the medium itself, so that characteristic aspects of the medium and artistic form are inse- parably united." p.72.

Taylor, J. (1981). Learning to look:A handbook for the visual arts. Chicago: University of Chicago Press. Copyright 1957, 1981 by The University of Chicago. By permission.

P Why would finger paint help an artist show a windy March day? a sculptor has metal rods and some sandstone from which to make a bear sculpture. Why is one media better than the other?

I Glittery metallic gold thread contrasts sharply with the soft deep black of velvet in some Mexican paintings. Why might these media fit with certain events or moods of traditional Mexico?Does this make each work an artwork?

J Is there more value in etchings than woodcuts or lithographs? Is the finer linear quality sufficient to value art of one process over another? What else could be considered?

H Does visualization in a particular medium and completion as visualized make an artwork more legitimate (than if the artist adds or changes media during the creative process) or not?

3.2 VIDEO ART DEMANDS VIEWER TIME COMMITTMENT 227

"Video art asks for the kind of concentration that we are expected to give to painting and sculpture, and it also asks us to give up our time to it." p.97.

From Post -to-neo: The artworld of the 1980's by Calvin Tomkins, Copyright 1988 by Calvin Tomkins. Reprinted by permission of Henry Holt and Company, Inc.

P Some movies are considered art and you look at them. How is looking at video art different than looking at painting, sculptures, etc.

I How is watching a video art film like certain non-visual art forms and unlike certain visual art forms?

J How could viewing of video art be like trying to contemplate art at a gallery opening? Why might it **not** be so?

H How might the nature of video art effect the viewer and/or the impact of the artwork? What variables could enter into the art experience because of the viewing over time?

3.2 APPRECIATING ARTISTS' CHOICE OF MEDIA AS PART OF THE CREATIVE ACTIVITY IS ENHANCED BY KNOWING PROCESSES AND THE EXPRESSIVE POSSIBILITIES OF MEDIA   228

"An appreciation of the particular nature of these experiences may be enhanced by a knowledge of the actual processes involved and by a recognition of the expressiveness artists have found in some established materials and methods." p.7.

Taylor, J. (1981). Learning to look: A handbook for the visual arts. Chicago: University of Chicago Press. Copyright 1957, 1981 by The University of Chicago. By permission.

P Why would a sculptor who wanted to make a "big stretch" look choose huge sheets of curved metal rather than toothpicks?

I Why do art teachers have students do more than just learn to draw... important as that is?

J How would knowing that acid eats metal help a chemist to understand something about an artist's etching? Why? Would that be enough to appreciate the print?

H Why might breadth of exposure to art materials be advantageous to the high school student?

3.2 POPULAR ART INVOLVES THE SURPRISE OF RECOGNITION ENHANCED BY THE FORCE OF AN ARTIST'S PERSONAL STYLE   229

"Popular art... restates, in an intense form, values and attitudes...known; which reassures and reaffirms, but brings...the surprise of art as well as the shock of recognition...in common with folk art genuine contact between audience and performer; but it differs...it is an individualized art." p.66

Hall, S. & Whannel, P. (1964). The popular arts. New York: Pantheon Permission granted by Random House, Inc.

P If an artist created a life size Barbie and Ken painted wood sculpture for an art show, would it be "art"? What if it was made from plastic and materials identical to the Barbie and Ken dolls?

I An artist made a jack knife so large that it looked like a boat. Is the surprise of the common object and its size enough to be "art"?

J Why might an artist (Red Grooms) make "art" of life size plywood cut-outs of people in places (grocery stores)?

H What is it that surprises people when they see common objects promoted to the status of art? Should people be surprised? Should artists offend peoples' sensibilities?

3.2 EXPRESSION OF IDEAS IS INFLUENCED BY THE MEDIA USED   230

"Only where material is employed as media is there expression and art... Everything depends upon the way in which material is used when it operates as medium." p.63

From Art as experience by John Dewey. Copyright 1934 by John Dewey, renewed 1973 by The John Dewey Foundation. Used by permission of G.P. Putnam's Sons, a division of Penguin Putnam Inc.

P   What about the way a slinky is made and its material allows it to smoothly flip down steps? Why might a yarn slinky not work? Why would another artist choose yarn for an art product?

I   If someone wanted a wintery table decoration, why might that person spray pricky branches with silver and use a crystal bowl?

J   Why might an artist choose to make a plate out of hammered metal than clay? Why might the choice be clay rather than metal?

H   What is a general rule of the thumb for selection of media to use in art?

3.2   CULTURAL TRADITIONS MAY LIMIT MEDIA OR TECHNIQUES EMPLOYED   231

"...theory should be adjusted to limiting conditions that certain characteristics of style (e.g., the depth dimension or particular colors) do not exist as technically realizable alternatives in some cultural traditions."p.163.

Kavolis, V. (1968). Artistic expression: A sociological analysis. Ithaca, NY: Cornell University Press. By permission and fair use.

P   If an eagle feather was part of an Indian dance costume, why do you think it would be okay or not okay to substitute a pretty aqua one for it?

I   Why could an artist depict "Uncle Sam" as a farmer in overalls or could he or she not take that liberty?

J   How could it help to know about the social taboos of a culture before drawing conclusions about its artwork? How could images, colors or positioning of images be limited? Is that bad?

H   Why do you suppose Japanese china is thin and subdued in coloring? What about the nature of the homes and people's behavior is compatible? Where does that hold true in other cultures or does it?

3.2 NEW MEDIA ART MAY PRESENT QUESTIONS ABOUT THE ROLE OF THE VIEWER   232

"Does video art exist? The question sounds naive, considering the large number of people currently working as video artists...for purely visual rather than dramatic, narrative, or documentary ends." "But how does one take part in a viewing process...?" p.92.

From Post-to-neo: The artworld of the 1980's by Calvin Tomkins, Copyright 1988 by Calvin Tomkins. Reprinted by permission of Henry Holt and Company, Inc.

P Video tapes are common place. Are they important now? Why might one video be "art" but not all?

I Does video art need sound or can it be a purely visual experience? Why? How is video art more like a painting? How is it more like a TV newscast? How is it more like an opera?

J Two weavers may do quite different things with fibers and weaving. Why do various intents of video artists affect judgment by the public about the quality of their video art work?

H Why might the audience of video art vary from film audiences? To what extent does the audience impact on the media as "art"? Why? How?

3.2 TECHNIQUE MUST CONTRIBUTE TO THE QUALITY OF ARTWORK   233

"A knowledge of techniques as the ordering of means toward an end may be relevant to the discovery of an aesthetic value-- whether by an artist or by a viewer--but without an experience of the ends-in-view [perception of the aesthetic quality pervasive of the artistic creation] guiding the use of available means, there would be no way of evaluating their use." p. 186.

Kaelin, E. F. (1989). An aesthetics for art educators. New York: Teachers College Press. By permission.

P Why would you draw some things in pencil, but use a large brush and paint for other things? Are artist fussy about using the right tool?

I Why might a painter choose to do drawings or prints as art work sometimes? How many reasons can you give?

J Artists can draw with many tools and use each tool in many ways to vary the stroke. Is an artist uninventive to choose to use a single tool and a stroke by which his/her style is characterized? Why or why not?

H When might an artist make choices to vary tools or a stroke in the same artwork? Why might it be appropriate and contribute to the aesthetic quality and when not?

250

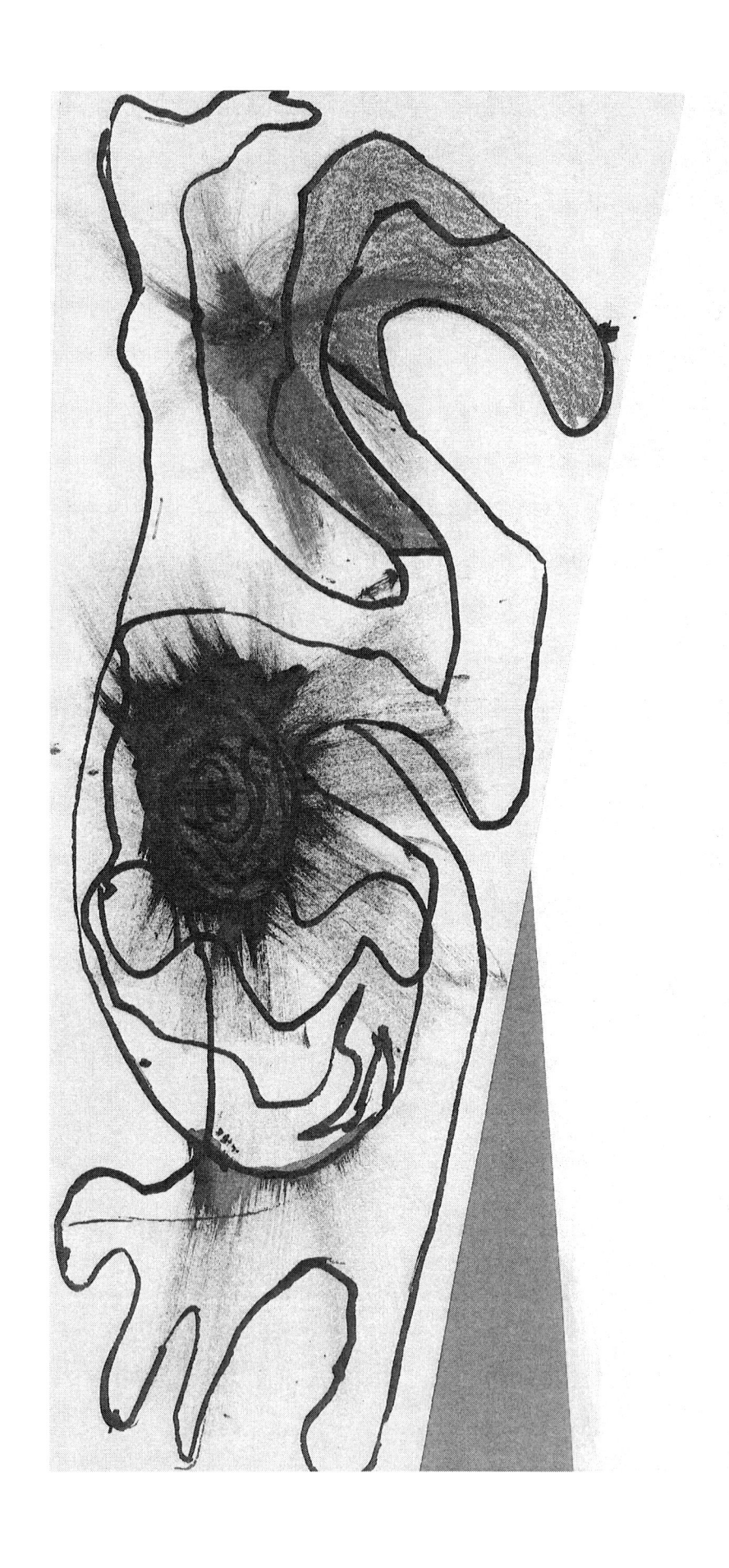

AN AESTHETIC ATTITUDE

3.3 AESTHETIC ATTITUDE: INTENSELY ABSORBED IN ART 234

"...the aesthetic attitude...disinterested and sympathetic attention to and contemplation of any object of awareness whatever, for its own sake alone."p. 34-35"... 'disinterested' is very far from being '<u>un</u>-interested'. " p.36.
Stolnitz, J. (1960).<u>Aesthetics and the philosophy of art criticism</u>. Boston: Houghton Mifflin Company. By permission of the author.

P How is looking at art like enjoying the taste of a sucker (as opposed to eating food that makes you grow)?

I How might thinking about works of art be different from studying about vegtables whose vitamins keep you healthy?

J What could constitute objective viewing of art? How could a degree of disinterestedness be positive?

H What role has personal involvment, if any, in the objective motive of an aesthetic attitude?

3.3 AESTHETIC ATTITUDE DEPENDS ON PRIOR VISUAL ANALYSIS 235

"He [Stolnitz] maintains criticism plays an important and necessary role in preparing a person to appreciate the nuances, detail, form, and so on of works of art." ..."...'<u>prior</u> to the aesthetic encounter', or it will interfere with appreciation." p.62.
Dickie, G. (January,1964). The myth of the aesthetic attitude. <u>American philosophical Quarterly</u>, 1 (1), 56-65. By permission.

P If you had the same facts about a work of art, what difference might there be in seeing it quickly on TV and standing before it to look at it ?

I Once you knew the artist's name, when and where he/she lived, and what the work of art was made with, what else could you find out to understand a work of art?

J What different opinions could come from being an art detective who gets dates,media, size, and historical period information about a work of art, from, an artist who imagines him/herself being the artist in the process of making all the choices and feeling as the artist did about the object being created?

H What kinds of information exist in works of art that can, by visual analysis, contribute to grasping the meaning or significance of works of art?

3.3 HAVING AN AESTHETIC ATTITUDE MEANS APPRECIATING WITHOUT RECOGNIZING A PERSONAL MEANING 236

"...Distance is produced...by putting the phenomenon,..., out of gear with our practical, actual self; by allowing it to stand outside the context of our personal needs and ends- in short, by looking at it 'objectively'...and by interpreting even our subjective affections...as characteristics of the phenomenon." p.89.

Bullough, E. (1912). "Psychical distance" as a factor in art and an aesthetic principle. (1966) British Journal of Psychology, 5, 87-118. By permission of the British Psychological Society.

P If a work of art is about something you have seen, is that a good enough reason to like it?

I How important is it to remember that you have actually seen the subject of a work of art compared to other benefits from looking at art?

J What do you think about the statement: "If art doesn't look like something I know and care about, it isn't worth much!"?

H How can being too "close" to the subject matter in works of art be problematic, and what alternative focus could you suggest for viewing familiar subject matter in art?

3.3 AESTHETIC ATTITUDE MEANS SEEING CERTAIN SENSORY QUALITIES 237

"Attitude determines how we perceive through a 'set' i.e., selective attention. It becomes an aesthetic attitude of perception when..."(p. 32)"... we pay attention to a thing simply for the sake of enjoying the way it looks or sounds or feels." p. 32,34.

Stolnitz, J. (1960). Aesthetics and the philosophy of art criticism. Boston: Houghton Mifflin Ccompany. By permission of the author.

P If you wanted to imagine how parts of a work of art would feel, but could only ""touch with your eyes", what would you have to notice?

I How is looking at art different from looking at billboards as you ride down a highway in the car?

J Scientists look at things with a magnifying glass. How is the "looking closely" that artists do similar or different?

H How would you compare the role of viewer at an art fair with that viewer at a science fair?

3.3 AN AESTHETIC ATTITUDE IS A SPECIAL RECEPTIVITY TO VISUAL PROPERTIES OF WORKS OF ART UNASSOCIATED WITH NEEDS OF EVERYDAY LIFE 238

"This fundamental attitude consists in the separation of the aesthetic experience from the needs and desires of everyday life and from the responses which we customarily make to our environment as practical human beings." p.4.

From Meaning and truth by John Hospers. Copyright 1946 by the University of North Carolina Press and renewed 1974 by John Hospers. Used by permission of the publisher.

P Does it make any difference whether an artist paints a beautiful red apple or a sculptor carves a grey one out of stone if they are both well done? Why might it make no difference?

I Two people are loking at an approaching storm. How and why might an artist-type person describe that view differently from the person thinking about the fact that farmers need rain?

J How would a person with an aesthetic attitude react to a "food art" exhibit differently than a hungry person without an aesthetic attitude? Why?

H To what extent can people attend to aesthetic qualities of art or of their environment if they lack their basic needs? Why?

3.3 AESTHETIC ATTITUDE MEANS BEING ALERT AND THINKING 239

[discriminating, alert, and vigorous] "...aesthetic attention is accompanied by activity...which is either evoked by disinterested perception of the object, or else required for it." p.37).

Stolnitz, J. (1960). Aesthetics and the philosophy of art criticism. Boston: Houghton Mifflin Ccompany. By permission of the author.

P If every art work had a secret, how would you go about finding the secret?

I Suppose that works of art were really mystery stories. How would you, the detective, go about looking for clues?

J Today's society emphasizes the speed of cars, of getting some jobs done or running a race. How does the value of speed fit with giving appropriate attention when viewing works of art? Why?

H To what extent could familiarity with the subject matter or the artist of a work of art detract from a discriminating, thinking attention to aesthetic qualities? Is familiarity an asset?
Why? Why not?

3.3 AESTHETIC ATTITUDE IS MENTAL, NOT PHYSICAL OR PSYCHOLOGICAL 240

An aesthetic attitude is a kind of attitude not closely associated with bodily needs towards objects or situations, but an inclination to be responsive to qualities and relationships.
(unknown)

P What does it take to appreciate art... doing something, feeling some way or thinking?

I When you visit an art exhibit that offers a taped explanation of the work shown, why would anyone bother and pay for that?

J How do you approach understanding a new art form that is totally different than anything you thought of as art?

H How would you differentiate between preference and appreciation of art and what does each demand from the viewer?

3.3 IF "AESTHETIC ATTITUDE" IS A MYTH, IS IT WORTHLESS? 241

"...the notion of aesthetic attitude has played an important role in the freeing of aesthetic theory from an overweening concern with beauty."
"...people have been encouraged to take an aesthetic atitude toward a painting as a way of lowering their prejudices, say, against abstract and non-objective art." p.64,65.
Dickie, G. (January,1964). The myth of the aesthetic attitude. American philosophical Quarterly, 1 (1), 56-65. By permission.

P If you always saw calendar pictures as art, how would a person be able to enjoy all the other kinds of art in the world?

I How many reasons can you give for looking at art besides looking for beauty?

J Not all art fits with our previous ideas about what it is. How is art like changes in the world of technology -- computers, guided missiles, or space exploration? Why should art remain the same or should it not?

H What qualities of viewers would be desireable to make a society in which the arts could flourish?

3.3 AN AESTHETIC ATTITUDE INVOLVES DETACHMENT, AWARENESS, AND FULL EXPERIENCING OF AN OBJECT   242

" It [Art] invites us to take up a certain attitude. Yet the attitude does not depend on the object...the attitude implies a certain detatchment...An aesthetic response,...implies no more than a heightened present awareness ..the attitude itself is no more than the full experiencing of any given thing." p. 101-102.

Pole, D. (1957). What makes a situation aesthetic? The Aristotelian Society. (1957). Proceedings of the Aristotelian Society, Supp. Vol.XXXI, 101-102. Fair use.

P   How important is it to have had your own dog in order to know whether a painting or sculpture of a dog is a good painting or sculpture?

I   When might it help and when might it hurt to now about or have a feeling for the subject of a work of art when you are the judge of a show?

J   Can you think of reasons why viewers who know something about the subject of a work of art would be more fair or less fair judges of the worth of that work of art?

H   To what extent does judgment of a work of art depend on familiarity as opposed to unfamiliarity with the subject of the work in terms of detached objectivity?

3.3 "...THE ACT OF JUSTIFYING ONE'S JUDGMENTS IS AN ESSENTIAL FEATURE OF APPRECIATION." p.8.   243

Ecker, D. (1967). Justifying aethetic judgments. Art Education, 20 (5), 8. By permission of NAEA.

P   If you think something is "art", what do you have to do to convince someone else that it is "art"?

I   If you and your friend disagree about whether some work of art is good or not, why isn't it
enough to just agree to disagree saying <u>anything</u> is okay if you like it?

J   How would you attempt to resolve disagreements about whether a sculpture on a building should be called art?

H   Is it necessary to verbalize reasons for appreciating works of art in order to appreciate them? Why or why not? Is the human capacity to reason a factor? Is some concensus for a cohesive society a consideration for justifying judgement? Why or why not?

3.3 AESTHETIC CRITERIA MUST BE CONSIDERED IN A CONTEXT OF KNOWLEDGE OF THE VISUAL ARTS SPECIFICALLY   244

"...there is no substitute for an intimate knowledge of whatever the field of art under criticism... must first perceive what he is judging before he can judge responsibly." p. 15.

Pepper, S. (1945). The basis of criticism in the arts. Cambridge, Mass: Harvard University Press. Copyright 1945 by the President and Fellows of Harvard College. Reprinted by permission of the publisher.

P   What is wrong if someone, who never heard of or saw a sculpture that moves, sees one, and immediately says that it isn't art?

I   Ten years from now, if someone calls something art that we never even imagined, what could you try to find out to help you decide if it should be considered art?

J   Is knowing the history of visual arts in the world necessary to having a basis for judging unimaginable art of the future? Why or why not?

H   If not everyone can be well-informed about art, must judgment be left to the scholars? Why or why not? To what extent can less informed persons make judgement about art?

3.3 ARTISTIC JUDGMENT DEMANDS A UNIVERSAL IDEA OF ART PLUS APPRECIATING THE INDIVIDUALITY OF THE ARTIST IN EXPRESSING THAT UNIVERSAL   245

"To appreciate a work of art we need bring with us nothing but a sense of form and colour and a knowledge of three dimensional space." p.27.

Bell, C. (1913). Art. London: Chatto & Windus. Public domain and by permission of Chatto & Windus.

P   If you had to pick one work of art that your whole school would admire, what would it need to be like?

I   If all art had to meet certain standards why wouldn't it all look alike?

J   How can the leaders in art set basic criteria by which works "qualify" as art and yet not limit the artist's license to be unique?

H   How far can an artist's license be extended before it exceeds the universal parameters of "art"?

3.3 BEAUTY IS OBJECTIVELY JUDGED AND AGREED UPON; TASTE/ PREFERENCE IS AN INDIVIDUAL DECISION BASED ON PERCEIVING THE FORMAL RELATIONS IN A WORK   246

[Kant]The judgment of beauty is "disinterested" i.e. independent of the interest in real existence, is therefore "universal", and demands agreement ("necessity"), but judgments of taste are made singularly and require "recognition of the *form* [formal relations] of purpose...which evokes the beauty experience." p. 27-29.
Dickie, G. (1971a). Aesthetics. New York: Bobbs-Merril Pegasus Division of Prentice-Hall, Inc. Fair use.

P Why might you like some of the art works we've learned about more than others? Why is that okay? What does that mean about art that you don't like as much?

I If you learn about many kinds of art, for what reasons might you feel that some are more special to you than others?

J Can you explain why thinking that something qualifies as "beautiful" for certain reasons that are basic to a work of art, is, or is not, the same as liking it?

H How would you explain the difference between understanding or appreciating many kinds of beauty in art, and, preference for certain kinds of beauty?

3.3 AESTHETIC ATTITUDE MEANS EXAMINING WHERE VALUES OPERATE   247

"...interpretation itself is evaluation... because it concerns how we think we should look at art works. ...giving reasons for giving that sort of reason!" p. 112.
Eaton, M. (1988). Basic issues in aesthetics. Belmont, CA: Wadsworth Publishing Company. Copyright 1988 by Wadsworth, Inc.. By permission of Wadsworth Publishing Company.

P What happens if you ask yourself "why" three times after picking a "best" art work?

I If you live in a new modern city, what might you think that a painting of a deteriorating, run-down houses means? Why?

J How do values enter into giving reasons in interpretating art?

H Can one have value-free interpretation of artworks? Why or why not?

3.3 CONTEMPLATION OF VISUAL QUALITIES IN ART CONTRIBUTES TO AWARENESS 248

"...when we consider anything as an end in itself we become aware of that in it which is of greater moment than any qualities it may have acquired from keeping company with human beings." p. 69.
Bell, C. (1913). Art. London: Chatto & Windus. Public domain and by permission of Chatto & Windus.

P   If we see a knight's armor on display in the art museum, is it there to help us see how it worked or other reasons? Why?

I   A group of secretaries decide on a quick lunch hour trip through the art museum. Why might that way of seeing art bother you?

J   What would be better for someone who knows very little about art when visiting an art show... to rent the cassette and ear phones that explain the pictures in the exhibit, or to spent the same time carefully looking?

H   A person looks a long time at a work of art and sees more in that extended time. Why can't it all be seen at once if it is present? if the viewer is reading into the work more that what the artist intended, is that okay? Why or why not?

3.3 ARTWORKS ARE TREATED SPECIAL....THEIR PURPOSE IS TALKED ABOUT 249

"We protect...,...revere...,...display....talk about [artworks]...What is special about discussions of art is not their content, but their purpose--not *what* is said, but *why* it is said." p.94.
Eaton, M. (1988). Basic issues in aesthetics. Belmont, CA: Wadsworth Publishing Company. Copyright 1988 by Wadsworth, Inc.. By permission of Wadsworth Publishing Company.

P   We mat and frame works of 2-d art. Is it only to protect them or for other reasons?

I   Why do people in most countries have art museums? Is all art in museums? Why or why not?

J   How safe is it to assume that an artwork **is** "art" if it is given recognition, or special display? Can people be fooled? Why could this not happen, or could it?

H   Is the special treatment that befalls art a sufficient reason to assume that all "art" is so recognized? What problems do you see that could be addressed?

3.3 AN AESTHETIC POINT OF VIEW IS TAKING AN INTEREST IN THE AESTHETIC VALUE OF A THING   250

"To adopt the aesthetic point of view with regard to X is to take an interest in whatever aesthetic value that X may possess." p.19.

Beardsley, M. (1970). The aesthetic oint of view. In H. Kiefer & M. Munitz (Eds.) Perspectives in education, religion, and the arts. pp.219-237.Albany, NY: State University of New York Press. Fair use.

P You paint your mother a picture of roses because she loves them.Might she appreciate your painting for reasons other than that she likes you and roses?

I Someone hung a black painting in an art museum, at least, viewers who settled for that conclusion quickly never saw the subtle changes in the composition. What could that tell us about looking at art?

J Why would an art critic view nudes in art as some would calendar pin-ups or why not? How can we tell the purpose of the artist in such works of art? What could a viewer who's interested in painting for its aesthetic value see?

H A story on a quilt has more value than the story. How might the choice of a quilt art form fit the cultural value of group communication? ... the aesthetic value as a work of art?

3.3 THE CRITERIA FOR DECIDING ON THE MERITS OF WORKS ART ARE FLEXIBLE   251

"Works of art are not judged by general rules..."p.186 "Critical canons are, perhaps, more like rules of etiquette than morals and very unlike scientific laws or logical principles." p.187.

MacDonald, M. (1949). Symposium: What are the distinctive features of arguments used in criticism of the arts, III. In The Aristoteoian Society. (1949). Proceedings of the Aristotelian Society, Supp. Vol.XXIII, 186,187. Fair use.

P What kinds of things do you see in works of art to which everyone can agree? Should everyone be able to see these things? Why might someone not notice what other people see?

I What type of thing would you look for in works of art to support what you think a work of art means?

J What could you use from what you know about history, geography, literature or life experiences to help understand what works of art mean?

H How could you determine the value of information derived by looking at the work of art and other background information as you try to decide on the worth of the artwork?

3.3 ART KNOWLEDGE AND SYMPATHETIC UNION WITH A WORK YIELDS TRUE UNDERSTANDING 252

"We who participate in art...may indeed need to know about a great deal...in order to enter into a work of art. But once we are in it...we can be said to know...by sympathetic union with what is known." "This intimate, participative sense of being is a far truer guide to... art than any cognition can ever be." p. 27.

Morgan, D. (Fall, 1967). Must art tell the truth? <u>Journal of Aesthetics and Art Criticism</u>, <u>26</u>, 17-27. By permission of the editor.

P How could you help yourself understand an artwork that looks different to you?

I What would someone mean if they said to put yourself into a work of art you are viewing? They didn't mean climb onto the sculpture, but what could that advice mean?

J Skateboarders used a metal sculpture as a ramp for testing their skills. Why does this "involvement" constitute a sympathetic union with their knowledge of art or does it not? Is theirs an aesthetic attitude?

H Is knowledge about an artwork sufficient to appreciate it? Must one have empathy for the work? Would empathy alone be possible or sufficient for appreciation? Why?

AN AESTHETIC EXPERIENCE

3.4 "AN AESTHETIC EXPERIENCE NEED NOT BE EXPRESSIVE..." 253

"...and an experience involving expressiveness need not be esthetic."[Expression in art does not always evoke a parallel feeling nor constitute an esthetic experience for the viewer.] p.71.

From Meaning and truth by John Hospers. Copyright 1946 by the University of North Carolina Press and renewed 1974 by John Hospers. Used by permission of the publisher.

P If a work of art shows two creatures fighting, is the viewer supposed to feel like fighting?

I Should art arouse feelings in people who view it?

J Can viewers fully appreciate art if they separate or detach personal feelings from the depicted feelings?

H To what extent must art (a) arouse any feelings in viewers and (b) arouse common feelings in multicultural populations of viewers?

3.4 THERE ARE DEGREES TO WHICH AN EXPERIENCE MAY BE AESTHETIC 254

"Life values [the world of experiences outside art] play an important part in the artistic appreciation of most persons...they figure more largely than the formal or surface values." "..concerned with surface- and form-values...I should like to call the thin sense of the word...previous experience of life...be called the thick sense of 'esthetic'." p.12, 13-14.

From Meaning and truth by John Hospers. Copyright 1946 by the University of North Carolina Press and renewed 1974 by John Hospers. Used by permission of the publisher.

P Artist often experiment with new ideas. Does that mean that old ideas like paintings of family scenes cannot be art or appreciated by people? Why or why not?

I Is it okay for people to prefer good art that they relate to, eg. a mechanic likes a found object collage of gears, a carpenter likes an additive wood sculpture, etc. Why?

J If an artist designs an innovative and aesthetically pleasing costume for a party, could it be a work of art or would its practical function negate its quality?

H What conditions influence whether persons have a strong aesthetic response or mild aesthetic response to art? Why?

3.4 SENSUOUS SURFACES OF ART OBJECTS AROUSE AESTHETIC EXPERIENCES IN US   255

"...first level...of esthetic experience...esthetic surface...we are enjoying simply the look, the sound, the taste, the sensation, without making distinctions and without considering meanings or interpretations or significances..." p.9.

From Meaning and truth by John Hospers. Copyright 1946 by the University of North Carolina Press and renewed 1974 by John Hospers. Used by permission of the publisher

P If a work of art makes you feel wonderful or excited about the way it looks, but it doesn't affect your friend that way, can it be beautiful art and not beautiful art at the same time?

I "If you enjoy something aesthetically one day and not the next, is it beautiful one day but not the next?"

J What is the effect of a person's unpleasant association with the content of a work of art on the aesthetic value (beauty) of that work?

H Is every object that arouses aesthetic experiences, beautiful?

3.4 PERCEPTION OF RHYTHM IN ART IS SUBJECT TO THE INFLUENCE OF EXPERIENCES BEYOND THE WORK OF ART ITSELF   256

Although rhythm is fundamental to composition, rates of perception and feeling may influence its importance in judgment of particular art works.p.70,71.

Paraphrased from Prall, D. (1929). Aesthetic judgment. New York: Thomas Y. Crowell, Company

P Heart beats have a rhythm or regular repeat. What can be regularly repeated in works of art? Why do we look for rhythm in art?

I How could the many rhythms of junk sculpture form rhythms as a work of art? What do artists manipulate to create rhythm?

J Why might a ballroom waltz dancer respond to different cues to visual rhythm in a work of art than a tap dancer might?

H When an artist plans a work of art to change because of the presence of a viewer, is the viewer part of the work of art?

3.4 THE AESTHETIC VALUE WITHIN WORKS OF ART EVOKE PLEASURE 257

"Aesthetic value is the ...capacity [of art] to evoke pleasure... arising from features in the object traditionally considered worthy of attention and reflection." p.143.

Eaton, M. (1988). Basic issues in aesthetics. Belmont, CA: Wadsworth Publishing Company. Copyright 1988 by Wadsworth, Inc.. By permission of Wadsworth Publishing Company.

P Why could you like an artist's picture of a storm even if you do not like storms?

I Why would we like a flower picture where the long slender petals were perky, the long, slender leaves also were erect and they were in front of a tall window in a tall, slender vase?

J Why might one like an art work of lacey transparencies with sweeping curvilinear forms and subtle greyed tones of lavenders, blues and tans even if the subject matter is not identifiable?

H Why can many interpretations of the Madonna and Child theme exist as art? What evokes pleasure when the subject has no individuality?

3.4 FOCUS ON SENSORY QUALITIES TO FEEL BEAUTY IN ART 258

A highly developed, accurate perceptual distinction singularly identifies felt beauty. p.57.

Paraphrased from Prall, D. (1929). Aesthetic judgment. New York: Thomas Y. Crowell, Company

P Why is looking at art like looking through a magnifying glass?

I Why would you try to ignore subject matter in favor of noticing visual qualities of surfaces, backgrounds, or the overall art work?

J Why can beauty be found in very ugly subject matter in art?

H Can the beauty of functional art be appreciated without valuing its purpose or use? Why or why not?

3.4 BEAUTY IS IN THE NATURE AND POSITION OF THE BEHOLDER 259

Spatial forms exemplify well that beauty is perceived as such in the context of everything about the one who is perceiving a work of art. p.74.
Paraphrased from Prall, D. (1929). Aesthetic judgment. New York: Thomas Y. Crowell, Company

P   Why do you think that people can or cannot appreciate fully a fine rug from an old banquet hall of a castle if they stand at one corner of it?

I   Why would art museums place a huge sculpture so that people could view it from a balcony?

J   Does the beauty of a building depend on seeing it from a certain angle? Does the beauty of an art form depend on being viewed by someone? Why?

H   What constitutes the "eye" of the beholder? Why does that saying about beauty mean more than the viewer's physical eye? Why does a viewer's location in space influence perception of a work of art?

3.4 ART HELPS PEOPLE SEE DETAIL AND RICHNESS OF THINGS BETTER THAN LIFE   260

People perceive more richly and specifically when viewing a work of art than when viewing the actual object or scene due to the richer awareness and organization of the experience provided by the artist.   (unknown)

P   Why could you compare looking at works of art to putting on a pair of glasses that help you see more?

I   If people can see a sunset, or a tree, or a city, why are they impressed by art works that have these as subjects?

J   Why can a photographer-artist help people to see more through the camera lens than they see with their eyes?

H   What perceptual enhancement can come to viewers by way of works of art that are non-objective or "ready-mades"? Why?

3.4 AESTHETIC EXPERIENCE IS NON-PRACTICAL IN CHARACTER   261

"We are sympathetic and receptive and don't let moral concerns or economic worries... influence the [aesthetic]experience...marked by contemplation in absence of a goal." p.43.

Eaton, M. (1988). Basic issues in aesthetics. Belmont, CA: Wadsworth Publishing Company. Copyright 1988 by Wadsworth, Inc., By permission of Wadsworth Publishing Company.

P Why do you look at a work of art? Do you get paid to do so? Do you do so to get rid of a headache?

I Works of art might cause you to say "wow" or just admire or wonder. Why does this make it worthwhile to go to an art museum?

J Some people must see a use for everything. Why is that a good or not a good expectation when looking at art?

H Why is it good or not good for people to expect artist to: 1) promote high moral standards and 2) to be able to itemize costs that match the high dollar value that some art brings?

3.4 PEOPLE USE THEIR COGNITIVE AND AFFECTIVE SENSE IN SPECIAL WAYS TO DETERMINE "BEAUTY"   262

"...middle of the eighteenth century, theories began to appear in which the ordinary cognitive and affective faculties plus association constitute the apparatus of taste....[associationism] extending the range of things which can be judged beautiful." p.12.

Dickie, G. (1971a). Aesthetics. New York: Bobbs-Merril Pegasus Division of Prentice-Hall, Inc. Fair use.

P People can be special in many ways. Do you agree or not agree that some people know when something is beautiful better than others? Why?

I What reasons could you give to explain why all people don't have the same favorite color?

J What is implied by the claim "I have high priced taste' in regard to art? Why?

H Why is the concept of "taste" possibly problematic in regard to art?

3.4 THE STORY IN A WORK OF ART IS NICE, BUT NOT NECESSARY 263

The original story of a work of art is not necessary to appreciate it, but it may enrich one's aesthetic experience. p.322

Paraphrased from Reid, L. A criticism of art as form. In L.Reid, Ed. (1954). A study in aesthetics. New York: The MacMillan Company.

P Art in picture books helps tell the story. Is the story what makes pictures "art"? Could a picture book artwork be hung in an art museum and be worth looking at by people who don't know the story? Why?

I Why might you be able to enjoy art from India or from any other unfamiliar culture even though you do not know their customs and everyday life situation?

J To what extent can one interpret art from an unfamiliar country? What in the work might be universal enough to be clues? Is it necessary or just nice to know the story? Why?

H What **critical** bearing does contextual information have on interpretaion of art from cultures different from a viewers own? What might be universally capable of eliciting an aesthetic response, if anything? Why?

3.4 ART IS BOTH INSIDE AND OUTSIDE THE VIEWER 264

"An important distinction between visual form and aesthetic structure...aesthetic structure exists inside the viewer...visual form exists outside him in the art object." p.278

Feldman, E. (1967). Art as image and idea. Englewood Cliffs, NJ: Prentice-Hall. Fair use.

P Why can a cloudy day painting have different meanings for different people?

I Children come to school with different family backgrounds and experiences and learn to read the same. Why do adults look at the same work of art and receive different impressions.

J Why can the same work of art fit together differently for different people? Is that a negative for a work of art? Why or why not?

H Why is it the one organization of art elements fits together in the experience of viewers
differently?

3.4 ART DOES NOT SERVE AS SUBSTITUTE GRATIFICATION, SEDATIVE OR NARCOTIC WITHOUT SOME MERIT OF ITS OWN 265

"No body who is aware of the complexity of the artistic experience will be very content with Freud's description of the enjoyment of art as a substitutive gratification. Even non-formalists will prefer a definition that includes the autonomy of the work of art at least as an aspect..." p.63.
Hauser, A. (1985). The philosophy of art history. Evanston, IL: Northwestern University Press. Fair use.

P A nice lady said she liked to look at flower art because it made her think of her mother. Did she appreciate art for a good reason? Why or why not?

I A person goes to art galleries and parks to see sculptures of horses in order to imagine riding the horse. Does that person appreciate those works of art as much as the artists would want them to? Why or why not?

J Should artists have the responsibility for serving psychological needs (ie. helping people with mental problems) of viewers through their art works? Why or why not?

H Can people aesthetically respond to works of art without these works gratifying some psychological need? Why or why not?

3.4 ORGANIZATION AND UNITY ENABLE THE VIEWER'S EXPERIENCE OF ART 266

" But with the perceiver...there must be an ordering of the elements...the same as the process of organization the creator of the work consciously experienced." ..."In every integral experience there is form because there is dynamic organization." p.54 and 55.
From Art as experience by John Dewey. Copyright 1934 by John Dewey, renewed 1973 by The John Dewey Foundation. Used by permission of G.P. Putnam's Sons, a division of Penguin Putnam Inc.

P Traffic rules help people, cars and bikes save time and lives. How do rules in art help make better art, or should there be no rules, just freedom? Why?

I Someone said artists give people a map to find their way around a work of art. What could that mean? Do you agree? Why or why not?

J Suppose that by looking at hundreds of years of art, someone found that time-honored works consistently had certain organizational qualities. Is that a good reason for expecting art to follow those as "rules"?

H What relationship might exist between physiological and psychological comfort of viewers, and artistic merit of works of art? Can tipsy art be good? Can disturbing art be good? Can accidental work be "art" and affect an aesthetic experience?

3.4 AN AESTHETIC EXPERIENCE IS UNIFYING AND CONSUMING

"That which distinguishes an experience as esthetic is conversion of resistance and tensions, of excitations that in themselves are temptations to diversion, into a movement toward an inclusive and fulfilling close." p.56.

From Art as experience by John Dewey. Copyright 1934 by John Dewey, renewed 1973 by The John Dewey Foundation. Used by permission of G.P. Putnam's Sons, a division of Penguin Putnam Inc.

P We think of witches casting spells on people as bad. Why would it be good if an art work causes someone to be spell bound?

I Why might a work of art cause a passerby to take a second look and stop and return to gaze at it for a long time?

J What can be expected of people who go to museums... that they get excited about one favorite work?... look a long time at every work? ....enjoy the company of friends who came together? ...or what? Why should people respond to art as you say?

H Should every person have an aesthetic experience with all time-honored works of art? Why or why not?

3.4 ONE'S INTUITIVE EXPERIENCE OF ART, OR TASTE, IS NOT UNIVERSAL

" Intuitive experience of art is not the artist's intuition...it is...the individual direction, still too personal to have the right to universality; in a word, it is taste." p.339

Venturi, L. (1936,1964). History of art criticism. Translated from the Italian by Charles Marriot. New York: E. P. Dutton. Division of Penguin Putnam, Inc. By permission.

P Sometimes we know right away what we like. Why might someone go to see art that they think they might not like?

I I you "don't know much about art, but you know what you like", is it a good idea to keep you ideas to yourself? Why or why not?

J How might you respond to someone who says, "I only go see art that I know I'll like." ? Why?

H Where is the line between individual freedom to express opinion and recognition of limited expertise and basis for trying to influence others? Why can't just anyone practice medicine? ... or claim authority about art?

3.4 WORKS OF ART ARE APPRECIATED FOR THEMSELVES

" It is possible to experience every object... aesthetically... when we just look at it..without relating it, intellectually or emotionally , to anything outside of itself." p.11.

Panofsky, E. (1955). Meaning in the visual arts. Garden City, NY: Doubleday. By permission of Bantam Doubleday Dell Publishing Group, Inc.

P Why can we think a painting of a bare bone is beautiful even if we have never paid attention to bones before?

I Why might an artist paint a picture of one egg on a bare table?

J Why might an artist create a giant sculpture of a snap clothes pin or other such mundane object?

H Of what importance is the fact that the artist stumbled on a solution or was consciously pursuing a plan as the work of art progressed? What other things could be considered in your decision?

3.4 " WORKS OF ART PRESENT NO SELF-SUFFICIENT, FINAL CONCLUSION"

"...[The aesthetic experience] depends not upon 'discovering' the 'deposit' of the experience but on our perceiving and undergoing the producer's expression of his own doing and undergoing in visual or aural materials." p.81.

Leonhard, C. and House, R. (1972). Foundations and principles of music education. New York: McGraw-Hill Companies. Reproduced with permission of McGraw-Hill Companies.

P What can you enjoy about a picture in a picture book if it is shown to you alone, with no hints as to the story? Why is this okay?

I Why can one enjoy a work of art without "getting" a message?

J When viewers physically walk among the figures and objects of an artist's three dimensional construction (R. Groom's Supermarket) do they become components of the work of art even though the artist could not predict their positions and characteristics exactly? Why or why not?

H Is audience participation or involvement physically in the work of art the ultimate in aesthetic experience? Why? Why not?

3.4 SITUATIONS MAY HAVE BOTH AESTHETIC AND ANALYTICAL FEATURES

"Every human situation has a certain proportion of both of these sets of features." [aesthetic features, i.e., quality, intuition, fusion, unity and analytical features, i.e., relations, analysis, diffusion, detail] p. 58.

Pepper, S. (1945). The basis of criticism in the arts. Cambridge, Mass: Harvard University Press. Copyright 1945 by the President and Fellows of Harvard College. Reprinted by permission of the publisher.

P A whole tree may be beautiful but so is one leaf examined by a rubbing or under a microscope. Why should people look at works of art up close and from a distance?

I Some artists stand afar off to take a look at their art. Others examine it very closely. Why would people look at art closely or at a distance?

J Which is better, to get a global or overall impression of artworks or to look analytically at their composition and detail? Why?

H Why could one argue that analytic features of a work of art are encompassed by consideration of aesthetic features, or are they distinct as used by Pepper?

3.4 PEOPLE RESPOND TO WHAT THEIR SENSES PICK UP AND WHAT THE WHOLE WORK OF ART MAKES THEM THINK ABOUT

"The perception of works of art involves the *creative integration of the sensory excitations and psychological expectations aroused in the viewer by the organization of elements embodied in a visual form.*" p.280.

Feldman, E. (1967). Art as image and idea. Englewood Cliffs, NJ: Prentice-Hall. By permission.

P Can you explain why students in our class notice different objects in the same picture? Why do we say that the same picture has different meanings?

I Why should people people see different meanings in the same work of art, or should what an artist shows mean the same to everyone?

J Of what importance is noticing all the details of a work of art to achieve an accurate interpretation? Details noticed, will there be one interpretation?

H How does extended contemplation (like repeated, thoughtful viewing of a film) relate to accuracy in interpretation of works of art? Will extended contemplation overcome initial selective perception and premature conclusions?

3.4 AESTHETIC PERCEPTION INVOLVES SUBJECTIVITY, OBJECTIVITY, AND SYNTHESIS 273

"Empathy...the subliminal awareness of feelings which are experienced as qualities...of the work of art"p.283. "...psychic distance...the degree of persnal involvement of a viewer in a work of art" p.284."We can think of funding as including remembered perceptions and the accumulation of separate perceptions of the same work and fusion as the process of integrating those perceptions into a whole so that it is characterized by a single dominant quality."p.287.

Feldman, E. (1967). Art as image and idea. Englewood Cliffs, NJ: Prentice-Hall. By permission.

P If an artist's picture reminds uss of things we remember, how could that help or not help us know what the artist thought?

I If a work of art reminds you of some experience you had, like a pleasant walk across a bridge, will that help or hurt your understanding of what the artist intends to show in his/herpicture?

J How can our own life experiences help or hinder our interpretation of works of art?

H To what degree and why must one stay distanced from works of art when seeking to interpret ?

3.4 AESTHETIC EXPERIENCE DEPENDS ON SPECIAL PERCEPTIVENESS 274

"Aesthetic experience is experience of intrinsic features of things...traditionally recognized as worthy of attention and reflection." p.143.

Eaton, M. (1988). Basic issues in aesthetics. Belmont, CA: Wadsworth Publishing Company. Copyright 1988 by Wadsworth, Inc. By permission of Wadsworth Publishing Company.

P An experienced horse breeder can tell how good a performer a foal will be. What kind of experience, and why would that experience help a person tell if a work of art might become famous?

I You and your parent both like the same art work, but from art classes you can name many more reasons why it is good. Is your parent's experience as "rich" as yours? What is there to consider in making such a decision? Why?

J Must an aesthetic experience be immediate? If repeated exposure to an object brings persons to enjoy it, has it brought about an aesthetic experience?

H Is aesthetic response totally a personal reaction or has the art world influenced what we respond to? Why?

3.4 THE PURPOSE OF ART IS TO PROVIDE AESTHETIC EXPERIENCES

"...the only 'proper' aesthetic function of a work of art is to provide an aesthetic experience." p.184.
Kaelin, E. F. (1989). An aesthetics for art educators. New York: Teachers College Press. By permission.

P Does an artist make art for personal satisfaction or to have others enjoy it? What reasons can you give for your answer?

I An artist never shows an art work created to anyone, but views it with excitement and satisfaction. Is that a good enough reason to have made it? Would someone else have to appreciate it? Why?

J What purpose should art serve and for whom? Why?

H Must art be appreciated to have served it's reason for existence? How does context and time enter into this debate?

3.4 ANY FEELING EXPERIENCED CAN BE ACCEPTED, BUT NOT ALL UNDERSTANDINGS

"All sentiment is right; because sentiment has a reference to nothing beyond itself...But all determinations of the understanding are not right; because they have a reference to something beyond themselves, to wit, real matter of fact; and are not always conformable to that standard." p.208.
Hume, D. (1757,1970). Four dissertations. New York: Garland Publishing Company. By permission.

P If you do or don't like a work of art, does that say that you do or don't understand it? Can you like something and not understand it? Why could understanding art help one to like it?

I What must one get to know about a work of art to understand it? Can general knowledge about art be "understanding"? Why or why not?

J Can persons uninformed about art enjoy it? Of what help is a title in understanding art? Shoud titles contrubute to understanding? Why is the title sufficient or not for understanding?

H How does "Everyone has a right to an opinion" fit in reference to art? When is opinion an inadequate basis for judgement of quality in art? Can people misundersatan art? Why?

3.4 ALL ASPECTS OF AN AESTHETIC EXPERIENCE COINCIDE 277

"...it [aesthetic experience] is an experience that hangs together, or is coherent, to an unusually high degree." p.528.
Beardsley, M. (1958). Aesthetics: Problems in the philosophy of criticism. New York: Harcourt, Brace. Fair use.

P Parades excite us by what we see, hear, the way our heart beats and body rhythmically responds. What all fits together when we see art that we like especially well?

I A perfect friend has many good qualities that together, make a perfect friend. If you are responding to art in a perfectly wonderful way, what would you be seeing and feeling that would make it a super experience?

J What does it take to impress a teenager? If a work of art really impressed you, how would you describe your feelings in relationship to what you saw?

H Could contradictions be a part of an aesthetic experience if aesthetic experience is defined as "coherent"? Why or why not?

3.4 "SEEING" SENSORY QUALITIES DEPENDS ON SOME PRIOR KNOWLEDGE 278

[on awareness and perception as aesthetic apprehension] "...we rarely apprehend sense-data without knowing something about them and interrelating them, so that they become meaningful." p.41.
Stolnitz, J. (1960). Aesthetics and the philosophy of art criticism. Boston: Houghton Mifflin Ccompany. By permission of the author.

P Why do we try out many tools and media in art? Why do we talk about what we can see happen when we experiment in art?

I Why can art experiments using different tools and media to get different effects help you to talk about artists' work?

J After art lessons on noticing detail, a perfectly sighted 20-year-old claimed to have been blind for that many years. How could you explain what this person meant? How could this be so? Why?

H People gradually learn to use information provided by their senses. Are people the same in perceptual development? Can anyone appreciate art works to the same degree? Why or why not?

3.4 AESTHETIC EXPERIENCE: DRAWN TO UNLIKE BUT RELATED PARTS IN ARTWORK

"... an asthetic experience is one in which attention is firmly fixed upon hetergeneous but interrelated components of a phenomenally objective field..." p.527

Beardsley, M. (1958). <u>Aesthetics: Problems in the philosophy of criticism</u>. New York: Harcourt, Brace. Fair use.

P One artist put a small red spot in a mostly green landscape painting. What might that spot of red do when someone saw the painting? Why might it fit the idea of the landscape?

I A red cardinal looked almost luminous on the fresh spring lawn still yet from a rain. Why would an artist use this color relationship in a painting?

J Why would an artist incorporate actual silk flowers in a painting?

H Artist have broken traditional boundries of what is a painting, an embroidery, a sculpture by mixing these art froms in the same work. What principles are operating as they incorporate what would seem to be discrepant elements?

3.4 AN AESTHETIC EXPERIENCE HAS INTENSITY

"...it [aesthetic experience] is an experience of some intensity...aesthetic objects give us a concentration of experience ." p.527.

Beardsley, M. (1958). <u>Aesthetics: Problems in the philosophy of criticism</u>. New York: Harcourt, Brace. Fair use.

P Why do people stop to look at a sunset? Why are artworks similar in making people stop and look?

I Why do highway departments mark off areas as "vistas"? What reasons can you give for art works needing "vistas"?

J What is it about certain ideas portrayed by artists that compel people to pause and study... or to see a film over and over?

H How does the idea o beauty in art fit with compelling, but abhorent subject matter in some art?

3.4 AN AESTHETIC EXPERIENCE HAS A BALANCE OF AROUSALS AND RESOLUTIONS 281

"...it [aesthetic experience] is an experience that is unusually complete in itself...impulses and expectations aroused by elements...are...counterbalanced or resolved by other elements." p.528.

Beardsley, M. (1958). Aesthetics: Problems in the philosophy of criticism. New York: Harcourt, Brace. Fair use.

P When you play hard then rest, you feel great. How might a work of art be like playing... active and resting parts for the viewer?

I Rollercoasters or ferris wheels go up and down and around, but bring you back to a comfortable level. Why is looking a art somewhat like carnival rides for you eyes and thoughts?

J Life is full of anticipation and realization, as is the **approach to** and **reflection** about a work of art. How could you explain this?

H Why is viewing art a satisfying experience? Is it an even, consistent involvment or are there irregularities? How can you explain your opinion?

3.4 SUBJECT MATTER AND FORM ARE FUSED IN THE AESTHETIC EXPERIENCE 282

Psychological values of a work of art become embodied in forms that are perceived for their expressiveness just as the forms become perceived for their psychologically expressive qualities. p.323

Paraphrased from Reid, L. A criticism of art as form. In L.Reid, Ed. (1954). A study in aesthetics. New York: The MacMillan Company.

P Many artists have clowns in their art, but each clown art work tells a different story. Why?

I How can artists use body language to get a message across in art work? Can the body language give the whole message? Of what importance is the figure or character or setting? Why?

J Is the setting and arrangement important to having a "wow" (aesthetic) experience with an art work? How? Why?

H What makes art valuable, meaningful or satisfying? ... subject matter? or visually pleasing arrangement of the art elements? Does subject matter interfere with a pure aesthetic experience? Why or why not?

276

a fox

going down

PLEASURE, PLAY/THERAPY, ESCAPE

3.5 ART PROPER HAS NO IMPORTANT RESEMBLANCE TO PLAY 283

"The artist as purveyor of amusement makes it his business to please his audience by arousing certain emotions in them and providing them with a make-believe situation in which these emotions can be harmlessly discharged." "If playing means amusing oneself...there is no important resemblance between play and art proper;..." p. 80,81.

Collingwood, R. (1958). Principles of art. New York: Galaxy Press. Oxford University. By permission of Oxford University Press.

P Is an artist's sculpture a jungle gym? Why or why not?

I When artists playfully experiment with new ways of using paint of new ideas about what form art can take, is that play? Why? Why not?

J How could one differentiate between play (as in tag), play (as in play the piano) and play (as in experimentation)?

H Why is artistic play serious? Why is that, or is that not, a contradiction?

3.5 GOOD ART CRITICISM FERRETS OUT AESTHETIC VALUE FOR US 284

"...criticism,...continuing on our own to notice features and organize and relate them. ...criticism can help... if we think that other people's insights... can help us to participate in activities that we will find rewarding." p.122.

Eaton, M. (1988). Basic issues in aesthetics. Belmont, CA: Wadsworth Publishing Company. Copyright 1988 by Wadsworth, Inc.. By permission of Wadsworth Publishing Company.

P If you go to a museum, a docent might tell you about an artwork or ask you questions about it. Why could this help you see more about a work of art in the next room?

I Why would a book like, Let's Get Lost in a Painting series help you to look at another work by the artist?

J Why could wanting to make up your own mind about art short change you in the long run if you are at an art ixhibit where headphones to listen to critiques of the artwork are available? What disadvantage is the critique?

H What is more likely... an innocent insight or ignorance as an uninformed viewer confronts innovations is art? Why?

3.5 ART CRITICISM POINTS TO THINGS AND INVITES US TO FIND PLEASURE IN ART 285

"We cannot be reasoned into taking pleasure, but we can have reasons for believing that things will be pleasurable." p.121.

Eaton, M. (1988). Basic issues in aesthetics. Belmont, CA: Wadsworth Publishing Company. Copyright 1988 by Wadsworth, Inc.. By permission of Wadsworth Publishing Company

P How is looking at art like having fun playing a mystery game? Why?

I Why can talking about art be a mystery game?... a time machine? ... a fantasy trip?

J Why can talk about art help the viewer to seem to experience being a part of it? Why does it help to talk about more than story?

H If you drove fast through the mountains yu probably didn't contemplate or enjoy and can't describe the scenery. What would be a parallel situation as one visits an art museum? Why?

3.5 ART IS WORK IN MEDIA THAT IS ORGANIZED WITH INTENT TO CREATE AN EFFECT 286

Art results from human effort, is associated with a discipline, and is intended to produce an aesthetic effect due to material, formal or associational aspects.
(unknown)

P Why might someone want to touch a sculpture or painting or fabric because of something the artist did? Is it good to want to touch art? Why? Why not?

I Why is a painting of a mountainous scene "art" and the actual scene is not art even though you are in awe of the beauty looking at both the painting and looking directly at the scene?

J When is novelty insufficient to qualify a product as a work of art?

H How would you differentiate between reaction to novelty-but-not-art and a truly aesthetic and unique work that, in a disciplined way, results in visual pleasure or has an aesthetic effect?

3.5 SOME SAY, "ART IS PLAY"...SENSORY RELIEF FROM REAL LIFE 287

"It is only in periods of cultural and spiritual decadence, periods characterized by a loss of inner assurance in spiritual values, that the 'aesthete' (in the narrow and derogatory sense) has made his appearance and proclaimed that art is *reducible* to aesthetically agreeable patterns of sound and color and is therefore in essence an escape from reality, mere play, an object of delight and nothing more." p.233.

Greene, T.(1940). The arts and the art of criticism. Princeton, NJ: Princeton University Press. Copyright 1968 by Princeton University Press. Reprinted by permission of Princeton University Press.

P What would you see in a movie called "Art beyond scribble designs"?

I How is being playful in creating art different than thinking of art as playtime?

J Color and mixing colors intrigues many people. What does this have to do with art, or does it have nothing to say about art? Why?

H Does the human capacity to respond to sensory qualities contribute to greater value for art that is non-objective experimentation with the element of art? Why? Why not?

3.5 ART PROVIDES PSYCHOLOGICAL FREEDOM TO EXPRESS...TO "BE" 288

"Art as pleasure, art as play, art as the recovery of childhood, art as making conscious the unconscious, art as a mode of instinctual liberation, art as the fellowship of men struggling for instinctual liberation...fit into the system of psychoanalysis...[and]wear the stigmata of the romantic movement--the Romantic agony." p. 65-66.

Brown, N. (1959).Life against death, Midlothian, CT: Wesleyan University Press. By permission of the University Press of New England.

P Is art play? Is all play fun? Is all fun, play? Why could art be fun but not **just** play?

I Why is play different from "play with an idea"? How is it alike?

J How is "letting it all hang out" different from expressing personal views in works of art?

H Do artist make art for therapeutic reasons? Why? Why not? Can art viewing and/or art production have unplanned therapeutic side effects? Why Why not?

3.5 IMAGES IN ART MAY BE LINKED TO VALUE ORIENTATIONS

"If art forms and value orientations are linked by psychological congruence, the former may be construed as subconscious images of the latter." p.160.

Kavolis, V. (1968). Artistic expression: A sociological analysis. Ithaca, NY: Cornell University Press. By permission and fair use.

P If an artist did many family portraits, would that mean that families were important to the artist? Why? Why not?

I If an artist usually puts plants in paintings, what does that suggest to you about the artist? Why? How sure can you be of your reason?

J Why might candles or doorways frequently enter into an artist's work? What meaning is fair to assign to such an observaion? What other evidence would be necessary to conclude anything?

H What kinds of evidence would lend support to or disprove the idea that art reveals the artist's subconscious values?

3.5 ART IS NOT AMUSEMENT NOR HARMLESS RELEASE OF EMOTIONS

"The work of art.. which provides amusement, is...strictly utilitarian.Unlike a work of art proper, it has no value in itself;it is simply a means to an end." "...please his [the artist] audience by arousing certain emotions in them and providing them with a make-believe situation in which these emotions can be harmlessly discharged." p. 81.

Collingwood, R. (1958). Principles of art. New York: Galaxy Press. Oxford University. By permission of Oxford University Press.

P If someone makes a big sculpture that is so gross and scary that it frightens everyone away and it is displayed at Halloween, does the fact that it is a sculpture make it art? Why could it or might it **not** be good art?

I Do artists play? Is making art fun? If so, what kind of fun or play? Why would artists' play be like or different from playing ball?

J Film is an art form. Many art films are dramatic. Is the degree of terror aroused in the audience a good criterion for calling a film "art"? Why or why not?

H Kaleidoscopes are intriguing and colorful. Are they art? Why or why not?

3.5 ART IS NOT TO STIMULATE EMOTION AS AN END IN ITSELF 291

"If an artifact is designed to stimulate a certain emotion, and if this emotion is intended not for discharge into the occupations of ordinary life, but for enjoyment as something of value in itself, the function of the artifact is to amuse or entertain." p.78.

Collingwood, R. (1958). Principles of art. New York: Galaxy Press. Oxford University. By permission of Oxford University Press.

P Why might a pet store show sculptures of people loving animals? Is that a good reason to have art around?

I Do artists paint landscapes so people want to take vacations? How do or should beautiful landscapes or cityscapes affect viewers?

J Why is propaganda art good or bad? Should artists paint ideas that a government wants to affect people?

H An artist got the idea to allow motivated onlookers to help create a found object sculpture from audience participation theatrical performances. Is the result art or entertainment, and why?

3.5 ART IN ART MUSEUMS: SOMEWHERE BETWEEN ELITISM AND MOBOCRACY 292

"Our first responsibility is to the object, and the person who wants to respond to it in a private way. Art is not therapy or fashion, or social uplift, and a museum is not a community center." p.83 (quote attributed to Sherman Lee by Tomkins)

From Post-to-neo: The artworld of the 1980's by Calvin Tomkins, Copyright 1988 by Calvin Tomkins. Reprinted by permission of Henry Holt and Company, Inc.

P In an art museum, seeing a cat sculpture makes you feel good as you remember you own cat's playfulness. Is that why the artist made the sculpture or why it is good?

I Many art museums offer Saturday and after school programs. Why do children attend them? Why is each reason you give good or not?

J Imagine that art museums became as popular as baseball stadiums. Why would that be good or not?

H What is a desirable degree of community support for the visual arts? Visualize the effect of that support. Why is that support desirable and for whom?

3.5 ART IS NOT JUST AN EMOTIONAL RELEASE FOR PEOPLE INVOLVED

"A person who...paints...in order to blow off steam, using the traditional materials of art as a means for exhibiting the symptoms of emotion, may deserve praise as an exhibitionist, but loses for the moment all claim to the title of artist." p.122-123.

Collingwood, R. (1958). Principles of art. New York: Galaxy Press. Oxford University. By permission of Oxford University Press.

P You can splash and jump in a swimming pool if you are excited. Is that the reason why artists splatter or dribble paint in making art? Why or why not?

I Do potters throw clay to release emotions or to make beautiful forms? If a potter threw soft lumps of clay on a piece of pottery being made, could you assume that was a display of anger? Why or why not?

J How can someone tell what an artist's emotions were as a work of art was created 100 years prior to its critique? Is that an important consideration? Why or why not?

H Is it permissible to flaunt your emotions in a work of art in the name of artistic freedom? Why? Why not?

CHARACTERISTICS OF THE ARTIST, ARTISTIC STYLE, THE ARTIST'S INTENT

3.6 ART STYLES AND RULES ARE FLEXIBLE 294

"Artists today are not easily intimidated, and they regard art genres as loose guidelines rather than as rigid specifications." p. 107.

Dickie, G. (1971). Art and the aesthetic: An institutional analysis. Ithaca, NY: Cornell University Press. By permission and fair use.

P Why is it okay for artist to show birds as regal and still, fluttering, soaring, scratching or even with exaggerated parts or disconnected parts?

I Is it okay for an artist to combine parts of birds with other animals? Why or why not?

J What are the possible consequences of an artist breaking the rules in art?

H Would it make a difference if artists broke aesthetic compostional rules or if they broke
unwritten decency rules of a society? Is one more important or encompassing than the other? Which? Why or why not?

3.6 DOES ART MAKES PEOPLE FEEL WHAT THE ARTIST INTENDED? 295

"We might... revise the theory so as not to require that the audience should feel what the artist felt, but only what the artist *intended* the audience to feel." p. 339.

Hospers, J. (1955). The concept of artistic expression. Proceedings of the Aristotelian Society, 1954-1960, 55, 313-344. Fair use.

P If an artist's picture makes you think of something sad that happened to you, did the artist intend to make people feel sad?

I Can one tell by looking at a work of art what the artist tried to make a viewer feel? How, or why not?

J How could viewer experience or value system throw off what the artist thought would happen when an artwork is viewed? Why? Why not?

H In a good work of art, to what extent could a viewer stray from the artist's intent? How could a "stray" feeling devalue the work as "art"...for the viewer? for others?

3.6 THE ARTIST'S INTENTION DOES NOT ESTABLISH THE WORTH OF ART WORKS 296

"any attempt to support the goodnes of a work of art because it fulfilled the artist's intention or the badness of it because it failed to realize the artist's intention is misguided." because, according to Beardsley, the artist's intention is not part of the work of art. p. 112

Dickie, G. (1971). <u>Aesthetics</u>. New York: Bobbs-Merrill Pegasus Division of Prentice-Hall. Inc. Fair use.

P What could you enjoy about art even if you had no idea of why the artist did it? Why?

I What would make something good art if you knew nothing about its purpose or the intent for which it was make? Why?

J Can art be art without intention on the part of the person who made it? Why or why not?

H Do artist care if viewers correctly read their intent in visual artworks? Why should they or not? Why should viewers try to discern the artist's intention or should they not?

3.6 ARTISTS EXPRESS DISCONTENT WITH CONFORMITY 297

"In my country the artist is supposed to be provacative--an outsider whose job it is to transgress." p.1.

Quote attributed to Cohen-Solal. In B. Rose. (November, 1990). How Europe stole back the idea of modern art. <u>The Journal of Art,</u> 3 (2), 1-2. Fair use.

P At home and school we learn to do what is "right". Why don't artist always do in their art what everyone thinks is right?

I When can artists break laws and why is it okay to do so?

J In how many directions can artists change from what gets to be "old hat" in art. Why would artists change? Why is change good or when is it not? Why?

H Should artists who have developed an individual style change their style regularly to avoid conformity to themselves? Why or why is this not a concern?

3.6 EVEN IF IT IS POSSIBLE TO KNOW THE ARTIST'S INTENTION, THE JUDGMENT MADE WOULD BE ON THE ARTIST, NOT HIS WORK   298

"Genetic reasons, and in particular, the appeal to intention, cannot be good, that is, relevant and sound, reasons for critical evaluations..." p.458

Beardsley, M. (1958). Aesthetics: Problems in the philosophy of criticism. New York: Harcourt, Brace. Fair use.

P If the artist claimed to want to show friendship, would the artwork be good **because** two figures stood close like friends might? Why might that **not** be a good reason?

I Does the value of an artwork depend on people seeing in the work what the artist indicated by the title? Why?

J How can someone like some work of art where the point being make by the artist isn't clear? Can that be good art? Why or why not?

H Titles may give hints as to the artist's intent. How can "compostion" suggest artist intent? Why?

3.6 ARTISTS GIVE FORM TO THEIR IDEAS ACCORDING TO THE WAY THEY SEE LIFE   299

An artist's interpretive reflection on life experiences, including other artist's interpretations, influence the art form created.   (unknown)

P Would a starving child look at a painting of a Thankgiving dinner differently than a child who always had plenty to eat? Why? What kind of a dinner would each child see?

I How might an artist who has always been poor show "dressed up" compared to a young well-to-do prince? Why?

J Does one's background show in the artworks created? How? Can an artist shrug off early formed attitudes and values? Why? Why not?

H To what extent can artist fake a view of life?... change a view of life? What effect might it have on the quality of their work... or would it?

3.6 ARTISTS MANIPULATE ELEMENTS IN A WORK OF ART TO SERVE A THEME 300

"Every element in a work of art is indispensable for the one purpose of pointing out the theme, which embodies the nature of existence for the artist." p. 422.

Arnheim, R. (1966). Art and visual perception. Berkeley, CA: University of California Press. By permission of University of California Press.

P If an artist wanted to include a tree branch in a picture having many triangles, would a ginko tree, maple tree, or pine tree fit best? Why?

I How might artists alter a rectangular shape to make it fit a spooky forest theme? Why?

J If an artist designed a ballet program cover, why might the artist choose long curved lines and spirals and transparent colors?

H Computer graphic capabilities allow selection and alteration of shapes, textures and lines. Why is this important for narrative artworks?

3.6 ARTISTS ARE SENSITIVE TO THE UNCOMMON QUALITIES OF COMMON OBJECTS IN NATURE 301

"I conceived the form of the work of art to be its most essential quality, but I believe this form to be the direct outcome of an apprehension of some emotion of actual life...special and peculiar kind and implied a certain detachment." p. 194.

Fry, R. (1920). Vision and design. New York:Chatto & Windus. Public domain.

P An artist chose to paint just the gnarly rough bark of a tree trunk rather than the whole tree. Why might the artist have done that?

I We walk over grass without a thought. Why might an artist make a four foot square painting of a one inch square of grass?

J Why might artists make clothespins, or pocketknives into oversize sculptures or wrap tree branches with toilet tissue?

H Why do some ordinary objects "turn on" artists? Do the artists discover common objects that are already art? What is it about artist sthat makes them make uncommon art?

3.6 EACH ART OBJECT IS THE PRODUCT OF THE INDIVIDUAL ARTIST'S INSIGHT AND SOCIOLOGICAL FORCES 302

"..neither the individuality and special talent of the artist by itself, nor the institutions and traditions of his social milieu by themselves suffice to provide an adequate explanation of the peculiar character of a work of art." p.200.

Hauser, A. (1985). The philosophy of art history. Evanston, IL: Northwestern University Press. Fair use.

P How might artists who paint farm scenes have grown up or lived differently from those who paint the desert? Why?

I Architects plan different kinds of homes. Why do we see everything from condos to apartment buildings to huge ranch homes?

J Is an artist compelled to rebel against society's expectations in order to be a real artist? Why? Why not?

H What relationships might exist between social values and individual artists' insight in works of art? Are the two forces compatible?

3.6 ARTISTS CREATE SUSPENSE-- ANTICIPATION AS TO THE OUTCOME OF EVENTS 303

(after Tolstoy, L.)

P Do artists provide answers or make you ask questions through their art? When?

I How are works of art somewhat like mysteries?

J What kinds of questions might arise from works of art?

H What creates suspense in non-imitative works of art?

3.6 ARTISTS PORTRAY IDENTICAL SUBJECTS BY DIFFERENT STYLES DUE TO THEIR INDIVIDUAL EXPERIENCES AND CULTURAL VALUE SYSTEMS 304

"...form and colour are always apprehended differently according to temperament, the style of the school, the country, the race [or]...'period style'." p. 2-3, 6, 9.
Woelfflin, H. (1932). Principles of art history: the problems of development of style in later art. Mineola, NY: Dover Publications, Inc. By permission.

P Why might it be that art showing adults with children differs so? Some artists show them in stiff-looking postions, some cuddling affectionalely, some caring, gently teaching, and some in jovial family group dinner scenes. Is it just what the artist has people doning or more?

I One artist painted a flower with curly edges and twisted petals. Another showed its shapes fanned out from a cylindrical center. Why can artists be so dfferent from each other?

J A sculptor and a lawyer visit a junk yard. Which one might stay longer? Why?

H How might artists of different cultures portray the idea of "justice"? What reasons support your projection?

3.6 ARTISTS FEEL A NEED TO SAY WHAT THEY HAVE TO SAY 305

"...artists ...have strong feelings that they want to communicate and...they...embody their feelings in publicly communicable ways." p. 21.
Eaton, M. (1988). Basic issues in aesthetics. Belmont, CA: Wadsworth Publishing Company. Copyright 1988 by Wadsworth, Inc.. By permission of Wadsworth Publishing Company.

P Why might an artist show a trapped animal in a work of art?

I Why might artst make sculptures of poor people in ragged clothing?

J Why might artists show scheming lawyers, threatening weather, or cheating card players in their art?

H What relationship do you feel must exist between the compelling message of an artist and the depiction of that message? Why?

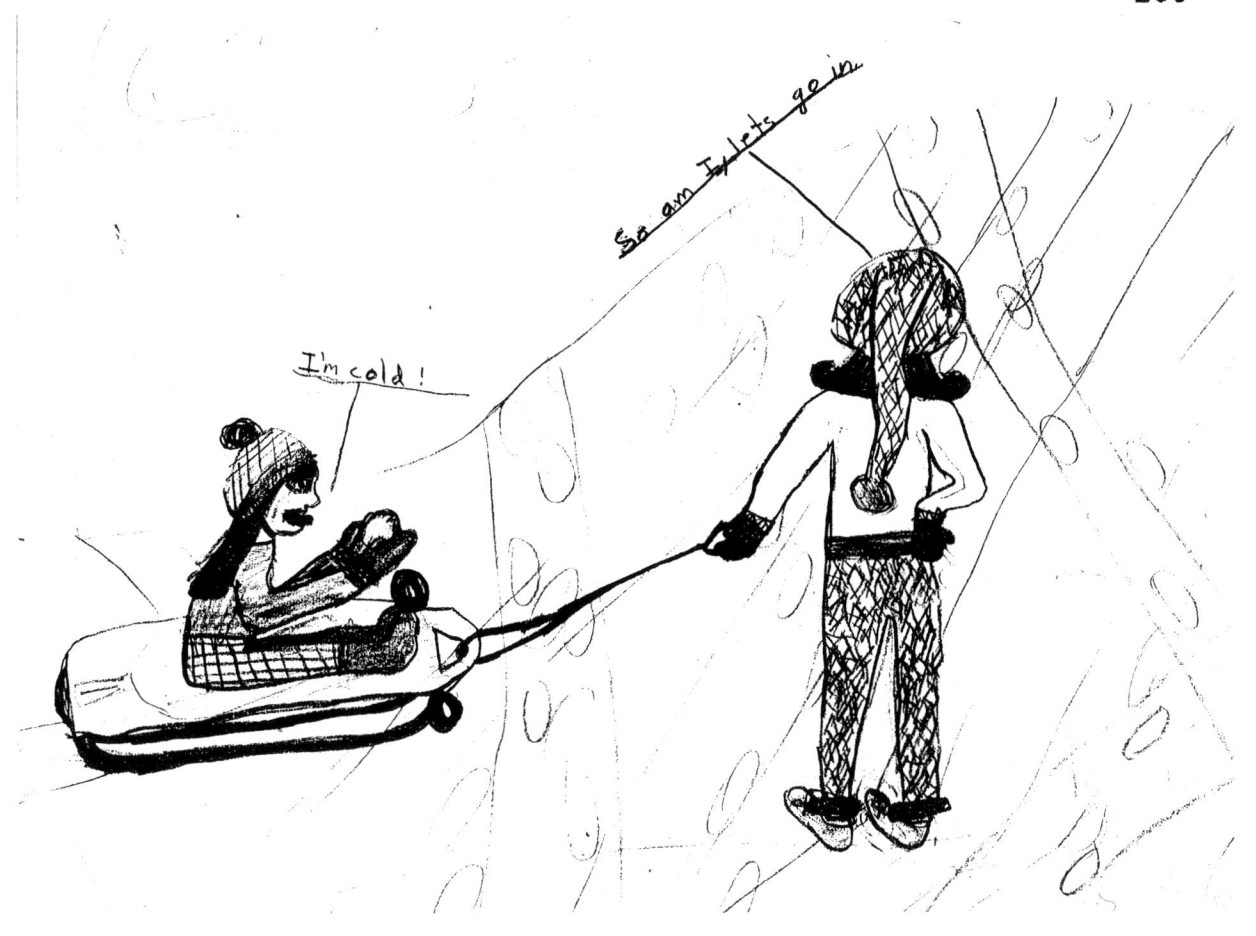

3.6 ARTISTS CREATE WHAT IS IMPORTANT TO THEM 306
"...the artist ...can...does, make decisions to create an environment consistent with his or her own creative desires." p.106.
Kaelin, E. F. (1989). An aesthetics for art educators. New York: Teachers College Press. By permission.

P How would an artist paint a child with curly hair if the artist wanted to say how perfectly well-behaved children are? Why? What would the artist show around that child? Why?

I If you bought a work of art but it didn't fit with other things you have, would you return the art or change your home to fit the art work? Why?

J Imagine a subdivision of identical houses. Soon artists, each with uniqe styles move in. Pick and artist and in your mind, visualize and describe the changes in that artist's house. Why?

H Why might the degree of committment to a client qualify the artists' decision to create environments consistent with the artist's own creative desires? When not?

3.6 ARTISTS OF CERTAIN PERIODS BECOME CHARACTERIZED BY AN EXPECTED STYLE 307

"Once an artistic style has become established, it tends (or it has tended, before the modern "cult of originality") to persist. A style that has been influenced by the social conditions of the past may thus continue on, even though conditions change." p. 8.

Kavolis, V. (1968). Artistic expression: A sociological analysis. Ithaca, NY. Cornell University Press. By permission and fair use.

P What happens to an artist who wants to show details in art, but is only sold the fat brushes that other use? Should the artist give up the idea of interesting details? Why? Why not?

I Why might an artist who draws very well but very realistic, not find much attention now?

J Is it important for an artist to learn to draw well realistically in the 1990's? Why, or why not, in view of art being given attention?

H How might the gallery world shape the artistic style by which a period is known? What are the merits of such art world influence? Why might this be detrimental to individuality?

3.6 ART STYLES MAY INFLUENCE VALUES 308

"... art styles may also function as a means of inducing change in established value orientations, and they may be successful or fail in this--intentional or unintentional--dynamic aplication." p. 161.

Kavolis, V. (1968). Artistic expression: A sociological analysis. Ithaca, NY: Cornell University Press. By permission and fair use.

P How might an artist's painting of flickering highlights of sunlight on objects influence what people chose to look at in nature? Why?

I What changes in people's ideas about art might come because of computer art?

J Why would artists glorify common environments like supermarkets, restaurants, or a corner store by depicting them as art?

H What kinds of effects does changing contemporary art have on concepts of art media, art subject matter, artists, art in life, art careers, art education? Why?

3.6 EVOLVED OR BORROWED ART STYLES MUST FIT VALUES OF THE CULTURE 309

"A culture which does not evolve or borrow styles of art that are psychologically congruent with its major value orientations seems likely to produce an inferior artistic tradition." p. 161.

Kavolis, V. (1968). Artistic expression: A sociological analysis. Ithaca, NY: Cornell University Press. By permission and fair use.

P We put on masks at Halloween for fun. Masks are for serious reasons in other cultures. Is it alright for us to make masks as art? Why? Why not?

I What are culturally appropriate subjects of art masks we would make in the 21st century in the USA?

J Picasso borrowed shapes of facial features from African masks for his art work as other artists have done. Is this culturally honest? Does it affect the value of such art? Why or why not?

H What reasons would support the borrowing of images that do not emanate out of an artist's cultural experience? Does calling it appropriation help? Why? Why not?

3.6 ARTISTIC SPONTANEITY IS OFTEN MODIFIED BY CONVENTIONS 310

""The spontaneous expression of value orientations in artistic style is likely to be circumscribed (i.e., forced into a conventional idiom) by the artistic traditions institutionalized in a culture, which may reflect an earlier value orientation profile." p. 164.

Kavolis, V. (1968). Artistic expression: A sociological analysis. Ithaca, NY: Cornell University Press. By permission and fair use.

P If one breaks a traffic rule, it is wrong. Can artists break rules in art? When? Why? When not? Whose rules?

I What good comes from learning rules to follow in making art? Are the rules always good? Why? Why not?

J Why is artistic spontaneity inherently good, or is it not? Is there reason to bridle spontaneity by traditional compositional rules? Why or why not?

H What are the pros and cons of traditional values in regard to artistic endeavors? Why?

3.6 VALUES TEND TO GUIDE STYLE PREFERENCES   311

"Value orientations merely create tendencies to favor particular stylistic characteristics, which are combined with other tendencies --some of them apparently caused by sociological factors--to form a style." p. 162.

Kavolis, V. (1968). Artistic expression: A sociological analysis. Ithaca, NY: Cornell University Press. By permission and fair use.

P Artists design fantasy creatures for childrens films. Do you think artists just imagine such characters or do they think about what children like? Why?

I Artists design all kinds of clothing for people. Why do they need to design bold, multi-colored jackets; solid-color plain ones; full, flaring ones; and clean, crisp ones? What kind of art might the jacket buyers like?

J How do teenage preferences and values influence visual art forms, or are they shaped by visual images brought into their homes? Why?

H What effect does the value orientation of the mass population of a culture have on the stylistic characteristics of art? Why?

3.6 LASTING STYLES REFLECT DOMINANT VALUES   312

"Styles that do not become popular at (or soon after) the time of their creation cannot, of course, be assumed to reflect dominant value orientations." p. 163.

Kavolis, V. (1968). Artistic expression: A sociological analysis. Ithaca, NY: Cornell University Press. By permission and fair use.

P Why do you suppose artist still make art about people even thought they did that in the oldest art we know?

I If artists in a group come up with a style that is very innovative, why might they stop making their kind of art? What might help people see what they invented? Why would that make them continue or not?

J Why could age relate to art preference? Why could where people live relate to art preference? Why might there be exceptions to either explanation you have given?

H Why does or doesn't, "popular" describe the dominant values of the total population of a country under current sysems for exposure of artistic work? Why is "dominant" values a good measure of art, or is it not?

3.6 ARTISTS PORTRAY ESSENCE RATHER THAN PHOTOGRAPHIC REALITY

"Being true-to the experienced quality of things, like being true to human nature, often involves distortion from the 'photographic reality'; one must leave the literal truth to get at the 'essence'." p. 178.

From Meaning and truth by John Hospers. Copyright 1946 by the University of North Carolina Press and renewed 1974 by John Hospers. Used by permission of the publisher.

P Why would the artist who designed E.T. make so many wrinkles? Why make Popeye with such big muscles?

I Why could a cartoon of important meetings of politicians tell more than an accurate photograph of that same situation? Are all cartoons art? Why? Why not?

J An artist photographer and a cartoon artist are both recording an important trial. What can each contribute by the art work produced? Which can tell more about the trial and why?

H Of what relevance is realistic, observational drawing skill to an artist who feels liberated from photographic reality? ...to the non-objective artist? to the texture dominant weaver? to the potter?

3.6 ARTISTS GIVE VISUAL FORM TO GENERAL PERCEPTIONS   314

"...the main sociological function of artistic <u>style</u> is the shaping or emotional re-inforcement of general tendencies to perceive situations of action in certain structured ways." p. 5.

Kavolis, V. (1968). <u>Artistic expression: A sociological analysis</u>. Ithaca, NY: Cornell University Press. By permission and fair use.

P   Why can artists weave flower shapes in fabric that are not a particular flower, yet no one objects? Are "non-flowers" okay?

I   An artist sculpted a child's head and called it "friend". Is it important to know whether the model was a boy or girl or whether there was a model at all? Why do you think it is important or not?

J   Some people tell more than a person wants to know. If people generally don't observe their world very well, how might that affect the art work of perceptive artists? Why?

H   What is the role of the critical thinking, perceptive artist in a society which blithely and unobservedly goes through life? What hard decisions about artistic style might the artist face and why?

3.6 ARTISTS BRING US ENRICHED PERCEPTIONS, NOT NECESSARILY LITERAL TRUTH   315

"... a work of art may exist without them [truths]."p.214 "Whether a given work is called a work of art depends generally upon a *combination* of characteristics, of which 'artistic truth' is only one." p. 217.

From <u>Meaning and truth</u> by John Hospers. Copyright 1946 by the University of North Carolina Press and renewed 1974 by John Hospers. Used by permission of the publisher

P   Why might an artist make a green face on a person in an artwork? Could that be true? Should art be true?

I   Little white lies are not exactly true but don't hurt. How might artists tell a lot about a situation by not showing things like a photograph?

J   There's a saying, "Tell it like it is" that implies a value to accuracy. Is it valuable for art to have photographic accuracy? If not truth, what qualities should art have? Why?

H   Can abstractions be "true"? What great perceptiveness can be brought about by an artist's non-objective work... or is that not logical?

3.6 "...SUBJECT MATTER CANNOT OF ITSELF MAKE A WORK OF ART EITHER TRIVIAL OR PROFOUND"   316

"But in *actual practice* those subjects which normally possess deep significance for us lend themselves more easily to a more profound interpretation than do those subjects which we normally judge to be petty and trivial." p.466.

Greene, T.(1940). The arts and the art of criticism. Princeton, NJ: Princeton University Press. Copyright 1968 by Princeton University Press. Reprinted by permission of Princeton University Press.

P Why is or is not a picture of an important person going to be important art?

I Why might an artist's picture of a family picnic have more meaning to people than a picture of a pencil by the same artist, or is that not true sometimes? Why?

J Why do people like different movies, or like different subjects in works of art (weather, battles, families, animals)? Does good subject matter make good art? Why or why not?

H To what extent is it true that the meaningfulness of subject matter of a work of art determines the depth of a person's understanding of it? What might limit that conclusion? Why?

3.6 ARTISTS SELECT ESSENTIALS BEFORE EMBELLISHMENTS   317

"The aim of the artist, therefore, should be first to seek the essential; when the essential hath been found, then, if ever, will be the time to commence embellishment." p.81.

Greenough, H. (1957). Form and function. Berkeley, CA: University of California Press. By permission of University of California Press.

P If an artist liked the long eyelashes of the person sitting for a portrait, why might that be one of the last details the artist painted?

I If an artist wanted to make a piece of pottery that looked like a section of a tree trunk, when would the bark texture be created and what would be the artists **reason** for doing it **then**?

J An artist is commemorating a national holiday celebration by showing a speaker addressing a crowd in a highly decorated hall. Why would the artist start with the speaker or would that not be likely?

H Seeking the essential structure of an animal must proceed drawing texture of the animal, but does this apply to conceptual art or to newer directions in art? Why or why not?

3.6 ARTISTS' PURPOSES GUIDE SELECTION FROM COMPLETE TRUTH 318

"...photographic truth is hampered by this fact that he [the artist] must select some details and not others, and in his selection some aim or purpose is already indicated..." p. 150.

From Meaning and truth by John Hospers. Copyright 1946 by the University of North Carolina Press and renewed 1974 by John Hospers. Used by permission of the publisher.

P If an artist titled a painting, "My strong Oak Tree" and the picture didn't show all the little brances of that tree, was the artist lazy? Was it fair to not show the whole tree, or why would that be okay?

I If a young artist's drawing of a friend showed the friend doing something that did not occur, does calling the drawing art make it okay? Why?

J A photograph captured the expression of the tough football player, but the football player claimed that was unfair because he is a oving father. Did the artist photographer have the right to be selective? Why?

H What is the artist's responsibility to truth? How does truth mesh with creative expression and the artist's license to portray a personal view of reality? What can the public expect from art? Why?

3.6 ARTISTS' CALM CONTRIBUTES TO SEEING ACCURATELY 319

"Only when the artist's mind is as calm as the surface of a mirror can the real nature of the outside object be grasped." p.117.

Kishimoto H. (1967).Some Japanese cultural traits and religions.pp.110-121. In C. Moore, (Ed.) (1967).The Japanese mind. Honolulu, HI: University of Hawaii Press. By permission.

P Sometimes art museums are very crowded when many people come at once. Sometimes few people are there. Why would you want many or few people if you want to see the art work clearly?

I How well could an artist see how to draw a clowns face if the artist were on a thrilling carnival ride? What would be a better way for the artist to see well? Why?

J Do you think artists should be involved in emotional scenes that they depict in art works, or work from models posing as photographs show the action? Why?

H How can the artist's state of mind contribute to accuracy in perceiving a subject? Would your answer apply to preliminary sketches as well as the final work of art? Why?

3.6 ARTISTS SHOULD BE MODEL HUMANS

"...consider the traditional conception of the artist in Chinese culture: He is a man 'who is at peace with nature...above all, his breast must brood no ill passions, for a good artist, we strongly believe, must be a good man'..." "The Chinese artist can only create beauty if he himself is a paragon of goodness, a model for everyone to emulate and revere." p. 246.

Anderson, R. (1990). Calliope's sisters: A comparative study of philosophies of art. Englewood Cliffs, NJ: Prentice-Hall. By permission of Prentice-Hall Division of Simon & Schuster.

P Why would you say that artists are good people?

I How can art influence people's beliefs and behavior? Would you want evil persons making art? What kind of person should an artist be? Why?

J When artists create works that surprise most people because they can't be easily understood, people might fear that the artist has bad intentions. How would you resolve this dilemma? Why?

H If artists can influence people's values and society progresses smoothest with cohesive values, what happens to the role of the artist as an individual critical thinker? What personal qualities should artists have?

3.6 INTENTIONS OF THE ARTIST CAN BE INFERRED

"...works of art are assumed to be the products of intention...and...can be intentionally produced without being the product of conscious deliberation." "In art too intentions are inferred from the observation of coherent patterns." p. 105.

Sheppard, A.,1987. Aesthetics: An introduction to the philosophy of art. New York: Oxford University Press. By permission of Oxford University Press.

P Can you read the mind of an artist by looking closely at the art work made by the artist?

I What kinds of things in works of art hint at what the artist wants viewers to think or feel when looking at the work? What reason do you have for saying so?

J To what extent do you believe that an art critic's assertion about what an artist intended can be true? Could the assertion be influenced by the critics background? Why or why not?

H If one considers debate about 1) an artist's **conscious** intent and 2) Viewers interpretation or misinterpretation of visual images, why can a viewer make a pretty good guess about the artist's intent in a work of art?

3.6 ARTISTS BELIEVE THEIR WORK TO BE TRUE AND SIGNIFICANT 322

"He [the artist] is concerned to express interpretations of his subject-matter which he believes to be both true *and* significant." p.477

Greene, T.(1940). The arts and the art of criticism. Princeton, NJ: Princeton University Press. Copyright 1968 by Princeton University Press. Reprinted by permission of Princeton University Press.

P Why would an artist make a sculpture of parents caring for their children?

I Artists paint portraits of important people and identify them by name. Why would an artist use a worker as a subject of a painting and name it "Fisherman" or "Postman" or "Child with a Pet"?

J Most people work in order to earn money. Why does an artist work? Why do artists sculpt or paint or make prints or draw?

H Is art, work or play? How does a common concept of work mesh with aritsts' concept of what they do?

3.6 ARTISTS ARE REBELS: UNQUALIFIED PROMOTION OF ORIGINALITY AND INDIVIDUALITY COULD CHANGE THEIR IMAGE 323

"...what is to become of the artist as rebel if every new work is instantly and unreservedly accepted?" p.33.

Millet, C. (November,1990). Nostalgia in the seventies: Hope for the nineties. The Journal of Art, 3 (2), 32-33.

P "Say no to drugs" is suggesting that people should think for themselves like artists do. When artists think about the way things go in our world and say "It's wrong" in their art, what do people who see it do?

I Should people say "okay" to anything artists call art? Should people change whatever artists show as bad about life? Why or why not?

J Why do artists take on the role of critic or rebel of society? What would happen to art if people agreed with the visual recommendations of artists?

H Is the role of the artist by default of society? Why do artists serve as defined critics of society and rebel against what seems to be expected, or do they?

THE CREATIVE PROCESS

3.7 ARTISTS INVENT BY CHANGING THINGS — 324

"Artists change materials and come up with something new. They are imaginative and inventive. They do not just tell us what the world is like...[nor] just hold up a mirror to nature..." p. 16).

Eaton, M. (1988). Basic issues in aesthetics. Belmont, CA: Wadsworth Publishing Company. Copyright 1988 by Wadsworth, Inc.. By permission of Wadsworth Publishing Company.

P Why do children have more than one jump rope game? How might that be like artists using different objects to paint a painting?

I An artist made the seeds in the center of the flowers in a painting seem to bounce around like styrofoam beads. Of course they did not do this in real life. Why is that okay to do or not in a work of art?

J Why do works of art surprise us by different views of familiar places, things out of ordinary positions like upside down cows, etc.

H At one time people believed that the world was flat or that earth was the only inhabited planet. Yet creative minds imagined the "impossible". Why are artists simialr to these other people who dared to think divergently.

3.7 CLARITY AND ORDER EMERGE OUT OF INITIAL STAGES OF THE CREATIVE PROCESS — 325

"Most accounts of the expressive process emphasize the confusion and chaos with which the process begins in the artist's mind: gradually replaced by clarity and order as it approaches completion." p. 314).

Hospers, J. (1955). The concept of artistic expression. Proceedings of the Aristotelian Society, 1954-1960, 55, 313-344. Fair use.

P If you are experimenting with new tools and ideas in art, why might it be good if you don't know what you are going to make exactly?

I An artist from the United States wants to make art about the jungle. Would it be best to go to a jungle, to look at many photographs of the jungle, or to imagine how a jungle looks? Why?

J Why is making art referred to as creative problem solving? How is it like math or science problems?...different from solving math or science problems?

H Why would an artist consciously seek information and organize it mentally, as an artwork is created?

3.7 CREATING IN ART MEANS INVENTING AND SELECTING

"There is the *inventive* phase [inspiration]...in which new ideas are formed in the preconscious and appear in consciousness. And there is the *selective* phase, which is nothing more than criticism, in which the conscious chooses or rejects the new idea after perceiving its relationships to what has already tentatively been adopted." p. 300).

Beardsley, M.(Spring,1965). On the creation of art. The Journal of Aesthetics and Art Criticism, 23(3), 291-304. By permission of the editor.

P What familiar object in nature is somewhat like this shape? Is it <u>exactly</u> like a _____? What did the artist do to change it? Is it still "art" if the artist chooses to change its looks?

I If you paint a dream exactly the way you remember it, does that inspiration ensure a good work of art or are there other considerations in making art?

J An artist is on location painting a naturalistic desert scene when a train passes through the scene being painted. If you were the artist why would you include or not include the train?

H Why would an artist not feel compelled to tell the whole truth and nothing but the truth in a work of art?

3.7 ARTISTS CREATE RELATIONSHIPS BETWEEN VISUAL QUALITIES TO COMMUNICATE TO OTHERS

"Art is the ordering, manipulating, refashioning of these qualities toward still further qualities....when art is conceived as the constructing and organizing of the qualities of experience, it may be thought of as man's <u>qualitative intelligence</u>." p.4,5.

Villemain, F. (Jan.,1964). Democrcy, education and art. Educational Theory, 14 (1),1-14,30. By permission.

P Some things are just neat to look at. Art is one of those things. What do artists do in art that makes us want to look?

I Why do we enjoy looking at art and at what nature has created? What do artists do that might happen by chance in nature?

J Artists and nature create sights that are inviting. Do artists copy natural objects or use rules of natural beauty or neither? Why?

H What, from either life experience or principles of beauty derived from nature, contributes to how artists create visual objects that intrigue people? Why?

3.7 THE VIEWER NEED NOT KNOW HOW AN ARTIST ARRIVED AT THE FINAL WORK 328

"There are many experiences which the artist undergoes in the process of creation-- the divine agonies of inception, the slow working through of ideas to fruition, and the technical details of execution-- which the audience need not and probably should not share." p.336)

Hospers, J. (1955). The concept of artistic expression. Proceedings of the Aristotelian Society, 1954-1960, 55 , 313-344. Fair use.

P If you don't need to know how clouds form in order to enjoy the way they look, why would you need to know how a sculptor goes about making a sculpture in order to enjoy it, or would it be good to know that?

I Of what importance would seeing the sketches of a finished weaving be, or to see the silk screen used for a fabric print to enjoy the work of art? Why?

J Can an art historian, who knows a great deal about art, appreciate a serigraph if he/she has never worked with that process enough to know all that the artist went through?

H One artist explains to viewers everything about the artwork--the inspiration, the intent, the visual study, the practice, the changes --and another artist explains nothing. Which approach can you defend, and why?

3.7 TRADITIONAL PIECES OF ART CAN BE CREATIVE 329

" A Greek vase was almost always a creation, although its form was traditional and its decoration deviated but little from that of its numberless forerunners." p. 41.

From Langer, S.(1953). Feeling and form Copyright 1953. Published by Scribner's & Sons, New York. Fair use.

P If a candlestick must be made to hold a candle, is it possible for an artist to make a creative candlestick? Why?

I Can an artist be creative with the idea of a Christmas tree? If so, would turning it upside down do? Why or why not?

J Must artists always be unique? Why might it be important for an artist not to change something? How creative can artists be in changing things that have meaning for people as they are?

H Does artistic license apply to all creative work of an artist? Why or why not?

3.7 FOLLOWING PROCEDURES MAY HELP, BUT PROCEDURES DON'T GUARANTEE, NOR NECESSARILY ACCOUNT FOR A WORK OF ART   330

"Even if all artists did in fact go through the process described by the expression theory, and even if nobody but artists did this, would it be true to say that the work of art was a good one *because* the artist, in creating it, went through this or that series of experiences in plying his medium?" p. 320.

Hospers, J. (1955). The concept of artistic expression. Proceedings of the Aristotelian Society, 1954-1960, 55, 313-344. Fair use.

P Does splashing paint make something art? Does drawing with a ruler make it art? Is the twentieth pot thrown on a wheel "art"?

I If an artist has an idea and uses what was learned correctly, will the result be "art"? Why or why not?

J Why are there art "classes" if art is not like math where correct procedures ensure correct answers?

H Why do people go to school to pursue careers in fine arts where individuality and originality count so heavily for success?

3.7 ART BEGINS WITH THE ARTIST'S NEED TO LOOK CLOSER   331

"'One paints a thing in order to see it'". [The subject defines itself in the artist's mind as he paints it]" You see something in your subject...It means noticing what you see." p. 303, 304.

Collingwood, R. (1958). Principles of art. New York: Galaxy Press. Oxford University. By permission of Oxford University Press.

P Why is it better if an artist smells a flower with open eyes?

I Why would an artist make a flower ten times larger than it is in nature? What reason might the artist have for doing so?

J Is it true that artists who paint abstractly have not veen able to clearly perceive an object and paint it realistically? Why or why not?

H Why might an abstract or nonobjective painter benefit from examing visual qualities of nature very closely?

3.7 THE ART PROCESS : USING HUMAN SKILL TO SHAPE EXPRESSIVE FORM 332

"...the art process is the application of some human skill to this [creation of expressive form] essential purpose." p.4.

From Langer, S. (1953). <u>Feeling and form</u> Copyright 1953. Published by Scribner's & Sons, New York. Fair use.

P People who take piano lessons or play ball need to practice. What would artist practice and why do they need to ?

I What are some reasons that certain people are able to make art that expresses ideas well?

J Why can't just anyone who has feelings to express make art? Is it some magical talent?

H How can you explain the self-taught artist? Is that a recommendation for anyone who wants to be an artist? Why might the self-taught artist obtain a sufficient background to make art?

3.7 THE NEEDS OF AN ARTIST INTERACT WITH THE IMAGE EMERGING IN THE MEDIUM 333

"Before his canvas the artist responds to his subjective needs and to the image he has created through a series of trials and errors like life itself."p.97.

Cherry, H. (Chapter: Mark Rothko, Kedzo O'Kada, Herman Cherry, Ad Reinhardt) in S. Rodman. (1961). New York: Capricorn Books. Copyright by Devin-Adair Publishers, Inc., Old Greenwich, CT. 06870. Permission granted to reprint the above quotation. All rights reserved.

P Even close friends may feel differently about some things. Why might artists make different pictures about the same scene?

I If you pretended to be the artist making a certain art work of a cat, why might you and the artist make the work differently from each other?

J When you decide if you like a work of art, on what **do** you, or **could** you make your decision?

H Why might a capable viewer be unable to "step into the artist's shoes" to relive the artistic process and decisions as the artist did?

3.7 PROCESS IS NOT THE BASIS OF FINAL JUDGMENT OF A WORK OF ART   334

"...when we make a judgment of aesthetic value upon a work of art, we are in no way judging the process, including any expressive process..." p. 321.

Hospers, J. (1955). The concept of artistic expression. Proceedings of the Aristotelian Society, 1954-1960, 55, 313-344. Fair use.

P A person asked an artist how hard it was to make the art work they were discussing. Why might the artist say that, "how hard it was to make" was not important?

I Throwing a pot on the potter's wheel looks easy but is isn't. Is that why a piece of wheel-thrown pottery is valuable? Why or why not?

J Dribbling paint on canvas or welding found objects together appears pretty effortless. Why is effort an inadequate measure of value of art?

H To what degree does effort, process, correctness or complexity enter into the value of a work of art and why?

3.7 INSPIRATION AND EXECUTION MERGE IN THE PROCESS OF CREATING ART   335

"...with the assumption that an artist has done what he actually intended to do, there is no difference between 'inspiration' and 'execution'." p. 25.

Kaelin, E. (1968). An existential-phenomenological account of aesthetic education. Penn State Papers in Art Education, No.4. University Park, PA: Pennsylvania State University, Department of Art Education. By permission.

P If an artist gets an idea from something real, why might the art work that results be different from the real object that started the artist's thinking? Why might an art work be exactly as the artist hoped?

I Why might a potter or weaver change the nature of a flock of geese that inspired the artist's work? Would that change be a surprise to the artist?

J Using flock of geese as theme for a design, how might a package designer change lettering of the package to fit different behavior of the geese? Why would the designer do so?

H Why is it a sign of quality if the execution of a work of art matches the artist's intention or inspiration? How would this be determined and by whom?

3.7 ARTISTS THINK ABOUT THEIR WORK AS THEY CREATE   336

"One of the weaknesses of the emotional/irrational theory of the artistic process is that it flies in the face of many artists' descriptions of their activity." p. 23.

Eaton, M. (1988). Basic issues in aesthetics. Belmont, CA: Wadsworth Publishing Company. Copyright 1988 by Wadsworth, Inc.. By permission of Wadsworth Publishing Company.

P   A car hit a puddle and splattered a fence. A person, thinking the splatters looked neat, stomped in the puddle to make thick and thin splatters that crossed and caused splattered- into spaces on the fence. Why might what the person did be "art"?

I   Why might an artist pay attention to thoughts about what is happening that occur while making art?

J   What role does reason play in art? Why? Does reason have a part in spontaneous or emotional art? Why or why not?

H   Why is a non-reasoning theory of the artistic process not necessarily true and an insufficient description?

3.7 ARTISTS LEARN FROM OTHER ARTISTS, BUT 'APPROPRIATED' IN THE CURRENT SENSE FLAUNTS TRADITIONAL CONCEPTIONS OF ART
   337

"Artists have always appropriated the work and ideas of other artists...in the sense of building on previous achievements, but the term entered art jargon and assumed a new dimension in the work of a number of recent American artists..." "...that questioned and commented on the issue of originality in art." p. 236.

From: Post-to-neo: The artworld of the 1980's by Calvin Tomkins, Copyright 1988 by Calvin Tomkins. Reprinted by permission of Henry Holt and Company, Inc.

P   Why is it not okay to copy your neighbor's art work when artists seem to copy comic strip artist's work in their paintings?

I   Why may an artist copy another's work of art, or is that dishonest? Why?

J   You are on a jury to decide whether one artist's work, appropriated by another artist was wrong. The offending artist's lawyer claims times have changed and really nothing is original. Do you agree? Why or why not?

H   Why might artists copy another's work and proceed to alter it in ways that change the meaning of the first work? Is that legitimate?

3.7 ARTISTS INVENT BUT REVISIT NATURE TO VITALIZE THE IMAGE INVENTED 338

Burchfield worked in his studio to create general images, then worked from observation to revise and enliven those images. p. 63.
Paraphrased from Bauer, J. (1956). Charles Burchfield. New York: MacMillan Co.

P Why might the "smiley face" designer wish that others who draw smiley faces would look at real smiling faces?

I A fabric designer was using abstract flower symbols in a pattern. Why might that artist examine real flowers again while creating the flower symbol?

J What might it mean that an artist revisits the actual location of an abstraction of a landscape while painting it in the studio. Why?

H Would all artists revisit nature anticipating a positive effect on their art work, or would they not?

oi
3.7 A WORK OF ART MAY DEVELOP IRREGULARLY, BETWEEN RESPONDING TO THE EMERGING WORK, VISUALIZATIONS, MEMORIES AND THE ARTIST'S INTENT 339

I [Burchfield] rely on partial studies and memory in creating a work of art that depicts an intent with unity. p.46.
Paraphrase of a quote attributed to Burchfield by Bauer, J. (1956). Charles Burchfield. New York: MacMillan Co.

P An artist made a "mistake" on a drawing, looked at it, and decided to change the drawing to keep the mistake. Why might this have happened?

I Some teachers say not to erase what you think is wrong in a drawing, but to make something of your mistakes. What do artists do? When and why is it good to change or not change an art work while working on it?

J An artist's intent changes in creating a work of art. How does such redirection affect the artwork? Why?

H An artist has a contract to produce a site-specific sculpture based on sketches in the proposal. As the artist proceeds, a decision is make to alter the sculpture. Is this a problem? Why? Should the artist be allowed to change?

3.7 ARTISTS DO NOT HAVE A PRECISE SOLUTION IN MIND, BUT ARE SENSITIVE TO WHAT POSSIBLE BEAUTY COULD RESULT   340

"Matisse had learned exactly the delicate order of shape in which the color and form of nature best agreed." p.19.
Gowing, W. (1966) henri matisse: 64 paintings. New York: Museum of Modern Art. Copyright, The Museum of Modern Art, 1966. Reprinted by permission.

P Have you had to add ust a bit more to a picture when it was time to put it away? Why might some artist work very late into the night?

I Why might artist step back from their art work to study it during and toward the completion of it? Is it bad it they don't know when the art owrk will be finished for sure? When **is** it "finished"?

J Why could it be different for artists to stick to a rigid time table for a client who has commissioned a work?

H How does an artist know when a work of art is finally completed? Is it possible that an artist would consider a work only tentatively completed? Why?

3.7 ARTISTS DELIBERATELY LOOK FOR WAYS AND THINGS TO CHANGE   341

"Why, then, should sculpture remain shackled by laws which have no justification? Let us break them courageously...Nothing is more stupid than to fear to deviate from the art we practice... look for ways to accomplish what is assumed impossible." p.54,55.
Boccioni, U. In R. Herbert, (Ed.) Modern artists on art. Englewood Cliffs, NJ: Prentice-Hall. Fair use.

P Children sometimes try to do exactly what adults say not to just to check out what was said. Are artists being childish when they try to break "art rules"? Why or why not?

I Laws are rules accepted as important for society. Are there such binding rules in art? What kind of rules are there in art? Why may artists break these?

J Do artists change rules in art by breaking them or do rules change as society changes? If it's okay for artist to break art rules, why do the exist?

H Is change for the sake of novelty, originality, or change in itself a value in art? Is it a sufficient reason for designating something as a work of art?

This one guy said to the other "I'll trade you my tail for your horse"

ART AND CONTEXT

3.8 WORKS OF ART ARE PERCEIVED BY A PERSON IN A CONTEXT 342

Spatial forms exemplify well that beauty is perceived as such in the context of everything about the one who is perceiving an object or work of art. p. 74.

Paraphrased from Prall, D. (1929). Aesthetic judgment. New York: Thomas Y. Crowell Co.

P If a painting is lost for a hundred years in an attic, then is discovered and shown in a home as "art" why was it, or was it not, art when lost?

I Why is a cluster of three cypress knees* arranged by an artist "art" when the knees, stacked on a table among 50 others, were not "art"? *Knobby growths (new trees) protruding out of the water which are cut off and sold as pleasing natural "sculptures."*

J If a stone sculpture is picked up by a person out of a pile of them in a warehouse because it would look special in a garden spot, when is the sculpture art... before or after it is placed in a special place?

H Sculptures of cavalrymen are displayed on high pedestals and sometimes at ground level in a more natural setting. Why might one display be a better choice than the other?

3.8 MARKETING INFLUENCES WHAT IS PROMOTED AS "ART" 343

"The inclusion of more crafts may be better for impulse buyers or people looking for less expensive works, Newton said, but she's not so sure it's good for art in general." p.6B.

(Context: an interview with artist Deborah Newton). Lee, E. (September 4,1997). Are crafts, commercialization dominating art fairs? The Rockford Register Star 1B, 6B. Rockford, IL: The Rockford Register Star. By permission of the Rockford Register Star and the artist.

P Why is a Navajo Indian rug or an oriental rug special and different from carpeting in your home or our school?

I If old Mexican bark paintings become popular and all kinds of people start making them to sell to tourists, why would someone buy the new ones as art or not buy them?

J What's right or wrong about the newspaper headline, 'What's 'in' and 'out' in art."?

H How does fashion impact on the definition of art e.g. if Navaho rugs become fashionable, are they no longer "art"?

3.8 ANY SUBJECT CAN BE INTEGRATED AESTHETICALLY IN A WORK OF ART 344

"Ultimately there is probably nothing that may not be drawn into an aesthetic integration. Politics and business, medicine, factory labor, collecting tickets, working on the railroad,...war and religion..." p. 79-80.

Pepper, S. (1945). The basis of criticism in the arts. Cambridge, Mass: Harvard University Press. Copyright 1945 by the President and Fellows of Harvard College. Reprinted by permission of the publisher.

P If artists tell stories in their art, what can art be about...(working, playing, animals, nature, trucks or cars)? What reasons can you give for why it is okay to make art about any of these?

I For what reasons, and under what conditions, can common everyday subjects be "art"?

J Is shock effect of the subject matter or of an object a legitimate and suffiecient quality for something to be a work of art? If not, what is necessary to be so?

H Can some set of rules about art provide guidelines for establishing some quality criteria for innovative candidates for "work of art"? What? Why?

3.8 ART OF YESTERDAY MAKES US REFLECT ON TODAY 345

"The art of the past molds in countless ways the attitude, responses, dispositions of our daily lives, including our moral ones." p 290).

Hospers, J. (1982). Understanding the arts. Englewood Cliffs, NJ: Prentice Hall. By permission and fair use.

P If, in a work of art, you see people that make others suffer long ago, why might "good" come out of that old art?

I Artists showed situations where people were good and evil. The events depicted are ancient history. Why would we venefit from discussing such works of art today?

J If ancient art showed ideas of good and evil, of what relevance is that for today? Can old art affect our ideas about right and wrong? Should it? Why?

H Why cna art serve as an influence on morality across time and cultures? to what extent can it do so? Should it serve a morality function? Can it be avoided- either positively or negatively? by presence or absence?

3.8 ART LETS US IDENTIFY WITH THE SUBJECT   346

"Art can have a moral influence by giving us imagintive insight into other people and by inculcating values and attitudes, often in subtle and indirect ways." p. 153.

Sheppard, A.,1987. Aesthetics: An introduction to the philosophy of art. New York: Oxford University Press. By permission of Oxford University Press.

P Artist have made art about families for a long time. what can we learn about families from art? Why do you think that what the artist showed was true about families of that time?

I Artists have shown ideas about people in their art from many countries. Why can study of art help us form our ideas about what is good in people?

J Why is it an artist's responsibility to create wartime art as the mirror and commentator of the world scene? Why should artists not feel obligated to produce wartime art in time of war?

H What is the social responsibility of an artist - to a country, to ideas, to social cohesion, to preserving human life and the environment? Why?

3.8 ART BROADENS OUR UNDERSTANDING AND ENCOURAGES TOLERANCE   347

"...hasty judgments, and the injustices that result from thinking of other people in stereotypes...tend to disappear through the reading of literature...a major moral achievement." p.288.

Hospers, J. (1982). Understanding the arts. Englewood Cliffs, NJ: Prentice Hall. By permission and fair use.

P If a person notices that artists of many lands put birds caringly in art, even from unfamiliar places and times, why did these works of art do some good?

I If works of art from many unfamiliar countries and times show people your age playing games, why is that a good reason for having art?

J Why might art created by an artist of the country depicted be least likely to reinforce misinformation or stereotypes about that country than if artist from another country depicted life there?

H Is art a reliable source of truth? Does art serve to reliably inform us about little known peoples? To what extent is the artist a factor? Why? Should an artist be held responsible for spreading visual information truthfully?

3.8 ART DERIVES SUPPORT FROM SOCIAL INSTITUTIONS -- HOMES, SOCIAL GROUPS, LIBRARIES, MUSEUMS, FAMILY, COMMUNITY SERVICES
348

"..works of art are described as created, preserved,and appreciated in a set of overlapping social institutions designed to liberate the human impulses that drive us to creative expression of feeling." p. xvii.

Kaelin, E. F. (1989). An aesthetics for art educators. New York: Teachers College Press. By permission.

P If a town has a pumpkin decorating contest, why might that be a way of approving (expressive) art?

I How many different ways does your town or city support art by events sponsored by community groups? Do you think they make the connection between their event and art? Why? Why not?

J To what extent is it important to recognize the artistic qualities that are effective in a TV commercial or social event? Why not just enjoy?

H What are the possible benefits or negative effects of the good intentions of families, churches or other social community groups who show "art" in their locations? Is anything better than nothing? Why or why not?

3.8 ART IS A VEHICLE FOR MORAL REFLECTION AND POSSIBILITIES FOR GOOD
349

"Yet this indifference to praise and blame because of preoccupation with imaginative experience constitutes the heart of the moral potency of art. From it proceeds the liberating and uniting power of art." p.349.

From Art as experience by John Dewey. Copyright 1934 by John Dewey, renewed 1973 by The John Dewey Foundation. Used by permission of G.P. Putnam's Sons, a division of Penguin Putnam Inc.

P How could art works of heros, religious events and gods influence people who are around them? Why?

I Comic strips dramatize good and evil. Pop artist created frames in large scale. What good might come from this art? What reasons are there for qualifying you answer?

J Is protesting war through art a moral obligation? Why or why not?

H To what degree does war provide the "new" subject matter and timely topic or moral issue for an artist or other motivation?

3.8 THE ARTS SERVE IN RELIGIOUS SITUATIONS TO BOND PEOPLE 350

"As the church developed, the arts were again brought into connection with human life and became a bond of union among men." "These objects and acts were much more than works of art to the worshipers who gathered in the temple...much less works of art to them than they are today to believers and unbelievers." p.328,329.

From Art as experience by John Dewey. Copyright 1934 by John Dewey, renewed 1973 by The John Dewey Foundation. Used by permission of G.P. Putnam's Sons, a division of Penguin Putnam Inc.

P Before you could read, you could tell that two people holding hands were friends. Why could works of art help people to understand ideas and believe the same?

I How might artist influence what people believe the world is like? Why can that be good? Why not?

J When people gather together, they tend to shape their beliefs. How and where can art contribute to shaping beliefs in your town or city?

H To what degree is belief in the religious significance of a work of art a contributing factor to its interpretation and appreciation by people when it was originally in use and by people today? Does it help appreciaion as "art" to believe in the meaning of an artifact?

3.8 THE ARTS CONTRIBUTE TO A DEMOCRATIC SOCIETY   351

"Freedom of the press, radio, and television, and, in general, freedom of information and expression, are essential conditions for the existence of a democratic regime." p.517.

Inter-American Commission on Human Rights of the Organization of American States(1991).Annual report of the Inter-American commission on Human Rights, 1990-1991.englewood Cliffs, NJ: Prentice Hall. By permission of the Commission.

P Why are art works of American flags or people voting "patriotic"? Why might it be patriotic ...because the flag is present? or how it is shown?

I How might artists serve their country through their art?

J What role or roles can artist be expected to play in support of the country which allow freedom of speech?

H How do you think that artistic freedom, a democratic society, patriotism can be supported and a positive regard of a nation by other nations influenced conguently in works of art?

3.8 ART MUSEUMS PRESERVE ART AND PERFORM A VARIETY OF SERVICES

"...nobody seems to question the idea of an art museum as a social center, a magnet for crowds of people with an hour to kill and a generalized belief in the benefits of high culture." p. 134.

From Post-to-neo: The artworld of the 1980's by Calvin Tomkins, Copyright 1988 by Calvin Tomkins. Reprinted by permission of Henry Holt and Company, Inc.

P Why might an art museum plan a show of art works of flowers in the spring?

I If you were planning an exhibit of art work for a children's art museum, what would you select to show and why?

J A museum director promotes art that is "inevitable" rather than that which is personally preferred. Why is this a good or not a good position?

H What are the pros and cons of art museums operating as a profit-making business? For what reasons should they be purist and tax-supported or offer attractive services as a business?

3.8 ART HELPS NATIONS AS THEY UNDERGO CHANGE

"...artistic content has the function of helping man to develop an emotional involvement with the objects of his social and cultural environment and that the creation of art, by providing new symbolic foci of sociocultural integration, contributes to the reintegration of society after the disturbance of a relative equilibrium." p. 5.

Kavolis, V. (1968). Artistic expression: A sociological analysis. Ithaca, NY: Cornell University Press. By permission and fair use.

P Many artists have shown people viewing patriotic parades. Why does art like this teach people?

I Why could big art of common everyday obfects teach people some new importance in life? What might people learn to see and think about that they overlooked as unimportant before?

J Depicting sensitive social issues in art is one step removed from people being directly involved. Is this sufficiently "distant" to claim that art helps people objectively view their social
changes? Why? Why not?

H To what extent is the art of today assisting people in making value changes in keeping with rapid economic and political changes in the world. Why?

3.8 VALUE ACCORDED ART DEPENDS ON WHAT PEOPLE CALL GOOD AND EVIL OF LIFE 354

"...the value of art...depends on men's perception of the meaning of life; depends on what they hold to be the good and the evil of life. And what is good and what is evil is defined by what are termed 'religions'." p. 127.
Tolstoy, L. (1962). What is art? New York: Oxford University Press. A Hesperides Book. By permission of Oxford University Press.

P When might a violent scene in an art work be "good" rather than "evil"?

I If a sculpture depicting a god who signals "peace" by the position of the hands is beside a painting of war victims being shot, why could both artworks be teaching about good and evil?

J What might influence whether works of art are valued or not in a religious country?

H What is the likely effect of a multicultural society on concepts of good and evil and balue of art as a depictor of religious values? How is multicultural or multi-ethnic different from multi-ethic?

3.8 ART REFLECTS BELIEFS OF RELIGIONS THAT CONTRADICT EACH OTHER 355

"...the art which sprang up on this perverted teaching [of Christ's teaching] was for all that a true art, since it corresponded to the religious view of life held by the people among whom it arose." p. 130.
Tolstoy, L. (1962). What is art? New York: Oxford University Press. A Hesperides Book. By permission of Oxford University Press.

P If someone truly believed that people become rabbits and painted that event, can such a falsehood be "art"? Why?

I If a work of art showing a person going to heaven in a fiery chariot is viewed by a person who believes that all dead are buried, etc., can teh art work be appreciated? How? Why?

J Of what significance is the belief of the artist? Is a sculpture of Christ by a Buddist true art?

H To what extent is belief in what an artwork represents or symbolizes, a factor in accepting the value of that work as art? Why?

3.8 GOVERNMENTS GUARD NATIONAL ART TREASURES BY TREATIES 356

"Article 36 of the Treaty of Rome allows the prohibition of the export from the country of origin of works considered to be 'national treasures possessing artistic, historic, or archeological value'." "At present each country interprets 'national treasures' differently and it will be difficult to establish common criteria." p.61.

Gowrie, G. (November, 1990). Will art move more freely in 1993? The Journal of Art, 3 (2), 61. Fair use.

P Why would it be okay or no okay to trade a very old necklace given to you by your grandmother for some popular, stylish bracelets and pins?

I Would it be okay for a rich person to give a work of art to people to see in a museum instead of paying taxes to the government to use to help people in other ways. Why or why not?

J Should an art museum be allowed to sell the only fine sculpture of a national hero in order to purchase a work by the latest artist "star"?

H What considerations determine the relative value of new and old art? Is a piece in storage still art of value?

3.8 GOVERNMENT PROJECTS SUPPORT PUBLIC ART 357

"The [USA one-percent] law, which reserves one-percent of a government's project total budget for art, is still used in many cities..." p.66.

Conger, S. (November, 1990). Corporate art in the Helms era. The Journal of Art, 3 (2), 66-67. Fair use.

P Why is it important to have art in places where people shop or work?

I If a business borrows government money to build a shopping mall, the government says, the mall must have some art. Why do you think this rule was made? Is it a good rule? Why?

J Does the government rule about budgeting 1% for art assure that the art selected is good for the people who confront it daily? Why is any art better than no art?

H Why does controversy arise over art in public places especially when the art was a budget item paid for by federal taxes?

3.8 ART CONTRIBUTES TO CONTINUITY BETWEEN AND WITHIN CULTURES 358

"Continuity of culture in passage from one civilization to another as well as within the culture,is conditioned by art more than any other onething." p.327

From Art as experience by John Dewey. Copyright 1934 by John Dewey, renewed 1973 by The John Dewey Foundation. Used by permission of G.P. Putnam's Sons, a division of Penguin Putnam Inc.

P If your great grandmother saved art that showed life when she was young, in her town, why would that help people today if the art was in an art museum?

I What does the most modern art we've seen say about today's world? Why could people who think about art understand change? Does "understand" make you change you ideas of right and wrong? Why or why not?

J What older people and younger people consider "right" or "important' can be different. How does art help young people understand why older people think the way they do? Can art of today help older people understand the way young peole think? Why or why not?

H What art form(s) are likely to contribute to understanding change in society most effectively-- architecture, painting, advertising art, site-specific sculpture, fiber arts, drawing or others? For what reasons?

3.8 AN AESTHETIC CONTEXT IS THE ENCOUNTER BETWEEN THE ARTIST'S WORK AND VIEWER 359

"The aesthetic context is a positive experiential interaction between a percipient (perceiving subject) and the artist's arrangement of the medium's counters." p. 76.

Kaelin, E. F. (1989). An aesthetics for art educators. New York: Teachers College Press. By permission.

P We remember special events in our lives because of what happened to whom and where. Why would someone think certain art works are special?

I For what reasons would some important works of art be more memorable than others?

J What besides subject matter might arrest the attention of viewers at an art exhibit? What are the components of such a memorable encounter?

H Keats wrote about a moment of creation between awake and asleep. what is involved in a moment of appreciation of an artist's creation? Why is each part you mention critical to such an aesthetic context?

3.8 ARTISTS WHO UNDERSTAND A COMMUNITY CAN CREATE ART THAT THE COMMUNITY CAN UNDERSTAND 360

"An insightful artist understands what the public wants and what the public needs even when the public doesn't...but if artists do go through the community, they understand a litle bit more about the environment...and soften [their work]...so the community sees it without being turned off." p.67
Conger, S. (November,1990). Corporate art in the Helms era. The Journal of Art, 3 (2), 66-67. Fair use.

P   Families differ in some ways. Why could an artist show situations from one's own family better than imagining all families?

I   Stepping into someone else's shoes means trying to see things from their point of view. How and why would an artist who is commissioned to do a public work of art for a town, try to "step into the community's shoes"?

J   What are the pros and cons of the argument that "public art" artists should take the values of the people into consideration and "soften" possibly offensive aspects planned?

H   Some artists have gone to unfamiliar countries and depicted that life in their art by "going native". What does that phrase mean and why might it contribut to truth in art?

3.8 ART IS RELATED TO THE TYPE OF SOCIETY THAT EXISTS 361

"...abstractionism, in some form, seems to be specifically related to industrial society." p. 17.
Kavolis, V. (1968). Artistic expression: A sociological analysis. Ithaca, NY: Cornell University Press. By permission and fair use.

P   Smiley faces are simple faces. Why might artists simplify objects in abstract art? Why are simple shapes in machines or motors?

I   People often think of natural forms as beautify. Why might artists see beauty inside of watches, at a steel mill, in a car motor, in the maze of tubing at a drive-up bank or a furnace?

J   Robots are abstract people. Why might artists lean toward abstract or non-objective art in today's society? Is that a positive direction or not? Why?

H   With the USA moving into an information society era and with societal changes that can be expected, why might art change and how might it change? How might innovative art affect people's exposure and attitudes about art of the past?

3.8 ART STYLES REFLECT ECONOMIC CONCERNS 362

"...a static economy, relatively lacking in trade, favors static and formal art styles. Conversely, dynamic processes, such as active trade and free competition, stimulate spontaneous and dynamic--informal--art styles." p. 20.

Kavolis, V. (1968). Artistic expression: A sociological analysis. Ithaca, NY: Cornell University Press. By permission and fair use.

P Why might the art of slowly changing times look different from art of fast moving, active times? What are all the ways art could be different in slow and fast times?

I Why might the question to an artist change in the 21st century change from "How long did it take you to make that artwork?" to "How fast did you turn out that artwork?"

J What will happen to traditional art forms, processes, media and tools in a society caught up in computerized instant answers? Why will the art look the same or different and why?

H How might more money for the arts mean more and better art? Why might there be no guarantees in an information society where status comes from winning computerized air battles? Why is better art possible in these times even?

3.8 HISTORY, INSTITUTIONS AND TRADITIONS INFLUENCE ART 363

"History, social institutions, ideologies and...traditions have all been identified as influential or essential to the nature of art and the aesthetic." p. 100.

Eaton, M. (1988). Basic issues in aesthetics. Belmont, CA: Wadsworth Publishing Company. Copyright 1988 by Wadsworth, Inc. By permission of Wadsworth Publishing Company.

P Some USA artists from Native American, Latino, or Asian families create art forms that look modern, but have the same feeling that works of their ancestors have. Why do you suppose that would happen?

I What message could a sculptor have for society by creating forms that look like industrial waste spills? Why would an artist seem to "fight" industrial progress?

J Why might artists revolt against social trends in a society through their art work?

H To what extent can or should descendents of particular cultural groups resist influence of their heritage in their response to modern trends in society and art? Why?

3.8 PEOPLE CAN "READ" SOMETHING IN ART, BUT CONTEXT INFORMATION HELPS 364

"If we must know everything about an object's context in order to 'get' it, it is easy to become skeptical about ever being able to understand anything." p. 88.

Eaton, M. (1988). Basic issues in aesthetics. Belmont, CA: Wadsworth Publishing Company. Copyright 1988 by Wadsworth, Inc.. By permission of Wadsworth Publishing Company.

P Why can you like something about art when you don't know why the artist make it like it is? What might you see and like?

I Can young people in mid-American States understand art by artist from Siberia or an African State? What can be understood? Why?

J Can third generation American-born ethnics understand the art of their great, great grandparents? Why or why not?

H What degree of direct or vicarious experience is critical to a viewer in order to understand art steeped in cultural traditions? Why can information about a cluture suffice or not?

3.8 ART IS A PART OF LIFE...INFLUENCING AND BEING INFLUENCED BY SOCIETY 365

"A work of art ...belongs to history"..."To appreciate particular works we need some understanding of their background, for the history of art raises problems...which these works may precisely seek to solve." p.152.

Pole, D. (1973). Presentational objects and their interpretation. Philosophy and the Arts. Lecture Series 6, 1971-1972. New York: St. Martin's Press.Copyrright royal Institute of Philosophy. Reprinted with permission of St. Martin's Press, Incorporated.

P Some people liked the sculpture in the front yard of a person's house and some didn't at first, but soon houses were identified by how near they were to the house with the sculpture. Does this mean people learned to like it? Why or why not?

I Art works are put in public plazas or gardens. Why might people miss them if they were removed after a year? Why might people learn about art by seeing a sculpture each day?

J Are public works of art an imposition on people that see them each day or a positive, free art education? Why?

H Should people be confronted with images that reflect artists' perceptive views of a future society? How can accuracy of perception of the future be verified except after-the-fact? What logic supports your position?

3.8 INTERPRETATIONS OF CHANGE EFFECT REFLECTION OF THAT CHANGE IN ART   366

"...there are, to be sure, some indications of an association between short-run severe upheavals in the community system and expressionism in visual art." "...the cultural interpretation of change--e.g., the image of the universe in terms of which change is conceptualized--determines how change will be reflected in art styles." p. 48,49.

Kavolis, V. (1968). Artistic expression: A sociological analysis. Ithaca, NY: Cornell University Press. By permission and fair use.

P Why might an artist-animal lover make posters supporting protection rather than endangering wild life?

I If an artist believes in keeping nature beautiful, why might art that criticizes the accumulation of more industrial waste be expected from that artist?

J Why might artists object to inclusive statements about artists and how they relate to society?

H How might the individual value systems of artists be reflected in their response to or perception of societal change in their art work? Why? Is it inevitable that some response to societal change would show in art work?

3.8 RULES FOR ART EMERGE AS SOCIETIES BECOME SETTLED   367

"Formalism--that is to say, such compositional devices as symmetry, parallel division, radial division and regular repetition of any kind-- only come into evidence when a nomadic existence gives way to settled agrarian communities." p.19.

Read, Sir H. Art in an aboriginal society. In M. Smith,(Ed.) (1961). The artist in tribal society. New York: The Free Press of Glencoe. Proceedings of a symposium held at the Royaal Anthropological Institute, London, 1857. By permission of the Royal Anthropological Institute of Great Britain and Ireland, 1961.

P Groups of people who roam may make art, but don't make rules about correct ways to make it. Why do you think this could be true?

I Cave paintings were art but did not show rules for organizing art that later societies accepted. Why might this be?

J Is it likely that rules for art making will be totally discarded in the name of individuality in the 21st century? Why or why not (considering art in relation to people in various stages of economic development)?

H What relationships might you propose between principles to which art should adhere and the stages of economic development of a group of people?

3.8 PUBLIC ARTISTS MODIFY INDIVIDUALITY WITH RESPONSIVENESS 368

"...to work successfully in the public area, an artist must be willing to change his entire approach--must to a certain extent relinquish his ego, and all notions of autonomous genius that go with it. The concept certainly hints at a new role for the artist in modern society..." p. 8.

From Post -to-neo: The artworld of the 1980's by Calvin Tomkins, Copyright 1988 by Calvin Tomkins. Reprinted by permission of Henry Holt and Company, Inc.

P Should the subject of art for a park be different that art for someone's private home? Why or why not?

I If people pay taxes to support public art, they essentially "buy" that art. Should artists change their ideas or approach to fit the ideas of the public who will view the art works and who pay for them? Why or why not?

J If corporations support artists if the art they produce shows a product in positive light, is that influence on individuality bad for art, or not? Why?

H Is there a ethical discrepancy between the traditional autonomy of the artist and the idea that artist smust be willing to modify ideas to accommodate a client or public? Why? Why not?

3.8 ARTWORLD PERSONS HELP TEACH THE PUBLIC ABOUT ART 369

"Everybody should be 'pedagogical' in the noble sense of the word: give the means to understand without substituting education for art." p.31.

(Interview with Dominique Bozo.) Millet, C. (1990) The structure of French art patronage. The Journal of Art, 3 (2), 31. Translated from the French by Alba Arikha. Fair use.

P Is it okay, or not okay, if some child of a wealthy person decided what things were beautiful for all children's bedroom decorations or toys?

I Why would art museums have written explanations besides identifying title and information by works of art?

J Do the audio tapes about art exhibits to which people listen by using earphones prejudice the viewer? Should viewers rely on what they can see by themselves? Why or why not?

H If corporations seek to avoid a negative image of greed by patronizing the arts, how might that support impact a cultures "natural" development in art for better or for worse?

3.8 WORKS OF ART REFLECT THE SOCIETY AND WHAT COMMUNICATES WITH ITS MEMBERS 370

"The form of a representation cannot be divorced from its purposes and the requirements of the society in which the given visual language gains currency." p.90.

Gombrich, E. (1960). Art and illusion. New York: Pantheon Books. Copyright 1960 by the trustees of the National Gallery of Art, Washington, D.C.

P If you see a painting of a Bald Eagle in the typical frontal pose with a side view of its head, why do you think of our nation?

I If you saw a portrait of a yung person wearing a crown, why would you not think it was someone from the USA?

J Why would it be unlikely to see a painting of a beach party with lunch spread out on what looked like a country's flag?

H WPA murals have subject matter and a mode of representation that reflect the values that the government supported. Why was this art promoted? Why are these works attributed some value and status today?

3.8 EXPLANATIONS PERMIT MORE THAN MERE SURFACE UNDERSTANDINGS OF ART 371

"what students and scholars of...photography need is a reexamination of historical imortance...and an inquiry into the reasonsfor the work's unerring effectiveness." p.22.

Russo, M.A. (November,1990). Is Kertesz a cliche?The Journal of Art,3 (2), 22. Fair use.

P An artist created a sculpture of a general on a horse. Why might the sculptor have chosen this general as a subject and portrayed him so proudly riding his horse?

I Two postcards are about the desert... one a sunset photo and the other a Georgia O'Keefe reproduction of a painting of bones on the desert. Why is there more to know about the painting reproduction?

J Artists have portrayed assassinations, massacres and battles. What about the context of these scenes helps in analyzing the effectiveness of the artwork? Why?

H To what degree is contextual information helpful or critical in interpreting a work of art and judging its quality? Why?

3.8 ART MAY BE SUPPORTED FOR OTHER THAN ARTISTIC MERITS 372

""The founders of the Metropolitan...bankers, railroad men and merchants ...seemed to think that art, like theology, had a built in moral value." p. 82.
From Post -to-neo: The artworld of the 1980's by Calvin Tomkins, Copyright 1988 by Calvin Tomkins. Reprinted by permission of Henry Holt and Company, Inc.

P Why do you think artists show heros standing or sitting proudly and cofidently in works of art?

I At one time, reproductions of art hung in schools showed national heros or religious scenes. Why might art work with these subjects have been chosen for schools? Is that a good use for art? Why or why not?

J Churches, leaders of countries, and wealthy people have supported artists throughout history. Why might they have done so? Would they have the same reason for doing so?

H What is the relative value given artistic quality compared to other reasons for which artists have been supported throughtout history? What is the basis for your position?

3.8 ART STYLE CHANGES FOLLOW ESTABLISHMENT OF ECONOMIC CHANGES 373

"A change in artistic style should perhaps be expected, not at the begining of an economic transformation but only after it has reached a certain point." p.16.
Kavolis, V. (1968). Artistic expression: A sociological analysis. Ithaca, NY: Cornell University Press. By permission and fair use.

P If people were poor, why might they want art about nature rather than kings and queens around them?

I How could changes in the amount of money that people in a nation have change the art style? Why would artists follow, rather that lead the way?

J When a home section of a newspaper has an article titled, "What's in and What's out in Art", to which economic level is the ariticle appealing? Why?

H Do you agree with the position that artistic style follows economic changes once established? How does this assertion fit with the idea that artists have a sencitive perception which precedes changes? Why? Does style coincide with artistic ice breakers?

3.8 "SHARP INCREASES IN MAN'S CONTROL OVER HIS ENVIRONMENT TEND TO BE ASSOCIATED WITH GEOMETRICISM IN ART STYLE." 374

"Naturalism in art reflects a relatively static adaption to nature." p.18.
Kavolis, V. (1968). Artistic expression: A sociological analysis. Ithaca, NY: Cornell University Press. By permission and fair use.

P Do you draw differently when you are excited than when you are calm? Do artists? Why could the way the world is going affect the art made by artists?

I People physically have growth spurts and plateaus. So do countries. Why might relaxing, naturalistic art characterize the stable plateau periods?

J Are artists individual enough to resist the influence of hunger or plenty, war or peace in their approach to art? Why? Why not?

H People have work time and leisure time. What parallels might exist to growth versus static economic periods of a country and controlled versus naturalistic art styles?

3.8 ARTISTS ARE MOTIVATED FOR ECONOMIC AND ARTISTIC REASONS 375

"..it would be sheer romanticism to assume that Navajo artists are indifferent to the income they derive from sales; but besides the profit motive, women also weave for the satisfaction they receive from successfully carrying out the creative synthesis that the craft represents in the Navajo culture." p. 110.
Anderson, R. (1990). Calliope's sisters: A comparative study of philosophies of art. Englewood Cliffs, NJ: Prentice-Hall. By permission of Prentice-Hall Division of Simon & Schuster.

P Is art play or work? If artists need to eat but can't sell art, then they would work at another job and not make art. Is that right? Why? Why not?

I Some art forms take a lot of time for a small object. Why would artists create this art? Should people pay the artist based on the time it takes to make an art work?

J Is there any problem if an art form becomes popular and profitable for the artist? Why or why not? What would be a good solution if so, and why?

H Why do cultural art forms outcast tourist trade or fashion fads and the financial rewards that may accompany that recognition? Do you feel that such irregular support is fair? Is it different for mainstream artists?

3.8 ARTISTS DO NOT DEPEND ON CORPORATE TASTE 376

"Art is still anti-bourgeois...Artists as a whole are not interested in corporate taste. They realize that unless you can go beyond selling to corporations you are nowhere." p. 216. (Jack Boulton. In Tomkins, C., 1988).
From Post-to-neo: The artworld of the 1980's by Calvin Tomkins, Copyright 1988 by Calvin Tomkins. Reprinted by permission of Henry Holt and Company, Inc.

P It is important for parents to approve of their children's art! If a parent likes a childs art, is it as much a compliment as if the art teacher displays it in the principal's office? Why?

I An artist sold a drawing of cows to a veternarian. Why is that an important indicator of artistic merit or not?

J Is it more meaningful for a bank or law firm to buy an artist's work that for a library to buy it? Why or why not?

H What measure of worth of art is a corporate purchase of art? Why?

3.8 AESTHETIC VALUE OVERLAPS WITH SOCIAL AND/OR ECONOMIC VALUE 377

"Archeological and ethnohistoric evidence reveals that it was fairly common for Aztecs to give craft items to those whom they asked for favors." p. 151 note 4.
Anderson, R. (1990). Calliope's sisters: A comparative study of philosophies of art. Englewood Cliffs, NJ: Prentice-Hall. By permission of Prentice-Hall Division of Simon & Schuster.

P Do you ever trade items with a friend? If you were an artist what would you trade, with whom and why?

I Farmers used to thatk the preacher for the church work by giving vegetables. What could the artist say, "thanks" with? Why would that be valuable to the preacher?

J We speak of "tourist trade" and that usually means trading money for art-like objects. Why do people buy objects from other countries or parts of their own country?

H How are aesthetic, social and economic values intertwined in art works? When is there an imbalance of these values? Is there danger in the imbalance you describe? Why or why not?

3.8 "MODERN" ART IS AN INAPPROPRIATE NAME FOR A SINGLE PERIOD 378

"All new art is modern for awhile; the mistake was to posit a style called 'Modern'." p. 57.

From Post-to-neo: The artworld of the 1980's by Calvin Tomkins, Copyright 1988 by Calvin Tomkins. Reprinted by permission of Henry Holt and Company, Inc.

P Once the Model T Ford car was modern. Is it now? Is art that was modern when your grandparents were in grade school still "modern"? Why? Why not?

I Why is calling an art period modern like naming a daughter, "Daughter" or a son, "Son" when other daughters and sons follow?

J Why is modern an appropriate or inappropriate name for a period of art?

H What might be a better name for the modern period to avoid awkward names of following periods, such as, "post-modernism" or "post-post-modernism"? What are good reasons for your suggested names?

3.8 MULTI/CROSS CULTURAL STUDY OF ART MANDATES MORE CONTEXT-SENSITIVE CURRICULAR APPROACHES 379

"...cash culture literacy...ignores the multicultural nature of our society and the diverse art communities which have taken on global dimensions through our expanding 'Museum without walls'." p.223.

Hamblen, K., 1990. Beyond the aesthetic of the cash-culture literacy. Studies in Art Education, 31(4), 216-225. By permission of National Art Education Association.

P If someone wanted to see all art by going to an art museum, why would that be difficult?

I Why would a city like Chicago have a Black Art museum, a Ukranian museum, a Jewish museum and a Polish museum?

J Why is a city like Chicago and outdoor art museum? Why does the architecture of a large city provide a history lesson as well as an art lesson?

H What might be the role of the art museum in an era characterized by the concept of a museum without walls? Why?

3.8 PRIVATE SUPPORT OF ART MAY MASK BASIC PHILOSOPHIC DIFFERENCES

"...it is within our power to debate and decide whether the private sector is to dominate the context of aesthetics...acceptance...suggests that art's core purpose may be precisely the denial of unresolvable tensions." p.9.

Narrett, E. (June,1987). Art consulting and the new patronage. Art New England, 8 (6), 8-9. Printed with permission from Art New England magazine.

P If artists need to think for themselves, why might an army general not be the best person to plan on supporting a free thinking artist?

I Why might it be dangerous for artists to find it easy to sell to people who can pay good prices for their work?

J Why would a doctor not buy artwork which is controversial or emotionally arousing for a medical office or clinic?

H What is the chance that people with the financial means to support art are philsohpically compatible with the artist whose ideas emerge in the art works created?

REFERENCES: TEXT

Anderson, T. & McRorie, S. (1997). A role for aesthetics in centering the K-12 art curriculum. Art Education, 50(23), 6-14.

Anderson, W. (1973). Art learning situations for elementary education. Belmont, CA: Wadsworth Publishing Company, Inc.

Armstrong, C. (1979). Planning art curriculum (PAC) K through 8 and Guidelines. DeKalb, IL: ABAFA Systems.

Armstrong, C. (1986). Stages of inquiry in art production: Model, rationale and application to a teacher questioning strategy. Studies in Art Education, 28(1), 37-48.

Armstrong, C. (1988) The visual arts in the self-contained classroom. educational Horizons, 66(3),126-128.

Armstrong, C.(1990a). Description of the development of an aesthetics resource. DeKalb, IL: Northern Illinois University School of Art.

Armstrong, C, (1990b). Integrating aesthetics, art criticism, art history, and art production in an elementary education majors' art methods course. In A. Coveny, (Ed.) Directions: Addressing art history, aesthetics, and art criticism in Illinois schools (pp.50-60). Aurora, IL: Illinois Art Education Association.

Armstrong, C. (1992). Evaluation of questions suggested to initiate aesthetics dialogues in an aesthetics resource prototype. In P. Smith, Ed.(1992). Research presentations. West Lafayette, IN: Purdue University.

Armstrong, C. (1993). Effect of training in an art production questioning method on teacher questioning and student responses. Studies in Art Education, 34(4), 209-221.

Armstrong, C. (1994). <u>Designing assessment in art</u>. Reston, VA: National Art Education Association.

Armstrong, C. (1996). A choice: Comfortable ambiguity or clearly translated standards. <u>Studies in Art Education, 37</u>(2), 253-256.

Armstrong, C. & Armstrong, N. (1977). Art teacher questioning strategy. <u>Studies in Art Education, 18</u>(3), 53-64.

Ausubel, D. (1965). A cognitive structure view of word and concept meaning. In R. Anderson & D. Ausubel (Eds.). <u>Readings in the psychology of cognition</u> (pp.58-75). New York: Holt, Rinehart and Winston.

Barkan, M. (1966). Curriculum problems in art education. In E. Mattil (Project Director). <u>A seminar in art education for research and curriculum development</u> (pp.240-255). University Park, PA: The Pennsylvania State University, Department of Art Education.

Barkan, M., Chapman, L. & Kern, E. (1970). <u>Guidelines: Curriculum development for aesthetic education</u>. St. Louis, MO: CEMREL.

Battin, M., Fisher, J., Moore, R., & Silvers, A.(1989). <u>Puzzles about art</u>. New York: St. Martin's Press.

Battin, M. (1988). The contribution of aesthetics. In S. Dobbs, (Ed.). <u>Research reading for discipline-based art education: A journey beyond creating</u>. (pp.126-129). Reston, VA: National Art Education Association.

Bruner, J. (1963). <u>The process of education</u>. Cambridge, MA: Harvard University Press.

Champlin, K. <u>Assessing curriculum guides for art education</u>. Reston, VA: National Art Education Association. (pamphlet)

Clark, G. & Zimmerman, E. (Winter,1978). A walk in the right direction: A model for visual arts education. Studies in Art Education, 19(2), 34-49.

Clark, G.; Day, M.; & Greer, W. D. (Summer,1987). Discipline-based art education: Becoming students of art. Journal of Aesthetic Education, 21(2), 129-193.

Day, M. (1969). The compatibility of history and studio art activity in the junior high school art program: A comparison of two methods of teaching art history. Studies in Art Education, 10(2), 57-65.

Day, M. (1985). Evaluating student achievement in discipline-based art programs. Studies in Art Education, 26(4), 232-240.

Day, M. (1987). Discipline-based art education in secondary classrooms. Studies in Art Education, 28(4), 234-242.

Dickie, G. (1971). Aesthetics. New York: Pegasus Division of The Bobbs-Merrill Company, Inc.

Doll, R. (1989). Curriculum improvement. Boston: Allyn & Bacon.

Dunn, P. (1995). Creating curriculum in art. Reston, VA: National Art Education Association.

Efland, A. (1974). Evaluating goals for art education. Art Education, 27(1), 8-10.

Efland, A. (1977). Planning art education in the middle/secondary schools of Ohio. Columbus, Ohio: State of Ohio, Department of Education.

Erickson, M. (1986). Is teaching aesthetics a reasonable goal for K-12 art education? In E. Kern (Ed.). Pennsylvania's symposium on art education, aesthetics, and art criticism (pp.37-51). Harrisburg, PA: State

Department of Education.

Erickson, M. & Katter, E. (1986). Teaching aesthetics K-12: Activities and resources. Conference presentation handout.

Feldman, E.(1967). Art as image and idea. Englewood Cliffs, NJ: Prentice-Hall.

Gagne, R. & Briggs, L. (1974). Principles of instructional design. New York: Holt, Rinehart and Winston, Inc.

Hamblen, K. Constructing questions for art dialogues. Art Museum/ Education Conference, February, 1986. Northern Illinois University Art Gallery in Chicago, IL.

Hamblen, K. (1988). Approaches to aesthetics in art education: A critical theory perspective. Studies in Art Education, 29(2), 81-90.

Hardiman, G. & Zernich, T. (1984). Curricular considerations for art education: rationale, Content and Evaluation. Springfield, IL: Illinois State Board of Education.

Hobbs, J. & Rush, J. (1997). Teaching children art. Upper Saddle River, NJ: Prentice Hall.

Hurwitz, A. & Madeja, S. (1977). A joyous vision. New York: Prentice Hall.

Hubbard, G. & Rouse, M. (19720. Art: Meaning, method, media. Westchester, IL: Benefic Press.

Hubbard, G. & Zimmerman, E. (1982). Artstrands. Prospect Heights, IL: Waveland Press.

Jinayon, S. (1989). Suggested themes for retrieval of art reproductions based on curricular theories. Unpublished masters thesis. Northern Illinois University, Art Education. DeKalb, IL.

Kaelin, E. F. (1989). An aesthetics for art educators. New York: Teachers College Press.

King, A. & Brownell, J. (1966). <u>The curriculum and the disciplines of knowledge</u>. New York: Wiley.

Lankford, L. (1992). <u>Aesthetics: Issues and inquiry</u>. Reston, VA: National Art Education Association.

Madeja, S. & Onuska, S. (1977). <u>Through the arts to the aesthetic</u>. St. Louis: CEMREL. Inc.

Massey, M. (1976). <u>What you are is where you were when...</u> Parts 1 and 2 [Film]. Twentieth Century -- Fox Video, Inc.

Moore, R.,(Ed.) (1995). <u>Aesthetics for young people</u>. Reston, VA: National Art Education Association.

National Art Education Association (1994). <u>The National Visual Arts Standards</u>. Reston, VA: The Association.

National Art Education Association, Task Force (1994). <u>Exemplary art education curricula: A guide to guides</u>. Reston, VA: The Association.

Parsons, M. & Blocker, H.G. (1993). <u>Aesthetics and education</u>. Urbana and Chicago: University of Illinois Press.

Russell, Robert. (1988). Children's philosophical inquiry into defining art: A quasi-experimental study of aesthetics in the elementary classroom. <u>Studies in Art Education, 29</u>(3), 282-291.

Russell, Robert. (1991). Teaching students to inquire about art philosophically: Procedures derived from ordinary language philosophy to teach principles of concept analysis. <u>Studies in Art Education, 32</u>(2), 94-104.

Russell, Robin Franz. (1985). [Effect of isolated, separated and simultaneous concept development in art and music instruction.] Unpublished master's thesis. Northern Illinois University, Art Education, DeKalb, IL.

Saylor, J. G. & Alexander, W. (1966). Curriculum planning for modern schools. New York: Holt, Rinehart and Winston, Inc.

Silverman, R. (1969). Developing and evaluating art curricula for disadvantaged students. Studies in Art Education, 11 (1), 20.

Smith, B. O., Stanley, W., & Shores, J. H. (1957). Fundamentals of curriculum development. New York: Harcourt, Brace & World, Inc.

Stewart, M. (1986). Aesthetics. Presentation at the University of Maine at Orono. April, 1986.

Stewart, M. (1988). Teaching the skills of philosophic inquiry in art. Paper presented at the 28th National Art Education Association Conference, Los Angeles, CA.

Stewart, M. Aesthetics and the art curriculum. In R. Moore, (Ed.), (1995). Aesthetics for young people. Reston, VA: National Art Education Association.

Stewart, M. & Katter, E. (1993). Building a foundation for the future. Paper presented at the 33rd National Art Education Association Conference.

Wilson, B. (1974). One view of the past and future of research in aesthetic education. Journal of Aesthetic Education, 8(3), 59-67.

Wilson, B. (1988). An assessment strategy for the arts. In N. Meyers Saitlin (Project Director). Education for the nineties: The arts in the curriculum (pp. 23-41). Springfield, Il: Illinois Arts Council and Illinois State Board of Education. Project of the Illinois Alliance for Arts in Education.

Woodruff, A. (1975). First steps in building a new school program. Unpublished manuscript.

REFERENCES: AESTHETICS RESOURCE

Allara, P. (June,1987). The writing of art criticism. Art New England, 8(6), 19.

Adams, R. (1990). Alain Locke revisited: The reconsideration of an aesthetic. In B. Young (Ed.). Art, culture, and ethnicity (pp. 231-240). Reston, VA: National Art Education Association.

Aldrich, V. (1963). Philosophy of art. Englewood Cliffs, NJ: Prentice Hall.

Anderson, R. (1990). Calliope's sisters: A comparative study of philosophies of art. Englewood Cliffs, NJ: Prentice Hall.

Arnheim, R. (1966). Art and visual perception. Berkeley, CA: University of California Press.

Arnstine, D. (1966). The aesthetic as a context for general education. Studies in Art Education, 8(1), 15.

Bauer, J. (1956). Charles Burchfield. New York: MacMillan Company.

Beardsley, M. (1958). Aesthetics: Problems in the philosophy of criticism. New York: Harcourt, Brace

Beardsley, M. (Spring,1965). On the creation of art. The Journal of Aesthetics and Art Criticism, 23(3), 291-304.

Beardsley, M. (1970). The aesthetic point of view. In H. Kiefer & M. Munitz (Eds.). Perspectives in education, religion, and the arts. (pp. 219-237). Albany, NY: State University of New York Press.

Bell, C. (1913). Art. London: Chatto & Windus.

Berndt, R. (1964). The world of the first Australians. Chicago: University of Chicago Press.

Boas, G. & Wrenn, H. (1966). What is a picture? New York: Schocken Books.

Boccioni, U. (1964). Futurist sculpture. In R. Herbert. (Ed.). Modern artists on art. Englewood Cliffs, NJ: Prentice Hall.

Bonenti, C. (June, 1987). Symbolism, message, and meaning. Art New England, 8(6), 17.

Booth, W. (1961). The rhetoric of fiction. Chicago: University of Chicago Press.

Brown, N. (1959). Life against death. Midlothian, CT: Wesleyan University Press.

Bullough, E. (1912). "Psychical distance" as a factor in art and an aesthetic principle. British Journal of Psychology, 5, 87-118.

Burchfield, C. (1956). In J. Bauer. Charles Burchfield (p.46). New York: MacMillan.

Burke, K. (1941). The philosophy of literary form: Studies in symbolic action. Baton Rouge, LA: Louisianna State University Press.

Cherry, H. (1961). Mark Rothko; Kenzo Okada; Herman Cherry; Ad Reinhardt. In S. Rodman. Conversations with artists (pp. 92-99). New York: Capricorn Books.

Conger, S. (1990). Corporate art in the Helms era. Journal of Art, 3(2), 66.

Cohen-Solai, A. (interview)(1990). In B. Rose. How Europe stole back the idea of modern art. Journal of Art, 3(2), 1.

Collingwood, R.G. (1958). Principles of art. New York: Galaxy Press. Oxford University.

Danto, A. (1964). The artworld. Journal of Philosophy, 61(19), 571-584.

Dewey, J. (1934, 1958). Art as Experience. New York: Capricorn Books. G. P. Putnam's Sons, New York.

Dewey, J. (1958). Experience and nature. New York, NY: Dover Publications

Dickie, G. (January, 1964). The myth of the aesthetic attitude. American Philosophical Quarterly, 1(1), 56-65.

Dickie, G. (1971a). Aesthetics. New York: Pegasus Division of Bobbs-Merrill.

Dickie, G. (1971b). Art and the aesthetic: An institutional analysis. Ithaca, NY: Cornell University Press.

Dickie, G. (1984). The new institutional theory of art. In G. Haller, (Ed.). Aesthetics: Proceedings of the Eighth International Wittgenstein Symposium, Part I. (pp. 57-64). Vienna, Austria: Holder-Pichler-Tempsky.

Dickie, G. (1988). Evaluating art. Philadelphia: Temple University Press.

Dickie, G. (1989). Reply to Stecker. In G. Dickie, R. Sclafani & R. Roblin (Eds.). Aesthetics: A critical anthology (pp. 214-217). New York: St. Martin's Press.

Dockstader, F. (1962). Indian art in America. Greenwich, CT: New York Graphic Society.

Ducasse, C. (1929). The philosophy of art. New York: Dial Press.

Eaton, M. (1988). Basic issues in aesthetics. Belmont, CA: Wadsworth.

Ecker, D. (1967). Justifying aesthetic judgments. Art Education, 20(5), 8.

Eisner, E. and Ecker, D. (1966). Readings in art education. Waltham Massachusetts: Blaisdell Publishing Co. Div. of Ginn and Company.

Feldman, E. (1967). Art as image and idea. Englewood Cliffs, NJ: Prentice-Hall.

Focillon, H. (1948). The life forms in art. New York: George Wittenborn, Inc.

French, C. (November, 1990). A taste for narraton at the Whitney: Conceptual sculpture for the 90's. The Journal of Art, 3(2), 15.

Fry, R. (1920). Vision and design. New York: Chatto & Windus.

Fry, R. (1956). Transformations. New York: Doubleday Anchor Press.

Garcia, A. (November, 1990). Interview by M. Brenson. Nothing but the truth. The Journal of Art, 3(20, 39.

Gombrich, E. (1960). Art and illusion: A study in the psychology of pictorial representation. New York: National Gallery of Art and Pantheon Books for Bollingen Foundation.

Gombrich, E. (1963). Meditations on a hobby horse. London: Phaidon Press.

Goodman, N. (1976). Languages of art: An approach to a theory of symbols. Indianapolis, IN: Hackett. New York: Bollinger Foundation. Parthenon Books Division of Random House for National Gallery of Art

Gowing, L. (1966). henri matisse: 64 paintings. New York: Museum of Modern Art.

Gowrie, G. (November, 1990). Will art move freely in 1993? The Journal of Art 3(2), 61.

Greene, T. (1940). The arts and the art of criticism. Princeton, NJ: Princeton University Press.

Greenough, H. (1957). Form and function. Berkeley, CA: University of California Press.

Hall, S. & Whannel, P. (1964). The popular arts. New York: Pantheon.

Hamblen, K. (Summer, 1990). Beyond the aesthetic of the cash-culture literacy. Studies in Art Education, 31(4), 216-225.

Hauser, A. (1958, 1985). The philosophy of art history. Evanston, IL: Northwestern University Press.

Hospers, J. (1946). Meaning and truth in the arts. Chapel Hill, NC: University of North Carolina Press.

Hospers, J. (1955). The concept of artistic expression. In The Aristotelian Society (1954-1955). <u>Proceedings of the Aristotelian Society</u>, <u>55</u>, 313-344.

Hospers, J.(1982). <u>Understanding the arts</u>. Englewood Cliffs, NJ: Prentice-Hall.

Hume, D. (1957, 1970). <u>Four dissertations</u>. New York: Garland Publishing Co.

Inter-American Commission on Human Rights. <u>Annual report of the Inter-American Commission on Human Rights. 1990-1991</u>. Washington, D.C.: Organization of American States.

Isenberg, A. (July, 1949). Critical communication. <u>The Philosophical Review</u>, <u>58</u>, 330-344.

Kaelin, E. F. (1968). An existential-phenomenological account of aesthetic education. <u>Penn State Papers in Art Education, No. 4</u>. University Park, PA: Pennsylvania State University, Department of Art Education.

Kaelin, E. F. (1989). <u>An aesthetics for art educators</u>. New York: Teachers College Press.

Kavolis, V. (1968). <u>Artistic expression--A sociological analysis</u>. Ithaca, NY: Cornell University Press.

Kishimoto Hideo (1967). Some Japanese cultural traits and religions. In C. Moore, (Ed.). <u>The Japanese mind</u> (pp.110-121). Honolulu: University of Hawaii Press.

Langer, S. (1953). <u>Feeling and form</u>. New York: Scribner & Sons.

Langer, S. (1957). <u>Problems of art</u>. New York: Charles Scribner's Sons.

Lee, E. (September, 4, 1997). Are crafts, commercialism dominating art fairs? <u>The Rockford Register Star</u>.1B, 6B. Rockford, IL: <u>The Rockford Register Star</u>.

Leonhard, C. & House, R. (1972). Foundations and principles of music education. New York: McGraw-Hill.

MacDonald, M. (1949). Symposium: What are the distinctive features of arguments used in criticism of the arts, III. In Aristotelian Society. Proceedings of the Aristotelian Society, Supp. Vol. XXIII, 186, 187. London: Harrison & Sons, Ltd.

Magill, F. (1961). Masterpieces in world philosophy: In summary form. New York: Salem Press.

McCorduck, P.(1991). Aaron's Code: Meta-art, artificial intelligence, and the work of Harold Cohen. New York: W.H. Freeman.

Millet, C. (November, 1990a). Nostalgia in the seventies: Hope for the nineties. The Journal of Art, 3(2), 33.

Millet, C. (November, 1990b). The structure of French art patronage. The Journal of Art, 3(2), 31. Translated from the French by Alba Arikha.

Morgan, C. (1958). The nature of dramatic illusion. In S. Langer. (1958). Reflections on art. Baltimore, MD: The Johns Hopkins Press.

Morgan, D, (Fall, 1967). Must art tell the truth? Journal of Aesthetics and Art Criticism, 26, 17-27.

Mumford, L. (1952). Art and technics. New York: Columbia University Press.

Narrett, E. (June, 1987). Art consulting and the new patronage. Art New England, 8(6), 9.

Ortega y Gasset, J. (1948, 1968). The dehumanization of art: And other essays on art, culture, and literature. Princeton, NJ: Princeton University Press.

Panofsky, E. (1955). Meaning in the visual arts. Garden City, NY: Doubleday.

Parsons, M.(1970). The concept of medium in education. In R. Smith (Ed.). Aesthetic concepts and education (p. 263-285). Urbana, IL: University of Illinois Press.

Pepper, S. (1945). The basis of criticism in the arts. Cambridge, MA: Harvard University Press.

Pepper, S. (1949). Principles of art appreciation. New York: Harcourt, Brace & World.

Plato. (1941, 1945). How representation in art is related to truth. The republic of Plato. Translated by Francis Cornford. New York: Oxford University Press.

Pole, D. (1957). What makes a situation aesthetic? The Aristotelian Society. Proceedings of the Aristotelian Society, Supp. Vol. XXXI, 101-102.

Pole, D. (1973). Presentational objects and their interpretation (p.147-164). In The Royal Institute of Philosophy. Philosophy and the arts. Volume Six, 1971-1972. New York: St. Martin's Press.

Prall, D. W. (1929). Aesthetic judgment. New York: Thomas Y. Crowell Co.

Read, Sir H. (1961). Art in an aboriginal society: A comment. In M. Smith (Ed.). The artist in tribal society (pp.14-21). New York: The Free Press of Glencoe. Proceedings of a Symposium held at the Royal Anthropological Institute, London 1957.

Reid, L. (1954). A criticism of art as form. In L. Reid (Ed.). A study in aesthetics (pp. 312-325). New York: The MacMillan Co. (First published by George Allen & Unwin, 1931.)

Ringgold, F. (1995). We flew over the bridge. Boston, New York: Bulfinch Press Division of Little, Brown and Company.

Russo, M.A. (1990). Is Kertesza a cliche? The Journal of Art, 3(2), 22.

Schaper, E. (1968). Prelude to aesthetics. London: George Allen & Unwin, Ltd.

Shapiro, M. (1953). Style. In A. Kroeber (Ed.) (1953). <u>Anthropology</u>. Chicago: University of Chicago Press.

Sheppard, A. (1987). <u>Aesthetics: An introduction to the philosophy of art</u>. New York: Oxford University Press.

Sibley, F. (October, 1959). Aesthetic concepts. <u>The Philosophical Review, LXVIII,</u> 421-450.

Stolnitz, J. (1960). <u>Aesthetics and the philosophy of art criticism</u>. Boston: Houghton Mifflin Co.

Storr, R. (1990). Raiding the icebox at MOMA. <u>The Journal of Art,</u> 3(2), 25.

Streb, J. (1984). Thoughts on phenomenology, education and art. <u>Studies in Art Education,</u> 25(3), 164.

Taylor, J. (1957,1981). <u>Learning to look: A handbook for the visual arts</u>. Chicago: The University of Chicago Press.

Tolstoy, L. (1962). <u>What is art?</u> New York: Oxford University Press. A Hesperides Book.

Tomkins, C. (1988). <u>Post-to-neo: The art world of the 80's</u>.New York: Viking Penguin Books. Henry Holt and Co., Inc.

Venturi, L. (1936, 1964). <u>History of art criticism</u>. Translated from the Italian by Charles Marriot. New York: E. P. Dutton.

Villemain, F. (January, 1964). Democracy, education, and art. <u>Educational Theory,</u> 14(1), 1-14, 30.

Weitz, M. (1966). The nature of art. In E. Eisner & D. Ecker. <u>Readings in art education</u> (pp.49-56). Waltham, MA: Blaisdell, Division of Ginn.

Woelfflin, H. (1932). <u>Principles of art history: The problems of development of style in later art</u>. Mineola, NY: Dover Publications.

APPENDIX: WORKSHEETS

Art/General Education Outcome Statements (Goals Grid)

Goals/Aesthetics Alignment in Encounters

Course Structure

Generalizations Merging Curruculum and Aesthetics Theories

Structure of Visual Arts Encounters

Organizing Content within a Structure

Format for planning visual arts outcome statements that show compatibility between fine arts goals and general education goals of school districts

Fine Arts goals:1	2	3	4	5	6
General Education Goals					
1					
2					
3					
4					
5					
6					

(Select appropriate cells in which to write visual arts outcomes. Demonstrate how visual arts uniquely addresses general education and fine arts goals or standards. See figure 4.7.)

Format for showing where encounters dealing with aesthetics theories and issues contribute to visual art goals or student outcomes

ART GOALS: AESTHETICS THEORIES/ ISSUES	1	2	3	4	5	6
IMITATION						
EXPRESSION						
FORMALISM						
SOCIAL INSTITUTION						
PRAGMATISM						
NO THEORY						
NON-WESTERN						
META-CRITICISM						
MEDIA GENERATED						
AESTHETIC ATTITUDE						
AESTHETIC RESPONSE						
PLEASURE/PLAY						
ARTIST CHARACTERISTICS						
CREATIVE PROCESS						
ART AND CONTEXT						

(Enter numbers of the encounters that contribute to meeting visual arts goals by emphasis on aesthetics.

346

Format for planning a course structure

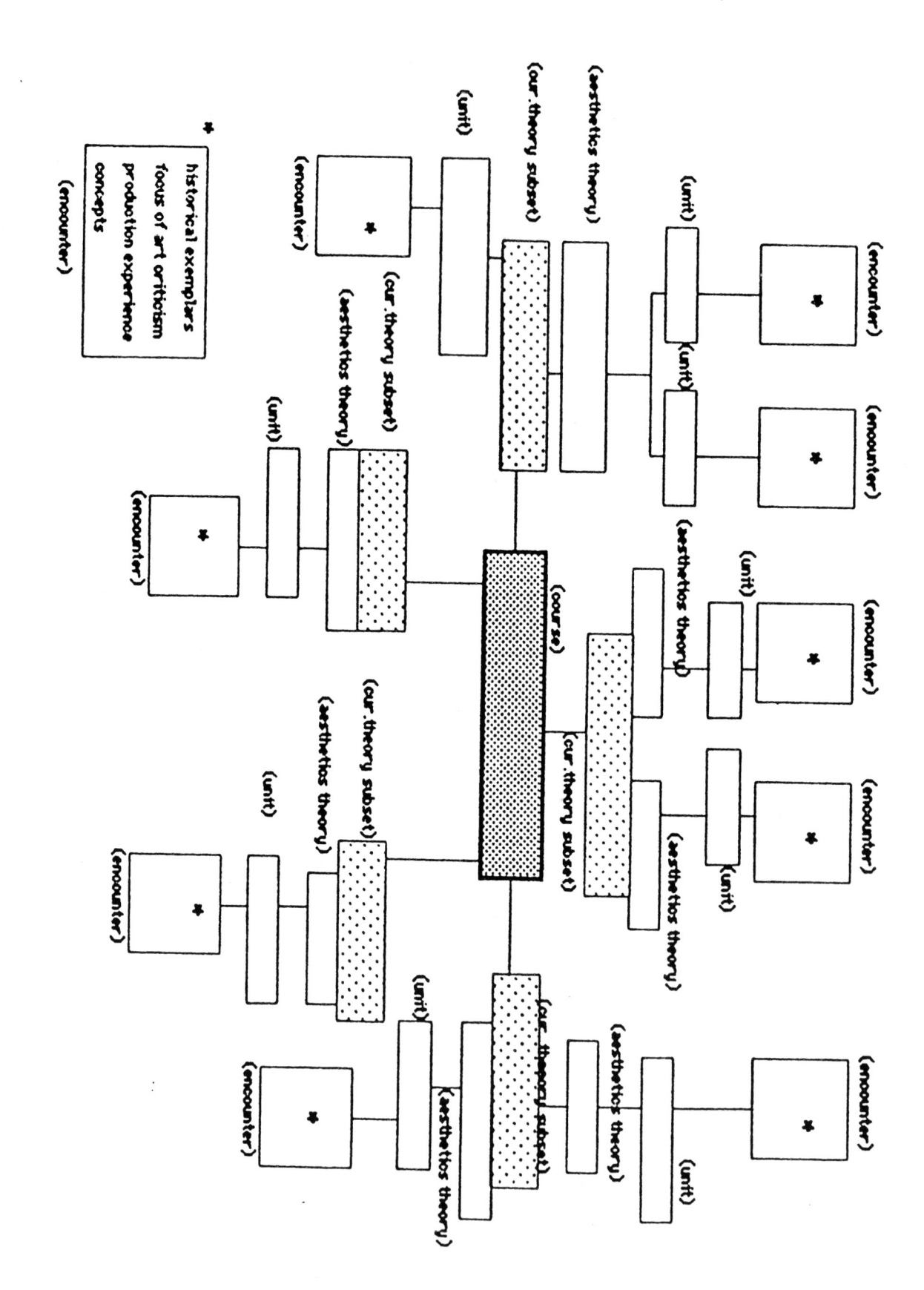

*historical exemplars
focus of art criticism
production experience
concepts

347

Format for creating universal aesthetics generalizations by merging subsets of the institutions curricular theory and aesthetics theories/issues

AESTHETICS THEORIES/ ISSUES	INSTITUTIONS: 1 SOCIAL	2 POLITICAL	3 ECONOMIC	4 PHILOSOPHICAL
IMITATION				
EXPRESSION				
FORMALISM				
SOCIAL INSTITUTION				
PRAGMATISM				
NO THEORY				
NON-WESTERN				
META-CRITICISM				
MEDIA GENERATED				
AESTHETIC ATTITUDE				
AESTHETIC RESPONSE				
PLEASURE/ PLAY				
ARTIST CHARACTER-ISTICS				
CREATIVE PROCESS				
ART AND CONTEXT				

(Refer to Table 4.1, pages 42-43 and Figures 4.10 and 5.1 Write generalizations that could guide an art encounter based on compatible subsets of curricular and aesthetics theories.)

348

A format for initial organization of comprehensive visual arts content by connecting aesthetics theories ◯ and subsets of a curriculum theory ◯

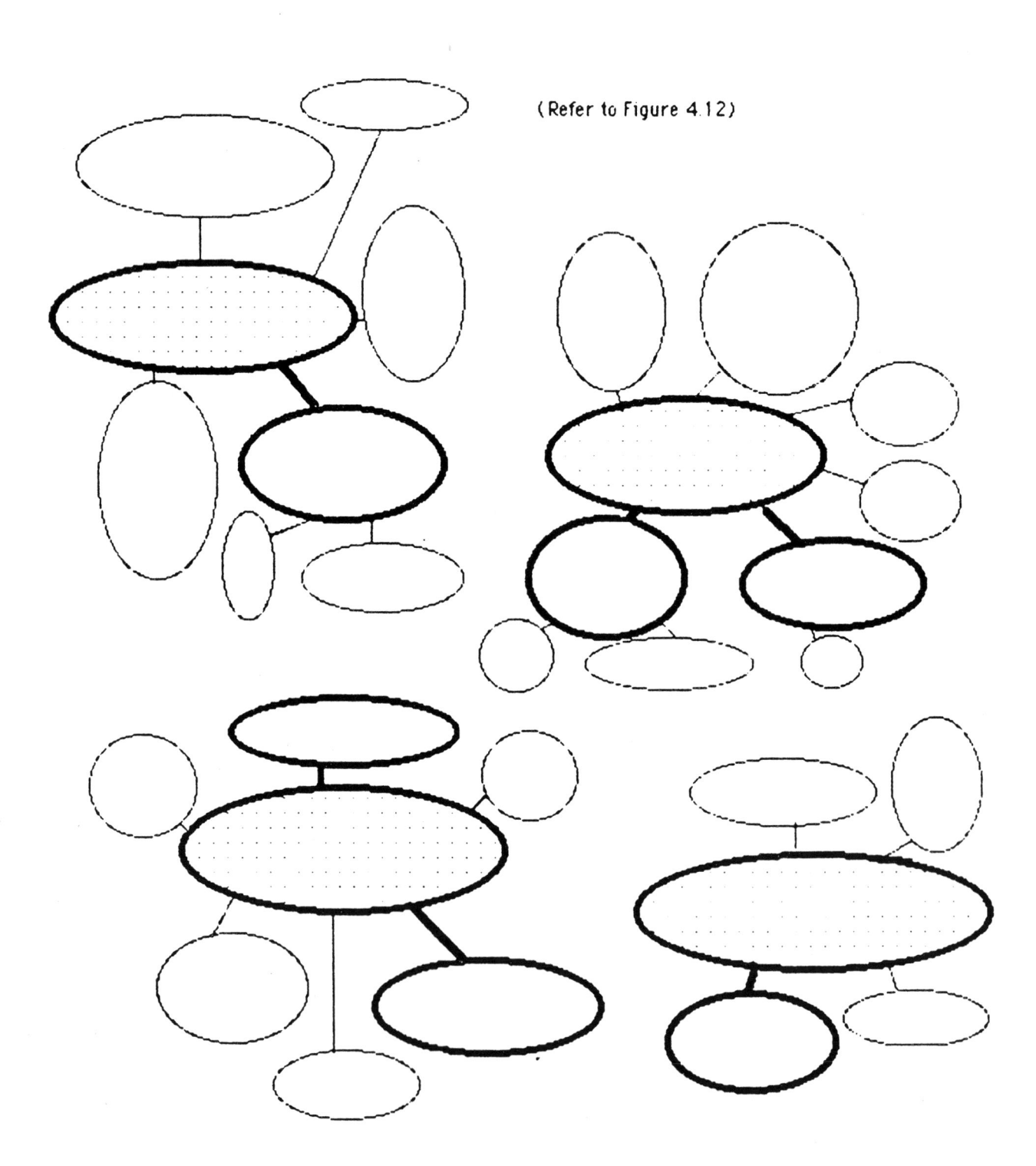

(Refer to Figure 4.12)

Format for planning a visual arts encounter

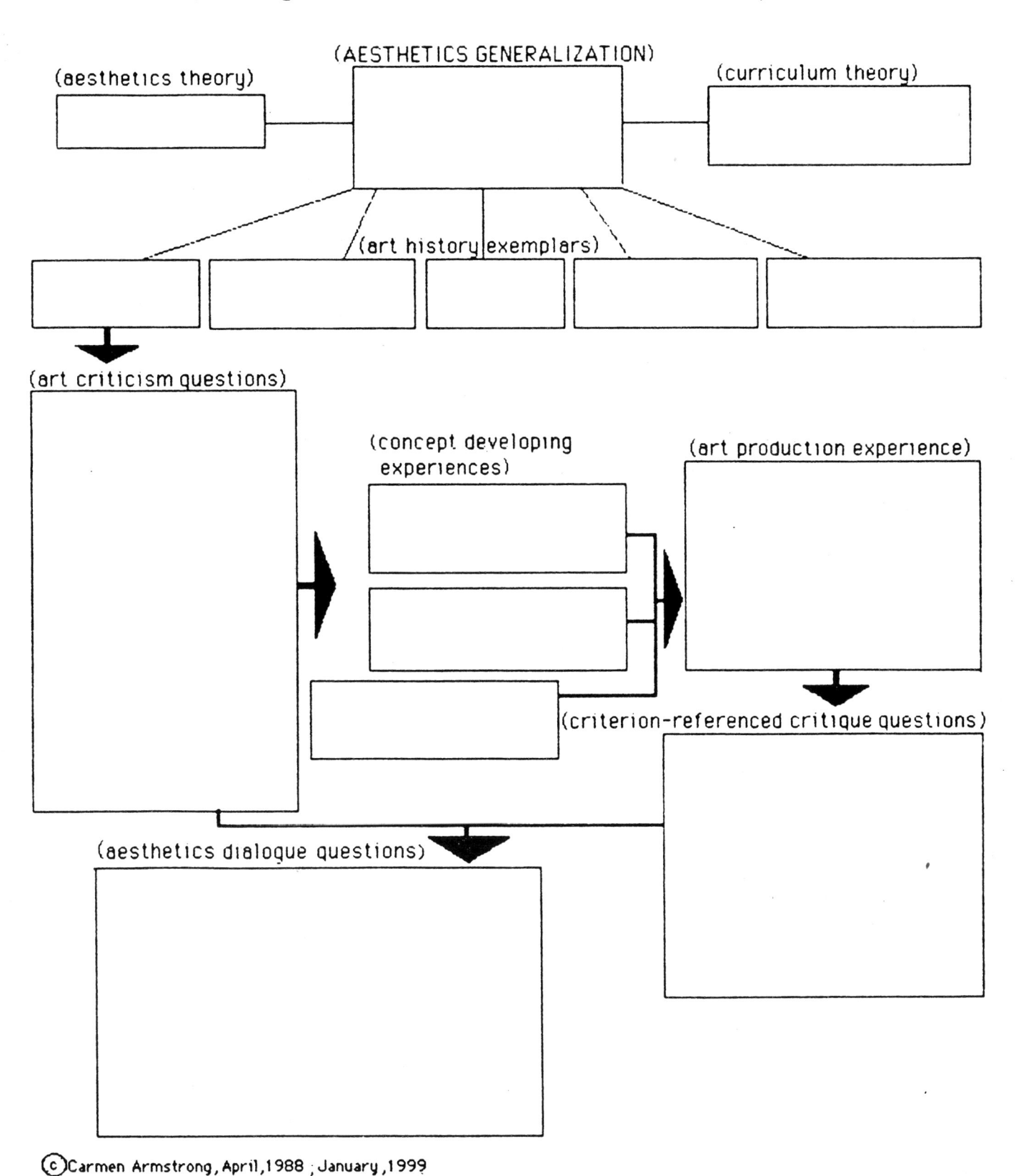

(aesthetics theory)

(AESTHETICS GENERALIZATION)

(curriculum theory)

(art history exemplars)

(art criticism questions)

(concept developing experiences)

(art production experience)

(criterion-referenced critique questions)

(aesthetics dialogue questions)

©Carmen Armstrong, April, 1988; January, 1999

Notes